ROXBURY LIBRARY

Books by Morris Schaff

THE BATTLE OF THE WILDERNESS. Large crown 8vo, $2.00, *net*. Postage extra.
THE SPIRIT OF OLD WEST POINT. Illustrated. Octavo, $3.00, *net*. Postage 20 cents.
ETNA AND KIRKERSVILLE, LICKING CO., OHIO. 12mo, $1.00, *net*. Postage 8 cents.

HOUGHTON MIFFLIN COMPANY
BOSTON AND NEW YORK

THE
BATTLE OF THE WILDERNESS

★ ★ ★ ★ ★

THE BATTLE OF THE WILDERNESS

BY

MORRIS SCHAFF

AUTHOR OF
"THE SPIRIT OF OLD WEST POINT"

WITH MAPS AND PLANS

BOSTON AND NEW YORK
HOUGHTON MIFFLIN COMPANY
The Riverside Press Cambridge

COPYRIGHT, 1910, BY MORRIS SCHAFF

ALL RIGHTS RESERVED

Published October 1910

SECOND IMPRESSION

This book is dedicated to the memory of my mother
Charlotte Hartzell Schaff
*buried in the little graveyard at Etna Ohio
and whose gentle clay has long since
blended with the common earth*

MORRIS SCHAFF

LIST OF MAPS

BATTLE-FIELD OF THE WILDERNESS . . . *Frontispiece*

COUNTRY BETWEEN THE RAPIDAN AND RAPPAHAN-
NOCK 52

COUNTRY SOUTH OF THE RAPIDAN 68

GENERAL MAP OF THE WILDERNESS 122

COUNTRY SOUTH OF THE RAPPAHANNOCK 144

★   ★   ★   ★   ★

THE BATTLE OF THE WILDERNESS

I

FROM time to time, one or two friends have urged me to write of the war between the States, in which, as a boy, I took a humble part just after graduating at West Point; but I have always answered that nature had not given me the qualifications of a historian, and that, moreover, every nook and corner of the field had been reaped and garnered. So, I kept on my way. But not long ago, while in a meditative mood, a brooding peace settled over my mind, and lo! across a solemn gorge, and far up and away against the past, lay the misting field of History. While as in dreamland my inward eye was wandering bewitched over it, a voice hailed me from a green knoll at the foot of which burst a spring whose light-hearted current wimpled away to a pond hard by. "Come over here," said the voice, beckoning; and seeing that I stood still, and wore a perplexed look, it added feelingly, "You have written your boyhood memories of your old home, and you have written those of your cadet days at West Point; am I not dear to you, too? I am your boyhood memories of the War." At once, from the fields of Virginia the Army of the Potomac lifted as by magic and began to break camp to go on its last campaign; its old, battle-scarred flags were fluttering proudly, the batteries were drawing out, the bronze guns that I had heard thunder on many fields were sparkling gayly, and my horse, the same wide-nostriled, broad-chested, silky-haired roan, stood saddled and bridled before my tent. The trumpets sounded; and, as their notes died away, I picked up the pen once more.

Upon graduating at West Point in June, 1862, I was commissioned a Second Lieutenant in the Ordnance Corps and assigned to duty under that loyal, deeply-brown-eyed, modest Virginia gentleman and soldier, Captain T. G. Baylor, commanding the Arsenal at Fort Monroe. Fort Monroe, or Old Point Comfort (which is the loving and venerable historic name of the place), at that time and throughout the war was the port and station of greatest importance on our southern seaboard. Situated practically at the mouth of the James, it not only commanded the outlet from the Confederate capital at Richmond, but also the navigation of the Chesapeake and the Potomac, and offered a safe point for the assembly of fleets and armies preparatory to taking the offensive. When I reached there, it was the base of supplies for the Army of the Potomac, then on the last stage of its disastrous Peninsula campaign, and also for Burnside's army operating on the coast of North Carolina. Moreover, it was the rendezvous of our Atlantic squadrons and of the foreign men-of-war, which, drawn as eagles to the scene of our conflict, came in, cast their anchors, and saluted the flag, though the hearts of most of them were not with us. The little Monitor was lying there, basking in her victory over the huge, ungainly Merrimac; and alongside of her, their yards towering far above her, lay the pride of the old navy, the Wabash, the Colorado, and the Minnesota. Vessels, sail and steam, were coming and going, and the whole harbor was alive with naval and military activity. Nor did it cease when night came on; at all hours you could hear the wharves' deep rumblings, and the suddenly rapid clanking of hoisting engines as ships loaded or discharged their cargoes; while from off in the harbor we could hear the childlike bells on the grim war-vessels striking the deep hours of the night.

It was my first acquaintance with the sea, and I think I was fortunate in the spot where I gained my first impressions of it. For never yet have I stood on a beach where the water, rocking in long, regular beats, as if listening to music in its dreams, spread away in such mild union with the clouds and sunshine.

The Army of the Potomac, whose fortunes I was to share on many a field, had just been through the fierce battles of Fair Oaks, Gaines's Mill, Glendale (or Frayser's Farm as it is called by the Confederates), and Malvern Hill. In these desperate engagements it had been driven from the Chickahominy, and was then huddled around Harrison's Landing on the north bank of the James, about twenty-five miles below Richmond. The army had suffered terribly in this campaign, known as that of the Peninsula; but the government, though cast down and sorely disappointed at the outcome, immediately responded with vigor to its needs, and the river and Hampton Roads were lined day and night with transports taking supplies of all kinds to it, and bringing back the sick and wounded, of whom there were very, very many. Its commander was McClellan, perhaps the war's greatest marvel as an example of personal magnetism, and one of Fortune's dearest children; yet one who, when Victory again and again poised, ready to light on his banner, failed to give the decisive blow. The authorities at Washington, never quite satisfied with McClellan and never confident that he would win, harbored, I am satisfied, a political dread of him should success attend him; and now, finding him cooped up at Harrison's Landing, organized an army to operate between Washington and Richmond, and had assigned to its command that really able and much abused soldier, John Pope, thereby hoping to get rid of McClellan.

When Pope's army on the upper Rappahannock was threatened with overthrow, the Army of the Potomac was recalled to Washington. It marched down the Peninsula to Old Point Comfort, where transports had been gathered to meet it. During that time McClellan and his staff were at our officers' mess for several days, and on one occasion I lunched almost alone with him. So sweet and winsome was he, that I ever after was one of his sympathetic and ardent admirers. Later on I served with Hooker, Burnside, Meade, and Grant, each of whom in turn followed him at the head of the Army of the Potomac; but were that old army to rise from its tomb, not one of them would call out such cheers as those which would break when "Little Mac," as it loved to call him, should appear. He was a short, compact, square-shouldered, round-bodied man, with a low forehead and heavily wrinkled brow.

It took three or four days to embark the troops, and meanwhile I visited the camps of many of my West Point friends, and for the first time heard the trumpets of the dear old army. At last they were all aboard, and I watched them heading off up the Chesapeake and longed to go with them, with my friends of cadet days, Custer, Cushing, Woodruff, Bowen, Kirby, Dimick, and others, — all of whose cheery, young faces seemed to diffuse the very air of glory, while the colors of Regulars and Volunteers seemed to beckon me to follow as they were borne away.

The Army of the Potomac had come to be recognized at home and abroad as the country's chief safeguard, the one firm barrier to be relied upon to hold

Washington. For, the National Capital once in the hands of the Confederates, the cause of the Union would be irretrievably lost. None saw this fact clearer than the cold-eyed commercial power of the North, yet whose heart throbbed with the common love of the country's ideals. So, all over the North, and especially in the region east of the Alleghanies where the most of its rank and file were reared, the people were proud of the Army of the Potomac; and at sunrise and sunset, and around every fireside, offered their prayers for it. Fearful indeed had been, and were to be, its trials. It had lost much blood, but the people knew that it was ready to lose still more before it would yield to a truce or ignominious peace.

From the parapets of Fortress Monroe I saw that army move away. It soon met its old antagonist, the Army of Northern Virginia, the flower of the Southern armies, on the field of Manassas, and then, just as autumn's golden glow began to haze the fields, at Antietam; and at last under Burnside in the short, cold days of December, it made its frightful assault on Lee's entrenchments along Marye's Heights, back of Fredericksburg. It never showed greater valor, and its losses were sickening. The army wintered on the Rappahannock, opposite Fredericksburg, and in sight of the lines it had vainly tried to carry.

Now and then I heard from my friends with the army, and day after day continued my duties in the shops, or testing big guns on the beach, wondering if the war would be over before I should see any active service in the field. Thus winter was passed and spring came — and nowhere does her face wear such a smile as at Old Point. The last of the migrating birds had gone over us, the days were lengthening, and I knew that the army would soon be moving again, and longed more and more to be with it. But my wonder and longing were soon to end.

On April 16, Captain Baylor called me into the office, and with a smile handed me the following: —

WAR DEPARTMENT,
ADJUTANT-GENERAL'S OFFICE,
WASHINGTON, *April* 15, 1863.

Special Orders No. 173

24. First Lieut. Morris Schaff, Ordnance Department, is hereby assigned to duty with the Army of the Potomac, and will report in person without delay to Major-General Hooker, Commanding.

By Order of the Secretary of War,
E. D. TOWNSEND,
Assistant Adjutant-General.

Great was my delight! I was in my twenty-second year, and what a mere, undeveloped boy! I bade good-by to Captain and Mrs. Baylor, and I never think of them without the tenderest emotion. He and a little group of friends, — in those days, as now, I made friends slowly, — all of whom were my seniors, went with me to the boat, and soon I was on my way.

8 THE BATTLE OF THE WILDERNESS

Hooker's headquarters were at the Phillips house on one of the hills known as the hills of Stafford, which shoulder up in array along the north bank of the Rappahannock. On reporting to him I was assigned as assistant to his chief of Ordnance, the big-hearted Captain D. W. Flagler (with whom I had been at West Point for three years), thereby becoming a part of the headquarters-staff of the army. I never saw Hooker's equal in soldierly appearance; moreover, there was a certain air of promise about him, — at least so he impressed me, — as he came riding up to headquarters just after I got there. His plans were made, and he was almost ready to move.

A few days after I had reported, he sent for Flagler, and gave him orders to have a supply of ammunition at the White House on the Pamunkey, which, as every one knows, is not far from Richmond, remarking that he had Lee's army in his grasp, and could crush it like *that*, — closing his hand firmly. When Flagler came back to the tent, and told me what the general had said, the big fellow smiled; and, in the light of what happened, well he might: for within a few weeks, at Chancellorsville (lying just within the eastern border of the Wilderness), Hooker met a crushing defeat, and his laurels, like those of his predecessors, McClellan, Burnside, and Pope, were permanently blasted.

The outlook from our headquarters, a truly venerable Virginia manor-house, was commanding and

THE BATTLE OF THE WILDERNESS

interesting. Before it, on the other side of the river, and dreaming of its historic past, lay the old colonial town of Fredericksburg, in whose graveyard Washington's mother is buried. At the foot of the hill was the Rappahannock, bearing on peacefully between its willow-fringed banks, the Confederate pickets on one, and ours on the other in open view. Starting at the river side is a plain running off level as a floor, nearly a mile, to a line of low encircling hills known as Marye's Heights. Fences, stone walls, and sunken roads mark the slopes of these hills, and on December 13, 1863, the ground in front of them was blue, but not with autumn's last blooming flower, the gentian, but with our dead. Back of the hills were fringes of timber, and then the rim of the bending sky. There lay Lee's intrepid army, under the command of Longstreet, Hill, and Stonewall Jackson. The view had a pensive charm for me, and I could look at it hour after hour.

At last all was ready, and Hooker, masked by the woods, moved up the river, crossed, and entered the Wilderness with boldness. He no sooner breathed its air than he lost all vigor, became dazed, and at Chancellorsville met his fate. In this savage encounter three of my young friends were either killed or mortally wounded: Marsh, Kirby, and Dimick.

It will be remembered that Stonewall Jackson, conceded by friend and foe to be the ablest and most formidable corps commander of modern times, lost his life by a volley from his own men at this battle of Chancellorsville, when on the very verge of delivering what might have proved a mortal blow to the Army of the Potomac. As the circumstances of this event, so momentous to the Confederacy, repeated themselves with startling fidelity just a year later on the same road, and not two miles away, in the battle of the Wilderness, stopping again, but this time for good and all, Lee's hour-hand of victory, there is established a mysteriously intimate and dramatic relation between the two battles, which will be revealed in its entire significance, I hope, as the narrative makes its way. On the day Stonewall was buried the bells of Fredericksburg tolled sadly, and across the river came to us the plaintive strains of their bands playing dirges.

After Chancellorsville the defeated army staggered back to its old encampments, and the writer returned to the ordnance depot at Aquia Creek. There I saw Abraham Lincoln for the first and only time. He was seated in an ordinary, empty freight-car, on a stout plank supported at each end by a cracker-box. Halleck, in undress uniform, was on his left, a big man with baggy cheeks and pop eyes. Mr. Lincoln was gazing off over the heads of the staring groups of soldiers and laborers white and black, to the silent, timbered Virginia shore of the Potomac. He seemed utterly unconscious of all who had gathered about him. He was on his way to Hooker's headquarters, and looked, and doubtless felt, sad enough. The world knows his features well. Plainer or more unpredictive externals nature never spread over the genius to govern; but then she put in his breast as kind and lyric a heart as ever beat.

Elated by his victory and urged on by the state of the Confederacy's resources and his natural inclination for the offensive, Lee, within a month, began the movements toward the upper Potomac which culminated in the battle at Gettysburg, where for a time I remained, collecting the arms that were left on the field. I little dreamed then, as I rode and walked over that famous field, what an epoch it marked in the history of the war. Through the vast amount that has been written about the battle, and the devoted spirit in which the field has been preserved, and the services of those who fell commemorated, an impression prevails that the fate of the Confederacy was sealed that day, — an impression which a comprehensive view of the situation will, I believe, challenge if not remove. Let me state the grounds of my disbelief, and, if they do not convince, they may at least serve as a background for the narrative, aiding us to weigh the issues hanging on the campaign of 1864.

When Grant was brought on from the West, and took virtual command of the Army of the Potomac, in the spring after Gettysburg, the war had been raging for three years. First and last, the North had put into the field rising two million men; and, although important victories, such as Vicksburg, Gettysburg, and Missionary Ridge, had been won, and obviously the North had had the best of it, yet there is no gainsaying that her condition was perilous and her disappointments great. She had hoped and had sincerely believed that long ere that time she would have put down the Rebellion, and keenly she felt the sneers of the old world as she struggled for existence. But, notwithstanding her supreme efforts, the South was in some respects closer knit than ever, and far from being conquered.

And now, at the end of three years of desperate war, she was staggering under a mighty debt, the Confederate cruisers had driven her commerce from the sea, volunteering, which had begun spontaneously and with burning enthusiasm, had stopped, and the administration had been forced to resort to the draft. Successive defeats had bred factions within and without the cabinet, — factions made up of governors, editors, and senators, all secretly denouncing Mr. Lincoln and his administration, and actively plotting to defeat him at the forthcoming convention.

To make matters worse, the government, fretted by repeated reverses, had become more and more irritable, and, as was natural with the continuance of the war, more and more arbitrary. Those in official life who criticised its policies were turned upon fiercely; the press, never an easy friend or foe to deal with in time of peril, was threatened with muzzling, and some papers were actually suppressed, and their proprietors imprisoned; the provost-marshals, of necessity invested with wide but delicate military authority, often became despotic in their arrests, and almost habitually haughty in parading of their office, — their haughtiness aggravated by ignorance, vanity, and bad manners. Under it all, discontent had grown and spread, until, by the time the campaign of 1864 was ready to open, in the states bordering on the Ohio there was a secret organization said to have had over four hundred thousand members, a coagulation of all phases of political hatred and tainted loyalty, only waiting for a substantial defeat of the Union army to break out into an open demand for an armistice, which, of course, meant the recognition of the South.

As a proof of the depth and reality of this overhanging danger, see the action of some of the courts, and the attempt of the legislature of Indiana to transfer the control of the state's arsenal, with its eighteen thousand arms, — directly, to be sure, to three trustees, but in the end to that ostensibly peace-seeking yet practically traitorous organization. Meantime throughout the North patriotism was smothering under the bitterness of faction, and the blighting evil of indifference to the country's glory, an indifference that nurses always at the breast of commercial prosperity. At the same time corruption in official life, and dissipation in various forms, ran riot and made their way, undermining civic morals and manly virtues. Never were gambling-houses so common, low theatres so crowded, streets gayer, or the rotundas of hotels and the richly furnished rooms of fashionable clubs more frequented by young, able-bodied, well-dressed "high rollers" and champagne-drinkers. Yet, let the sound of a drum be heard in the street at the head of some returning body of veterans,—whom not one of them had had the courage or manliness to join in defense of the country,—and lo! up would go the windows of the clubs, and they and the balconies of every hotel would be filled with cheering men.

This being the state of affairs, let us suppose that Lee, at the outset of the campaign of 1864, had defeated the Army of the Potomac decisively, and had driven Grant back across the Rappahannock, as he had driven Burnside, Pope, and Hooker, — how loud and almost irresistible would have been the cry for an armistice, supported (as it would have been) by Wall Street and all Europe! Where, then, would have been the victory of Gettysburg? In view of the disparity of numbers and the depleted resources of the Confederacy, was it possible for Lee to have given such a blow? Yes, and had not Fate registered her decree that at the critical moment Longstreet was to fall in the Wilderness as Jackson had fallen at

THE BATTLE OF THE WILDERNESS

Chancellorsville, he would have come near doing so. And so, great as was the victory at Gettysburg, I am not at all convinced that it was decisive, remembering, as I do, how the balance trembled more than once in the campaign from the Rapidan.

But, however this may be, it must not be forgotten that, counterbalancing the incongruous gayety and dissipation that prevailed in our large cities, the dying down of early ardor, and the disloyal hives that were ready to swarm, there were thousands of pure, high-minded, resolute men and women who remained faithful to their ideals and kept the national spirit alive; who, in sunshine and shadow, for the glory of the country and their generation, upheld Mr. Lincoln's hands and stood by him to the last most loyally. Neither defeat, pleas for peace, nor desire for ease prevailed against their heaven-inspired and steel-hardened determination to fight the Confederacy to an end; and on them and the army in the field, I think, the honors of carrying the country through its perils should fall.

It is true, and for the sake of history it should be recorded, that while a great majority of those steadfast, loyal people of the North had felt that slavery was wrong and altogether out of harmony with civilization and the spirit of a free government, yet in the beginning of the war they had no desire or intent to interfere with it in the states; so dear were the memories of the Revolution, and so deep their reverence for Washington and his fellow slave-holding compatriots who had joined Puritan New England in establishing the independence of the colonies. Moreover, and notwithstanding those galling irritations which always attend the concession of social and political dominance, the North had not inherited any active hates or vindictiveness, although it had felt deeply of late the repeated scorn and increasing arrogance of the political leaders of the South, manifested in the discussion of slavery that had been going on for twenty or thirty years. It is needless to say that the language in Congress grew more and more heated, or that it was marked more and more by asperity of criticism and ugliness of temper and insolence of bearing. Neither side was fair in judging the convictions or the situation of the other. The Disunionist was blind to the inevitable wreck of all that was dear in social and political life if he destroyed the Union; the Abolitionist was blind, utterly blind, to the immediate and lasting evils of having his way with slavery.

So it went on, till at last, burning with a raging fever over the John Brown raid, and lashed by a savage press, the South burst into delirium upon the election of Lincoln, and madly and vauntingly fired on the flag, that rippled out in joyful peace with every breeze that blew over Sumter. The arrogant leaders of the South meant that shot for a stinging challenge, and it was so understood. Every beech and maple and strong-limbed oak in the North, every one of her hills and streams, every one of the old fields and the liberty-enjoying winds that swept them, said, "Accept the challenge! Go, Northerners, go and assert your manhood!" But, Southerners! let me tell you that as they passed down the walks of the old home dooryards and out of the gates, followed by eyes that were dimmed with tears, the evils or the abolition of slavery did not enter the mind of one in a thousand. Their country and their honor were at stake, not the destruction of slavery. So it was generally, far and wide among the great body of the people.

But with the progress of the war, and under the severe defeats of one army after another, as the South, out of the depths of her resolution, struck again and again, the belief took root that God would not bless their arms while slavery had a recognized legal existence; and inasmuch as it became obvious that its death would be at the same hour as that of the Confederacy, the influence of long-accepted legal defense and the golden ties of friendship melted before the warmth of moral and patriotic emotion. As a result, Lincoln, sensitive in a marvelous degree to what was going on deep in the hearts of the common people, carved emancipation across the sky of those solemn days, and the army that had left home without pronounced feeling against slavery said, "Amen!" And, what is more, "Amen!" said all the civilized world.

There was also, coincident with this change, which

in a sense was political, another in the army, which was spiritual. Gradually, for in the divine ordering of progress consecrating spirits reveal themselves slowly, the consciousness broke at last on the minds of officers and men that the dearest hopes of mankind were appealing to them individually in the name of duty and honor and all that was sacred, not to despair or to yield, come weal, come woe, till the country's supremacy was unchallenged, and the way cleared for her future. Of nothing am I surer than of this visitation and the consequent serious, deep, and exalted mood; and I am fain to believe that every drop of blood that strained through a heart that listened to these spiritual heralds and welcomed the vow, was permanently heightened in its color. When we realize how meagre had been the advantages among the rank and file, and how generally humble and obscure their homes, the marvel grows, and our hands reach instinctively for garlands for every one of them who gave up his life or who bore his part manfully.

Now, a word as to the South. If the disappointments of the North over the outcome of three years of war had been deep, those of the South had been deeper. So sure was she of the poltroonery of the North, and the indomitable courage of her own sons, that she had expected at the beginning to achieve her independence long, long ere the date of the campaign of May 1, 1864. In fact, thousands and thou-

THE BATTLE OF THE WILDERNESS 19

sands of her soldiers believed, as they set off in the spring of '61 for the Potomac and the Ohio, that the southern banks of these beautiful rivers were to be the northern boundaries of their proud and victorious Confederacy; and this before the cotton, then ready to branch, should all be picked. But there had been Gaines's Mill, Malvern Hill, Antietam, and Gettysburg in the east; Shiloh, Missionary Ridge, Stone's River, and Vicksburg, in the west. No, they did not get back in time to see the cotton picked; many of them were never to see it bloom again. Year after year they had followed the drum, and were still far from home fighting for their wan, unacknowledged Confederacy, or sleeping in their graves.

There is pathos in the contrast, as we think of them walking their sentry-posts to and fro, half-fed and half-clothed, now under drenching rains, now shivering under northern winds, their hearts beating low, — so completely had the scene shifted and their hopes vanished. And what surprises they had had, too! Where was the evidence of that poltroonery in their enemies that they were so sure of? Lo, as when the heavens at night are troubled, and lightning from some black cloud flashes as from a suddenly opened furnace door, revealing to us across a field a wood standing resolute in burnished glory, so in the light of their own volleys again and again they had seen the North. More than once, also, they had witnessed Northern courage, as when the volunteers came on at Fort Donelson and Fredericksburg, leaving the ground they passed over blue with dead. No, they had discovered that there was steel and iron in the Northern blood when it came to battling for their self-respect and a cause which they believed to be holy.

Again, when the Confederacy was launched at Montgomery, the South had the keen pleasure of seeing it hailed by several of the governments of Europe as a coming sister in the family of nations. While in buoyant self-confidence she was sure that all of them would recognize her sooner or later, yet it was her chief expectation and desire that England, with whose landed aristocracy the slave-holders had made themselves believe there was a natural sympathy, would be the first to reach out a welcoming hand. But days, months, and years had passed, and no hand had been extended. On the contrary, either through fear or interest, all, including England, had yielded to the demands of her despised adversary and drawn the mantle of neutrality closely around them. Before the first day of May, 1864, she had seen through the sarcasm and mockery of their greeting smiles. The situation was humiliating to the last degree. Moreover, the North had driven the Southern armies back from the Potomac and the Ohio, it had wrested from them the control of the Mississippi Valley, and had overrun and desolated a great share of their home-country.

THE BATTLE OF THE WILDERNESS

In addition, the Confederacy's financial system, to their distress and mortification, had broken down completely, and about all their ports had been sealed up, thus cutting them off from both military and hospital supplies, and — at the time with which this narrative is dealing — humanity's pleading cry from their hospitals was heard day and night. They had the means neither to succor their own sick and wounded, nor to discharge their duties to the prisoners they held. The luxuries, too, once so abundant and so hospitably shared, were all gone; rich and poor were living from day to day on the plainest food. As in the case of the North, the high wave of volunteering for service in the field had passed, and the conscripting officer had become a visitor at every door, no matter how secluded in the woods or remote in the mountains the home might be. At his first visit he called for the boys of eighteen and the men up to forty-five. Later he came again, and demanded this time the boy of seventeen and the man of fifty. Northern men, who after engagements went over the fields where the Southern dead lay, will recall the young faces and the venerable gray hairs among the fallen. I saw a boy with a sweet face, who could not have been over sixteen or seventeen years old, lying on his back in a clover-field on the Beverly farm, within sight of Spotsylvania. He had just been killed. We had had two or three days of heavy rains, but that morning it had cleared off smilingly. Only a few drifting white clouds were left, and I am sure that they and the door of Heaven opened tenderly for his spirit as it mounted from the blooming clover. Well, so it was, — the boys and all the old men had been gleaned.

While these bitter experiences and disappointments were following one another year after year with their deepening gloom, a profound seriousness, which is reflected, I think, in the prayers, sermons, and diaries of the time, spread over the entire South. As a result, the war's passions and the grounds of its justification underwent a progressive metamorphosis in the minds and hearts of the Southern people, and especially of its armies, not unlike that which was going on simultaneously in the North. I sometimes think that a history of the Rebellion cannot be full, just, or truly enlightening, that does not try to give us as close and real a view as it can of these spiritual changes. In the case of the South, it accounts, or so it seems to me, for two very impressive things, namely, the gallantry with which Lee's army battled on, when the chance of success was almost hopeless; and the dearness of the memory of the Confederacy to all of them, notwithstanding that they see now, as we all see, that it was best that it should fail.

This change in the temper of the South in regard to the war and its issues embodied itself finally, as in the North, in a spirit of consecration. And to what? Her ports closed, her resources nearly exhausted, her dwindling armies suffering for food and clothing, a wide zone of desolation along her northern border, and unfriended by one of all the nations of the world, the South in her chagrin, humiliation, and despair turned for comfort to mind and heart, as we all do at last, invoking the guidance and help of her naturally religious better nature. In that solemn hour, banishing from her presence the hitherto baneful companions Arrogance and Disdain, who had caused her to drink of the full stream of trouble, she summoned back that master workman, Judgment, to whom in her delirium she had not listened; and behold, there came with him an immortal youth whose name is The Future. The former, facing the cold realities, pronounced slavery dead, whether the Confederacy lived days or years; and Lincoln's emancipation proclamation, not the decree of one man, but the fiat of the civilized world.

While Judgment's verdict grew weightier and more certain as clearer and clearer became the writing on the wall, the immortal youth slowly drew back one of his curtains, revealing slavery becoming more and more abhorrent as mankind rose in intelligence and gentleness. Honor and Manliness, those two high-minded brothers in the Southerner's character, shrank back at the sight, and declared their unwillingness to leave as the ultimate verdict of history that the Southland, the home of Washington and

Jefferson, had plunged the country into war for the preservation of an institution so repellent. Then up spoke that mighty, but not over-scrupulous advocate called Reason; yet on this occasion he spoke with sincerity unfeigned, saying: —

"If there are wrongs, there are also rights. Mankind knows that we of to-day are not responsible for slavery. It descended to us from our fathers, and through generations it has knit itself into our homes, our social and our political life. We cannot separate ourselves from it at once, if we would, without chaos and possibly universal massacre. But if our slaves are entitled to freedom, then we are entitled to govern ourselves; for that is the first of the heaven-born rights in the hands of freemen. In other words, we are asking only for our natural rights incorporated in the rights of our states, which underlie the foundations of the Union;" — and in majesty before the Southern mind the original sovereignty of the old colonies, with Washington and Adams at the head, passed in review. "No, whatever may have been our delirium at the beginning of the war, we are not fighting for the defense of property in human beings, but for the ineradicable and unconquerable instinct of self-government as states; and for our homes."

And lo! at this point of the argument, the light of their burning homes flashed across the scene; for hardly a day or night passed that somewhere the Southern sky was not lit by them. Whereupon, leader and officer and man in the ranks rose as one, and facing the immortal Youth, in whose eyes lay the question of justification, exclaimed resolutely: "On the ground of the right of self-government we will stand; and committing our souls to God and our memories to those who follow us, let history record what it may as to our justification in the years and days to come." And thus having answered the question in the eyes of The Future, reverently and calmly, they fell on their knees and asked God to bless them. There, reader, we have the spring of their fortitude, and there we touch the tender chords which keep the memory of the Confederacy dear.

And really, friends, sure of the grounds of their construction of the Constitution and in the shadow of the clouds that overhung them, addressed by all the voices of their and our common nature, and moved by those deep currents which flow in every heart, could any other possible conclusion be expected of a proud people? I think not.

And now, having set forth, I trust with fidelity, I know with charity, the state of affairs North and South, as well as I can; and having brought into view, as faithfully and vividly as lies in my power, the spirits which animated both armies, my narrative will go on.

After Gettysburg, Lee, with what must have been a heavy heart, led his sorely wounded army back into Virginia. Then, passing through the upper gaps of the Blue Ridge, he took his stand once more behind the Rappahannock, near whose banks lower down he had played as a boy. Meade followed him, and when I was recalled from Gettysburg and rejoined his headquarters, I found them near Fayetteville, a little hamlet between Bealeton and Warrenton. They were pitched on a rise in a heaving old plantation more or less shadowed by a scattered growth of young pines. I was glad to get back. The month I had passed at Gettysburg, however, was very interesting, and has left many memories, most of them dear to me. But after a battle is over and the army gone, you see the obverse side of glory so plainly that you long to get away from the blood-stained fields, and the ever-speaking loneliness of the shallow graves, to join your young, light-hearted friends around the cheering camp-fires.

A few days after my return an incident took place which I think I should have laughed over whether we had gained a victory at Gettysburg or not. The tent I occupied was nearly opposite that of Colonel Schriver, Inspector-General on the staff. The old Colonel was rather spare, stern, and always neatly arrayed. About church-time, one very sunshiny Sabbath morning, I noticed him walking back and forth before his tent in high and brilliantly polished cavalry boots, with prayer-book in hand, reading his prayers. I thought what a splendid example of a follower of Jesus! and wished that I had the courage to perform my devotions so openly, and acknowledge that while I was a soldier of the Army of the Potomac I was also a soldier of the Cross. Suddenly I heard him call out, "James! *James!!*" James was his strapping young colored boy, and had a very nappy head. I looked up. The Colonel had halted, and his eyes were glaring across his well-defined nose toward James, who, sprawled out and bareheaded, was sunning himself with several other headquarters darkies behind the tent, and had probably gone dead asleep. "What are you up to there, you damned black rascal!" roared the Colonel. "Lift those tent-walls!" James was on his feet with startling rapidity, and dived for the tent-ropes. Up came the prayer-book, out went the Colonel's left foot, and when I saw his lips begin moving again reverently, boylike, I tumbled down on my bed and nearly died laughing. Even now a smile ripples as I recall the scene. Surely, our inconsistencies are a blessing, for they are one of the perpetual fountains of amusement.

The army was occupying the north bank of the Rappahannock, from Kelly's Ford, a few miles below where the Orange and Alexandria Railroad crosses the river, up to Warrenton. It had almost recovered from its severe engagement, and was beginning to realize the magnitude and significance of the victory it had won. That mild and deep joy which a soldier always feels when he has met danger and done his duty was in the hearts of all. Camp was bound to camp, corps to corps, and officer to private, by the ties of a new sense of high fellowship which proved to be abiding. This inspiring relation, the most valuable in an army's life, had been smelted, so to speak, in those three trying days at Gettysburg when cavalry, infantry, and artillery, line-officers, staff-officers, and privates in the ranks had witnessed each other's steady, heroic conduct. And the result of this supreme test of courage was that officers and men of the Army of the Potomac felt that respect for one another and that pride in one another that only a battlefield can create. Whoever will read the story of Gettysburg will gain a notion how and why these ties were formed. Every living veteran who was there will recall Webb, Cushing, Woodruff, Haskell, and Hall; the latter carried as mild a face as graced the West Point battalion in my day. I saw Haskell frequently, and I have no doubt that Duty and Courage visit often, and linger fondly, around the spot where he fell at Cold Harbor.

Allow me to add what I know to be true, that no matter how high or how low may be an officer's rank, no matter where he was educated, what name he bears, what blood may be in his veins, or what wealth at his command, if, when he is going up under fire, mounted or dismounted, a private or non-commissioned officer near him advances beside him with undaunted face, — more than once it was a lad from a farm or humble walk in life, — all the claims of rank, wealth, and station are lost in admiration and sympathetic comradeship. What is more, he never forgets the boy.

In this connection I trust I may refer with propriety to what a member of the Supreme Court of the United States, a learned judge who carries some of the country's best blood, and who spilled some of it on several fields, told me one evening, before a quietly burning wood-fire, of an impression made on him at the Wilderness. In the midst of darkness and widespread panic, veteran regiments and brigades of the Sixth Corps breaking badly, an officer who had only casually gained his attention called out above the din, in a voice of perfect control, "Steady, steady — Massachusetts!" The gallant regiment steadied, and the incident left, as an enduring memory, the cool voice of the obscure officer still ringing across the vanished years.

Nay, we think, in fact we know, that the final test of the soldier is when the colors move forward or the enemy comes on at them. Thank God for all the tender and iron-hearted young fellows who have stood it!

From that camp dates my first deep interest in the unfortunate Warren, for it was there, while messing with him and his fellow engineer-officers on the staff, that I saw him day after day at close range. The glory of having saved Round Top was beginning to break around him, and shortly after, as a reward, Meade assigned him to the command of Hancock's corps, Hancock having been wounded at Gettysburg. But however keen and full may have been his inward joy, the joy of having done his duty, and saved a glorious field, it altered not his bearing, — which was that of the thoughtful, modest scholar rather than the soldier, — nor did it kindle any vanity in look or speech. It may have accounted, however, for the manifestation of what seemed to me a queer sense of humor, namely, his laughing and laughing again while alone in his tent over a small volume of "limericks," the first to appear, as I remember, in this country. He would repeat them at almost every meal, and, I think, with wonder that they did not seem nearly so amusing to others as they did to him. I am satisfied that it takes a transverse kind of humor to enjoy limericks.

There was a note of singular attraction in his voice. His hair, rather long and carried flat across his well-balanced forehead, was as black as I have ever seen. His eyes were small and jet black also, one of them apparently a bit smaller than the other, giving a suggestion of cast in his look. But the striking characteristic was an habitual and noticeably grave expression which harbored in his dusky, sallow face, and instead of lighting, deepened as he rose in fame and command. Now, as I recall his seriousness and almost sympathy-craving look as an instructor at

THE BATTLE OF THE WILDERNESS

West Point, and think over his beclouded, heart-broken end, I never see the name of Five Forks that I do not hear Sheridan peremptorily relieving him just after the victory was won, and while the smoke of battle still hung in the trees. From my youth, I have seen Fate's shadow falling across events, and I incline to believe that evil fortune took up its habitation in that deeply sallow, wistful face long before he or any one else dreamed of the great Rebellion. But, be that as it may, in that sunny field at headquarters of the Army of the Potomac, I gained my first boyhood impressions of Warren, whose sad fate haunts that army's history.

And now, on those soft mountain and valley winds of memory, which always set in when anything pensive warms the heart, are borne the notes of the bugles sounding taps in the camps around us on those long-vanished August nights. Camp after camp takes up the call, some near, some far. The last of the clear, lamenting tones die away sweetly and plaintively in the distance, and back comes the hush of night as of old. Again the sentinels are marching their beats slowly, most of them thinking of home, now and then one, with moistened eyes, of a baby in a cradle. Peace to the ashes of Warren, peace to those of the sentinels of the Army of the Potomac who walked their posts on those gone-by, starry nights.

II

AFTER several abortively offensive movements by each of the armies during the autumn of 1863, they went into winter quarters: Lee, with his army well in hand, on the south bank of the Rapidan; Meade, between the Rapidan and the Rappahannock. The former's headquarters were among some pines and cedars at the foot of Clarke's Mountain, near Orange Court House; the latter's were on a knoll covered with tall young pines about a mile and a half northwest from Brandy Station. The bulk of the army of the Potomac was around Culpeper and Stevensburg; one corps, the Fifth, under Warren, stretched northward along the Orange and Alexandria Railroad—at present the Southern—as far as Calverton; the Sixth was between the railroad and Hazel River, a little tributary of the Rappahannock, the Second around Stevensburg, the First and Third, consolidated before we moved with the other three, were about Culpeper. Lee's principal depot for supplies was at Orange Court House, ours at Brandy, where I passed the greater part of the winter in charge of the ordnance depot.

The town, about midway between Culpeper and the Rappahannock, then had only three or four houses and a one-story, unpainted, lonely sort of a building

THE BATTLE OF THE WILDERNESS 33

for receiving freight. A good deal of military history of interest is connected with Brandy; for in the rolling fields of the plantations about it, Lee, just before setting out for Gettysburg, reviewed Stuart's cavalry, ten to twelve thousand strong. The dew was still on his great victory at Chancellorsville, won in the month before, and the review, according to all accounts, was a pageant, drawing people from far and near. Ladies, young and old, of Culpeper, Charlottesville, and more distant points in Virginia, were there, and around some of the horses' necks, and hanging from the cantles of the saddles, and at the heads of the fluttering guidons, were bouquets and bunches of wild flowers which they had brought with them. They were proud, and justly so, of their sons, brothers, and lovers; and I really believe that the future of the Confederacy never looked so fair to them, or to those at its helm as on that June day.

It will be remembered that in the deep mist of the morning following the review our cavalry crossed the Rappahannock and gave Stuart desperate battle right around Brandy; and it is a matter of history that our mounted force had its baptism on that field. For two years it had been a negligible quantity, and scorned by its enemy; but from then on to the end our cavalry met the enemy sternly, with increasing bravery and effectiveness. The battle lasted nearly all day and was very severe; Buford, Gregg, Custer, Merritt, Kilpatrick, and the lamented Davis, were all there. My tent at the station, pitched after dark and partly floored, I discovered later was over the grave of some one who had fallen in those repeated charges. The other day I wandered over those same fields: cattle and sheep were grazing up the slopes where the squadrons had marched in the June sunshine; killdeers with banded necks and bladed wings, turtle-doves, meadow-larks, and serenely joyous little sparrows were flying and singing where the flags had fluttered and the bugles sounded.

In view of the fact that the bulk of the supplies to meet the daily wants of the army, then consisting of a hundred thousand men, and between forty and fifty thousand animals, were sent to Brandy, it is easy to imagine that it was a very busy place. Of course they all came by rail from Washington and Alexandria. Those for the ordnance, hospital, and clothing departments were put under cover in temporary buildings, while forage, and unperishable quartermaster and commissary stores, were racked up and covered by tarpaulins along the track and sidings. Some of the piles were immense, and from morning till night trains of army wagons were coming and going, or stood occupying all the open space around the station, waiting for their turn to load.

In the history of the Fifth Massachusetts is the following letter from one of the sergeants of the battery. It is dated April 30, 1864.

"The next battle will be a rouser! The rebels of

Lee's army are all ready for us, and are said to be ninety thousand. They will give us a tough pull if my opinion amounts to anything.

"To-day I was up to Brandy Station. You can form no idea of the bustle and confusion at this depot when the army is getting ready to move. It looked to me as if a thousand or more wagons were waiting to load, and there were immense piles of ammunition and all kinds of Ordnance Stores, etc., etc., and piles of boxes of hard bread as high as two and three-story houses. It reminded me some of a wharf in New York with twelve or fifteen ships loading and unloading."

The trains were generally in charge of sergeants, but were often accompanied by their brigade and division officers, so that those of us at the head of depots gained a wide acquaintance throughout the army. Frequently these officers staid with us for dinner; and as my fellow messmate was Dr. J. B. Brinton of Philadelphia, in charge of the medical supplies, and as surgeons, like certain aspiring young lawyers, never cease to talk about their cases, I knew a good many surgeons well, and understood at least a part of their professional lingo.

The wagons were generally drawn by six mules driven by negroes, who rode the nigh wheeler and managed the team by a jerk line to the nigh leader. In these days it may seem like a shiftless way to drive a team, but it worked well, and possibly because the darkies and the mules, through some medium or other, understood each other perfectly; at any rate, the drivers talked to their teams as if they comprehended every word said to them; and sometimes it was worth listening to, when the roads were bad and some of the wagons ahead of them were stuck in the mud. "Calline" (Caroline, the nigh leader), giving her an awakening jerk of the line, "stop dreamin' with dem y'ears o' yourn." "Jer'miah" (Jeremiah, the off wheeler), "you'll think the insex is bit'n you if you don't put dem sholdahs agin dat collah." "Dan'l" (Daniel, the wheeler he is on), giving him a sharp dig in the ribs with his boot-heels, the road getting heavier every minute, "no foolin', you old hahdened sinnah!" "Member, Mrs. N'nias" (Mrs. Ananias, off leader), "if dis yere wagon sticks in dat hole ahead o' you, you'll wish you're down in the dakh grave 'longside dat lie'n husband o' yourn." And, on reaching the worst place in the road, yelling "Yep! Yah!" loud enough to be heard half-way from Washington to Baltimore, every prophet and lady mule in the team knew what to expect if the wagon stuck, and generally the faithful creatures pulled it through.

In one of the teams of the ammunition-trains that came to the depot, there was a little bay mule, the leader, that wore a small and sweetly tinkling sheep-bell. I stroked her silky nose and neck often and was always glad to see her. On the Mine Run campaign,

THE BATTLE OF THE WILDERNESS 37

one of the abortive campaigns referred to above, in December, 1863, while riding from Ely's Ford to Meade's headquarters at Robertson's Tavern on the Orange and Fredericksburg pike, a road which will be mentioned over and over again later, I overtook a long train. My progress by it was necessarily slow, for it was a pitch-dark night and the road narrow and very bad. But when I got near the head of the train I heard the little tinkling bell, and soon was alongside the faithful creature tugging away to the front. It may seem ridiculous, but I felt I had met a friend, and rode by her side for quite a while. I do not remember seeing her again till the army was crossing the James near Fort Powhatan.

While I do not wish to encumber the narrative with a burden of figures, yet it may interest the reader to know that we had in the Army of the Potomac, the morning we set off on the great campaign, 4300 wagons and 835 ambulances. There were 34,981 artillery, cavalry, and ambulance horses, and 22,528 mules, making an aggregate of 57,509 animals. The strength of the Army of the Potomac was between ninety-nine and one hundred thousand men. Burnside, who caught up with us the second day of the Wilderness, brought with him about twenty thousand more.

My original telegraph book, now before me, shows that I called for and issued between April 4 and May 2, the day before we moved, in addition to equipments and supplies of all kinds for infantry, artillery and cavalry, 2,325,000 rounds of musket and pistol cartridges as a reserve for what was already on hand. When Sheridan returned from his Trevilian raid and battle, we then had gone as far on our way toward Richmond as the White House, Mrs. Washington's attractive old home on the Pamunkey. At the mention of the memorable place, back comes the odor of mint being brewed in a julep, mint gathered in the famous war-stricken garden; and back come also a squad of dust-covered soldiers removing tenderly the bodies of their gallant commanders, Porter and Morris, killed at Cold Harbor, from ambulances, and bearing them aboard the boat for home. While at White House I ordered 88,600 rounds of pistol and carbine ammunition for Sheridan's command alone. When we reached City Point a few days later — the Wilderness, Spotsylvania, and Cold Harbor lay behind us — I called, on one requisition, for 5,863,000 rounds of infantry and 11,000 rounds of artillery ammunition, this 11,000 in addition to a like amount received at White House.

I should be untrue to my memory of Brandy if I did not record my high regard for my messmate through all that long winter of '63 and '64, Dr. J. B. Brinton, an assistant surgeon in the regular army. Transparency in minerals is rare, and always carries a suggestion of refinement; in the characters of men it is supreme, overtopping genius itself. It was Brinton's steady characteristic, and in all the long procession of friends that have blest my way through life I recall no one more humanly real, or who had more natural sweetness, or who cherished better ideals. Moreover, there was a fountain of quiet joyousness about him, too, and I fondly believe that the recording angel has but little in his book against either of us for those winter days and nights. For I know we passed them without envy, hatred, or malice toward any one in the world.

There was an incident in our life at Brandy, connected with Gettysburg, which possibly is worth relating. Batchelder, whose map of the battlefield of Gettysburg is authority, and whom we had fallen in with while we were there, asked to join our mess at Brandy when he came to the army to verify the positions of the various commands. One night, just after we had sat down to dinner, he entered quite tired. "Well," he announced, taking his place at the table, "I have been in the Second Corps to-day, and I believe I have discovered how Joshua made the sun stand still. I first went to —— regiment and had the officers mark on the map the hour of their brigade's position at a certain point. Then I went to —— regiment in the same brigade; they declared positively it was one or two hours earlier or later than that given by the other. So it went on, no two regiments or brigades agreeing, and if I hinted that some of them must certainly be mistaken, they would set me down by saying, with severe dignity, 'We were there, Batchelder, and we ought to know, I guess'; and I made up my mind that it would take a day of at least twenty hours instead of thirteen at Gettysburg to satisfy their accounts. So, when Joshua's captains got around him after the fight and they began to talk it over, the only way under the heavens that he could ever harmonize their statements was to make the sun stand still and give them all a chance." Any one who has ever tried to establish the exact position or hour when anything took place in an engagement will confirm Batchelder's experience; and possibly, if not too orthodox, accept his explanation of Joshua's feat.

My duties called me daily to Meade's headquarters; and when his Chief of Ordnance, John R. Edie of Pennsylvania and of the class ahead of mine at West Point, was away on leave I took his place there permanently. Meade at this time was in his forty-ninth year, and his Gettysburg laurels were green. His face was spare and strong, of the Romanish type, its complexion pallid. His blue eyes were prominent, coldly penetrating and underhung by sweeping lobes that when cares were great and health not good had a rim of purplish hue. His height was well above the average, and his mien that of a soldier, a man of the world, and a scholarly gentleman. He wore a full, but inconspicuous beard, and his originally deep chestnut, but now frosted hair, was soft and inclined to wave on good, easy terms with his conspicuous and speaking forehead. His manners were native and high-bred, but, alas! they reared a barrier around him which cut him off from the love of his army, and I doubt if it would ever have rallied around him had he been relieved and recalled, as it did around McClellan. In social hours, when things were going well, no man in civil or military life would outshine him in genial spirits or contribution of easy and thoughtful suggestive speech.

He had, too, that marvelous instrument, a rich, cultivated voice. But nature had not been altogether partial: she had given him a most irritable temper. I have seen him so cross and ugly that no one dared to speak to him, — in fact, at such times his staff and everybody else at headquarters kept as clear of him as possible. As the campaign progressed, with its frightful carnage and disappointments, his temper grew fiercer — but, save Grant's, everybody's got on edge, and it was not to be wondered at. Nevertheless, Meade was a fine, cultivated, and gallant gentleman, and as long as the victory of Gettysburg appeals to the people he will be remembered gratefully, and proudly too. In camp his military coat, sack in cut, was always open, displaying his well-ordered linen, vest, and necktie; when mounted, he wore a drooping army hat, yellow gauntlets, and rode a bald-faced horse with a fox-walk which kept all in a dog-trot to keep up with him, and on more than one occasion some one of the staff was heard to say, "Damn that horse of Meade's! I wish he would either go faster or slower."

Hancock, who commanded the Second Corps, was, like Hooker, a very handsome, striking-looking man; both were of the military type and looked and moved grandly. He was symmetrically large, with chestnut hair and rather low forehead, but authority was in his open face, which, when times were storming, became the mirror of his bold heart; "so that in battle," says Walker, his distinguished Inspector-General, "where his men could see him, as at Williamsburg and Gettysburg, he lifted them to the level of his impetuous valor. But when he was surrounded by woods and he could not see his enemy, as at Ream's Station and the Wilderness, he was restless and shorn of much of his effectiveness, very unlike the great commander he was as he rode up and down his lines, inspiring them with his electrical energy, until severely wounded, when Pickett was coming on." When he returned to duty I happened to be at Meade's headquarters. Some one observed, "There's Hancock," who was just dismounting. Meade came hurrying out from his quarters, bareheaded and with illuminated face — I can hear his rich-toned voice as he said, "I'm glad to see you again, Hancock," and grasped the latter's outstretched hand with both of his. They had not seen each other since the great day.

Sedgwick, who commanded the Sixth Corps, was stocky, had short, curling chestnut hair, was a bachelor, and spent lots of time playing solitaire. His whole manner breathed of gentleness and sweetness, his soldiers called him Uncle John, and in his broad breast was a boy's heart. I saw him only a few hours before it ceased to beat at Spotsylvania.

Sheridan joined the army just before we moved and so I saw much less of him than of any of the other corps commanders. He was not of delicate fibre. His pictures are excellent, preserving faithfully the animation of his ruddy, square face and large, glowing dark eyes. With his close army associates he threw off rank and fame and made many a night memorable and loud, and Lee's final overthrow is due in great measure to him. He had a genius for war and his name will last long.

Meade's chief of staff was Humphreys, and as so much of the success or failure of an army hangs on that position, a word about him will not be out of place. Moreover, his services were great as a corps commander, for after we got in front of Petersburg, Hancock, on account of his Gettysburg wound, had to give up command, and Meade assigned Humphreys to succeed him at the head of the famous Second Corps. He was a small, bow-legged man, with chopped-off, iron gray moustache; and when he lifted his army hat you saw a rather low forehead, and a shock of iron-gray hair. His blue-gray dauntless eyes threw into his stern face the coldness of hammered steel. I never saw it lit up with joy but once, and that was long after the war, as he met an old classmate at West Point on graduation day. And yet off duty, by his simple manners, unfailing in their courtesy, and his clear, easy, and informing talk, he bound friends and strangers to him closely. Look at him well: you are gazing at a hero, one who has the austere charm of dignity and a well-stored mind. Like a knight of old, Humphreys led his division against the heights of Fredericksburg; and at Gettysburg, on the second day, he was only driven from the Emmitsburgh road salient after a most desperate defense, probably saving the line. He graduated in the class of 1831, Meade in that of 1835.

And now I come to two men on Meade's staff whose names like daisies in a meadow dot the history of the Army of the Potomac: Seth Williams, who was the Adjutant-General, and General Henry J. Hunt, Chief of Artillery. To set them forth so that the reader would see them and know them as they were, would give me keen pleasure, for there never was a sweeter-tempered or kindlier heart than Williams's, or a braver one than Hunt's. Williams's hair was red, his face full, open and generous, and always lit up as if there were a harp playing in his breast. At Appomattox, when Lee was going through the trying ordeal of surrendering his army, the only one of all in the room whom he greeted with anything like cordiality was Williams; for all others his face wore its native dignity. Williams was from Maine, and had been Lee's adjutant at West Point when he was superintendent.

Hunt, the chief of artillery, whose complexion was about the color of an old drum-head, had rather dull black eyes, separated by a thin nose. His West Point classmates loved him, and called him "Cupid." He was lion-hearted, and had won brevet on brevet for gallant conduct. At Gettysburg it was Hunt, riding through the storm, who brought up the fresh batteries and put them into action at the critical moment of Pickett's charge. Both he and Williams have long since made their bed in the grave.

There is a great temptation to dwell on other members of the staff. On Ingalls, the chief quartermaster, a classmate of Grant's: a chunky, oracular-looking man who carried sedulously a wisp of long hair up over his otherwise balding pate, and who, besides being the best quartermaster the war produced, could hold his own very well with the best poker players in the army or Congress, and in those days there were some very good ones in both Senate and House. On McParlin, the head of the medical department, Duane, the chief engineer, Michler, Mendell, and Theodore Lyman of Boston, of Meade's staff. All were my seniors, and their character and services I remember with veneration. Especially would I love to dwell on those who were about my own age, not one of us over twenty-five, mere boys as it were: Sanders, Bache, Bates, Edie, Cadwalader, Biddle, Pease, and handsome George Meade, with whom I passed many a pleasant hour. So far as our services or personalities had significance, we were like the little feathery clouds which sometimes fringe great ones as they bear steadily on. And, truly like them, we have melted away. The big clouds, on the other hand, that we accompanied, at more or less distance, with such light hearts, Grant and Meade, are lying richly banded low down across the glowing sunset sky of History. When I visited the knoll, a few weeks ago, where Meade had his headquarters, and where we all passed a happy winter, — it is now bare, clothed only in grass, with here and there an apple tree or a locust in bloom, that have taken the places of the young pines, — I thought of them all. It is needless to say that the scene from the old camp offered its contrasts. Where desolation had brooded, clover was blooming; in the fields where the bleaching bones of cattle, horses, and mules, had stippled the twilight, the plough was upturning the rich red earth with its sweet, fresh breath of promise. In short, the choral songs of Peace and Home had replaced the dirges which underlie the march of glory.

Grant had his headquarters in the Barbour house in Culpeper, now the site of the county jail. At this time he was in his forty-second year, having gradu-

THE BATTLE OF THE WILDERNESS 47

ated at West Point in 1843. I am not vain enough to think that anything I may say will add to the world's knowledge of him. Several of his personal aides, and many admirers, have written books about him which like sconces throw their beams on his personality and remarkable career, but neither they as friends or the predacious critics who have driven their beaks fiercely into him, have yet revealed to me the source of the fascinating mystery in his greatness.

When he came to the Army of the Potomac — I remember the day well — I never was more surprised in my life. I had expected to see quite another type of man: one of the chieftain-type, surveying the world with dominant, inveterate eyes and a certain detached military loftiness. But behold, what did I see? A medium-sized, mild, unobtrusive, inconspicuously dressed, modest and naturally silent man. He had a low, gently vibrant voice and steady, thoughtful, softly blue eyes. Not a hint of self-consciousness, impatience, or restlessness, either of mind or body; on the contrary, the centre of a pervasive quiet which seemed to be conveyed to every one around him — even the orderlies all through the campaign were obviously at their ease. I often looked at him as I might have looked at any mystery, as day after day I saw him at his headquarters, especially after we had reached City Point, — the Wilderness, Spotsylvania, and Cold Harbor, with their frightful losses, lying behind us.

There was nothing in his manner or his tone or his face that indicated that he had ever had anything to do with the victories of Fort Donelson, Vicksburg, and Missionary Ridge, or that his unfinished task, so momentous for the country, troubled him. There was certainly something evoking about him. What of the earth, earthy, what of exceeding greatness, what dim constellation of virtues, were looking out of that imperturbable but sadly earnest face? At one time, and not long before the period dealt with, lean Want had sat at his table. Few tried companions frequented his door or cheered his fireside then. The war comes on, the spirit of the age, as I believe, in the guise of Opportunity knocks at his door, and without powerful friends to back him, and with no social or political influence to clear the way for him, in less than four years, never courting advancement, never resenting malevolent criticism or ill treatment, tempted always, there he was aloft in the country's eye the winner of its telling victories, a Lieutenant-General in command of all the armies of the North, and with the destiny of the Republic hanging on him! Has Genius ever shown her transcendency more masterfully?

It is needless for me to add that, marvelous as this career had been, the future was to unfold it, rising far above the level of wonder. If his antagonist Lee be the culmination of the gentleman and soldier of our land, and of all lands, Grant made the splendor

THE BATTLE OF THE WILDERNESS 49

of his background for him by putting into the hitherto hard face of war two humanizing features, chivalry's posies so fragrant with glory, magnanimity and modesty in the hour of Victory.

There was one man on Grant's staff whose name should not be forgotten; in fact, it ought to be carved on every monument erected to Grant, for it was through him, Colonel John F. Rawlins, his chief of staff, that Grant's good angel reached him her steadying and uplifting hand. He was above medium size, wore a long black beard, and talked in a loud, emphatic voice. Sincerity and earnestness was the look of his face.

He had on his staff three of my West Point acquaintances, Comstock, Babcock, and Porter. Comstock had been one of the instructors in mathematics; Babcock and Porter had been in the corps with me. Captain Hudson of his staff I have good reason for remembering; for I was playing "seven-up," with him and the late Admiral Clitz of the navy, when my ordnance depot at City Point was blown up by a torpedo brought down from Richmond, and placed by a couple of daring Confederates clothed in our uniform on the deck of a barge loaded with artillery ammunition. Our innocent game was going on in the tent of Captain Mason, who commanded Grant's escort. First came the explosion of the depot, that shook the earth and was felt for miles; then a solid shot tore through the mess chest. I doubt if a game of cards ever ended quicker than that one. We fairly flew from the tent, and at once came under a shower of bursting shells and falling wreckage. One of the barge's old ribs, that must have weighed at least a ton, dropped right in front of Clitz. Changing his course, he uttered only one remark, the first half of the 35th verse of the 11th chapter of the Holy Gospel of Saint John. Then, with eyes on the ground, and wondering, I suspect, what would come next, he passed at great speed right by Grant, who in his usually calm voice asked, "Where are you going, Clitz?" The admiral hove to, and then streaked it for his war vessel, and we never finished the game.

The youngest and nearest my own age on Grant's staff was "Billy" Dunn, one of the best and truest friends I ever had. He had reddish hair and naturally smiling eyes, and died not long after the war. Peace, peace be on the spot where the brave and sweet-hearted fellow sleeps!

The looming gravity of the situation North and South, which I have tried to depict, left no doubt, I think, in the minds of Grant and Lee, that the coming campaign called on Lee to give Grant a crushing defeat at the very outset of the campaign; or at least a blow that would send him reeling back across the Rapidan, leaving him stunned and helpless for months, as Burnside and Hooker had been left before him. For he knew, and every observer of the times knew, that such a defeat would give to the dastard Peace Party, on whom the last hope of the Confederacy hung, immediate and bold encouragement to declare "the War a failure," and at the coming presidential election, Lincoln's administration, pledged to its continuance, would be swept away. In that case, every leader and private in the Confederate Army knew that, once their inwardly despised friends got hold of the helm, under the cowardly cloak of humanity they would ask for an armistice. That granted, the goal would be reached and their weary Confederacy, weighted down with slavery, would be at rest. The children of the leaders of the Peace Party of the North ought to thank God for balking their fathers' incipient treason; for where would their present pride of country be? The last hopes then of reaching a harbor called on Lee for a victory; our country's destiny on Grant, for the complete destruction of Lee's army; for until then there could be no peace with safety and honor.

Little would it avail or does it seem necessary for me to discuss the military problem that confronted these two great Captains. What they might have done by throwing their armies this way and that I'll leave to the bass-drum wisdom of theoretical strategists. The moves they made were determined primarily, as in all campaigns, by the natural features of the country, the safety and facility of obtaining supplies, and the exigencies of their respective governments.

As has been said, Grant's and Lee's armies were on the Orange and Alexandria, now the Southern, Railroad. Each was about the same distance from his capital, whose capture meant in either case the end of the war. The Confederacy would have its place among nations if Lee took Washington, its death beyond resurrection if Grant took Richmond. Grant's headquarters at Culpeper were about sixty miles southwest from Washington; Lee's at Orange Court House, sixteen or eighteen miles farther south, were in the vicinity of seventy miles northwest from Richmond; in geometrical terms, the armies were at the apex of a flat isosceles triangle, its base a line running almost due north and south from Washington to Richmond. Twenty-odd miles to the west, beyond the camps of both armies, rose in matchless splendor the azure sky-line of the Blue Ridge, behind which lies the Valley of the Shenandoah, Lee's gateway for his two invasions of the North, and availed of by him for repeated strategical movements whereby he forced the Army of the Potomac to fall back for the safety of Washington. We all see now that a point convenient to the Baltimore and Ohio road at the foot of the valley should have been fortified, garrisoned, and guarded as tenaciously as Washington itself.

Down from this beautiful range come the Rappahannock and the Rapidan, — rivers whose names we shall repeat so often, — which, after flowing through

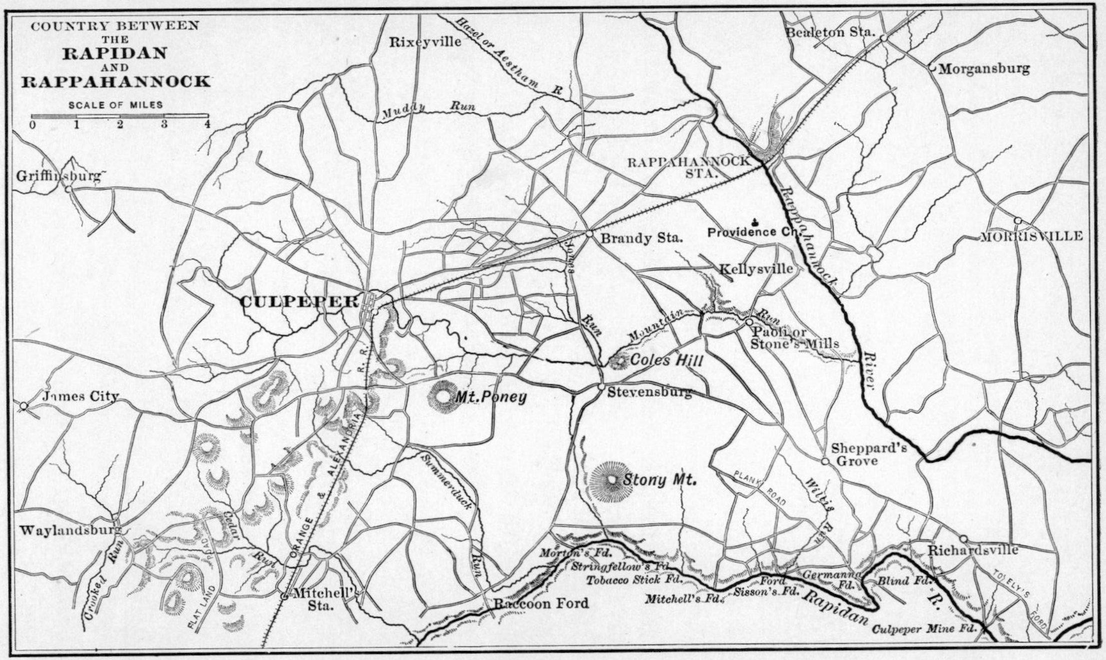
COUNTRY BETWEEN
THE
RAPIDAN
AND
RAPPAHANNOCK
SCALE OF MILES
0 1 2 3 4
Rixeyville
Hazel or Aestham R.
Muddy Run
Bealeton Sta.
Morgansburg
Griffinsburg
RAPPAHANNOCK STA.
Rappahannock River
MORRISVILLE
Brandy Sta.
Providence Ch.
Jones Run
Kellysville
CULPEPER
Mountain Run
Paoli or Stone's Mills
Coles Hill
R. R.
James City
Mt. Poney
Stevensburg
Sheppard's Grove
Stony Mt.
PLANK ROAD
Wilkis Run
ORANGE & ALEXANDRIA
Summerduck Run
Waylandsburg
Cedar Run
Crooked Run
FLAT LAND ROAD
Mitchell's Sta.
Raccoon Ford
Morton's Fd.
Stringfellow's Fd.
Tobacco Stick Fd.
Mitchell's Fd.
Sisson's Fd.
Ford
Germanna Fd.
Blind Fd.
Rapidan R.
Richardsville
TO ELY'S FORD
Culpeper Mine Fd.

THE BATTLE OF THE WILDERNESS 53

many an oak and chestnut wood and by many a smiling plantation, meet in the northern belt of the Wilderness, about twenty miles as the crow flies east of Culpeper, and nearly the same distance west of Fredericksburg. These rivers, the Rappahannock somewhat the larger, the Rapidan the faster, hold rich secrets of the struggle, for many a night the armies camped on their banks, and many a time crossed and recrossed them, sometimes in victory, and after Fredericksburg and Chancellorsville in dismal defeat. And now that I speak of them, I see them flowing in their willow-fringed channels and I hear their low musical tongues once more.

The country through which they run, and our corps' camps during the winter of 1863–4, can best be seen from the top of Mt. Pony, a wooded detached foothill of the Blue Ridge, that rises abruptly near Culpeper. From its top, looking north, the railroad is seen bearing on from the Rappahannock, through an undulating farming section, that is green and lovely: first past Elkwood, then Brandy, and by one plantation after another, on into the old and attractive town of Culpeper. Somewhat to the northeast, four or five miles away, and about equidistant from Brandy and Culpeper, is a hamlet of a half-dozen age-worn houses called Stevensburg, sitting at the foot of a bare hill that looks like a giant asleep. It is Cole's or Lone Tree Hill, so called from a single tall primeval tree that spread its leafless limbs against the winter's morning and evening skies. On and around this hill were the camps of Hancock. A short while before we moved, Sheridan assembled the second and third divisions of his cavalry near Stevensburg. Custer had his headquarters in the Barbour House, and Wilson at the old Grayson Manor, known as Salubria, where Jefferson on many an occasion was a guest and where Lady Spottswood is buried. Stevensburg, like so many of the old dreaming country towns of Virginia, has proud memories of distinguished sons.

From the northwest comes into the little village the road from Brandy, and from the west that from Culpeper; both are mighty pleasant ones to follow in May, when the rolling fields on either hand are dotted with herds of grazing steers and the meadowlarks are piping their clear, high, skyey notes. When we set off for the Wilderness, Meade and his staff, followed by the Sixth Corps, came down the one from Brandy; Grant and his staff, followed by Warren with the Fifth Corps, on that from Culpeper. At the village these roads enter the main one that was built in Washington's boyhood to connect Stevensburg with Fredericksburg. This old highway is narrow, and its course from Stevensburg is almost due east, sometimes skirting lonely clearings but warping its way most of the time through sombre woods, woods with a natural deep silence, but flaming here and there with clumps of azaleas in their season. At Ely's Ford it crosses the Rapidan, which three or four

THE BATTLE OF THE WILDERNESS 55

miles farther on falls into the Rappahannock. At Sheppard's Grove, midway between Stevensburg and Ely's Ford, a road branches off to Germanna Ford on the Rapidan.

Alone in the woods along this road, and standing close by it, is a little frame house painted white. In its narrow dooryard and under each window to the right and left of the door is a yellow rose-bush, and on passing it lately, attracted by the beautiful roses then in full bloom and the open door, I ventured to stop and make a call. I discovered that a pensioner, one of our old cavalry soldiers, lived there. He was not at home, but his wife, a frank, naturally pleasant gray-haired woman, seated in her rocking-chair, told me that she was born near by, her people rankly Southern, and that she fell in love with her Yankee husband while he was a sentinel at her father's house. After the war — and she remembered the volleys in the Wilderness well — her lover came back, they were married, bought the little farm, built the house, and transplanted the roses from the old home: and as I rode away I thought of the red rose of Lancaster and the white rose of York.

About a mile and a half beyond their little clearing is Germanna Ford on the Rapidan. From there runs a road to Stevensburg that crosses on its zigzag way a pretty brook and passes through the famous Willis plantation. All the roads that I have mentioned, and over which we moved, are intersected by many country roads that are but little more than tracks through the woods and fields.

There are two streams flowing through the landscape that spreads from Mt. Pony, which I should like to mention, for I am indebted to them for many a pleasant murmur, and because their mingled waters, pouring over the dam at Paoli Mills, now known as Stone's, told me where I was in the still hours of the night, when misled by a guide while carrying Grant's first despatches from the Wilderness. They are Jonas and Mountain runs. The former, much the smaller, rises in the fields beyond Brandy, the latter among the foothills of the Blue Ridge. They meet near Lone Tree Hill, and Mountain Run winds on northeastwardly to the Rappahannock, its course through stretches of oak, pine, and cedar forest, where wild turkeys breed and redbirds sing. When I was down there the other day, the miller at Clarico's Mill, three or four miles above Stone's, told me that a tame turkey, perfectly white, had joined a flock of wild ones and roamed the neighboring woods with them, — which suggests that our natures, like theirs, perhaps, are not changed by the feathers we wear.

Finally, before leaving Mt. Pony there is one more feature to which I wish to call attention. To the south, after traversing a gently sloping country sprinkled with farms and woods, the fences between the fields pomponed by small dark green cedars, the

THE BATTLE OF THE WILDERNESS 57

eye catches the top of a blue veiled peak. It is Clarke's Mountain, beyond the Rapidan, and was Lee's signal station. But the particular feature to which I wish to direct the reader's eye lies east of Clarke's Mountain, a vast expanse of forest green, in spots almost black, and reaching clear to the distant circling horizon. Gaze at it long and well, for that is the Wilderness, and when I saw it last from the top of the mountain great white clouds were slowly floating over it.

In its wooded depths three desperate engagements were fought between the Army of the Potomac and the Army of Northern Virginia, — Chancellorsville, Wilderness, and Spotsylvania, — in which, first and last, over sixty thousand men, whose average age did not exceed twenty-two years, were killed and wounded. A circle described from Piney Branch Church on the Catharpin road with a radius of five miles will take in all these fields.

What is known as the Wilderness begins near Orange Court House on the west and extends almost to Fredericksburg, twenty-five or thirty miles to the east. Its northern bounds are the Rapidan and the Rappahannock, and, owing to their winding channels, its width is somewhat irregular. At Spotsylvania, its extreme southern limit, it is some ten miles wide. There, as along most of its southern border, it gives way to a comparatively open country.

This theatre of bloody conflicts is a vast sea, so to speak, of dense forest — a second growth more than a century old. It is made up chiefly of scrubby, stubborn oaks, and low-limbed, disordered, haggard pines, — for the soil is cold and thin, — with here and there scattering clumps of alien cedars. Some of the oaks are large enough to cut two railroad ties, and every once in a while you come across an acre or two of pines some ten to twelve inches in diameter, tall and tapering, true to the soaring propensities of their kind. But generally, the trees are noticeably stunted, and so close together, and their lower limbs so intermingled with a thick underbrush, that it is very difficult indeed to make one's way through them.

The southern half of this lonely region may be designated as low or gently rolling; but the northern half, along the rivers, is marked by irregularly swelling ridges. Where the battle was fought, which is at about the heart of the Wilderness, and especially on Warren's front, the surface of the ground resembles a choppy sea more than anything else. There, like waves, it will heave, sometimes gradually and sometimes briskly, into ridges that all at once will drop and break in several directions. Soon recovering itself, off it will go again, smoothly ascending or descending for a while, then suddenly pile up and repeat what it did before, namely, fall into narrow swales and shallow swamps where willows and alders of one kind and another congregate, all tied together more or less irrevocably by a round, bright-green, bamboo-like vine.

THE BATTLE OF THE WILDERNESS

There is something about the scrawny, moss-tagged pines, the garroted alders, and hoary willows, that gives a very sad look to these wet thickets; and yet, for a few weeks in May and June, from them a swamp honeysuckle, and now and then a wild rose, will greet you joyously. As might be expected where the trees stand so thickly as they do in the Wilderness, a large number are dead. Here and there a good-sized oak has been thrown down by a storm, smashing everything in its way and pulling up with its roots a shock of reddish-gray earth, making a bowl-shaped pool on whose banks the little tree-frogs pipe the solitude. Others in falling have been caught in the arms of their living competitors and rest there with their limbs bleaching, and now and then is one standing upright, alone, with lightning-scored trunk and bare, pronged limbs, dead, dead among the living green. The woods everywhere abound in tall huckleberry bushes, from whose depending limbs hang racemes of modest, white, bell-shaped flowers.

As in all the woods of Virginia, there are many dogwoods scattered about. Both they and the huckleberries were in full bloom when the battle was going on, the dogwoods, with outspread, shelving branches, appearing at times through the billowing smoke like shrouded figures. I wonder how many glazing eyes looked up into them and the blooming bushes and caught fair visions!

Running through the Wilderness its entire length

is what is known as the Fredericksburg and Orange Court-House Turnpike, a famous post road in the old stage days. Leaving Fredericksburg, it bears almost due west till it reaches the heart of the Wilderness; there it crosses Wilderness Run, and then, diverting its course slightly to the south of west, aims straight for Orange Court House, some eighteen miles away. At the time of the war the stage-day glory of the road and its old taverns, Dowdall's at Chancellorsville, the Wilderness overlooking the run of the same name, Robertson's at Locust Grove, was all gone; most of the stables and some of the houses were mere ruins, and the road-bed itself lapsed into that of a common earth road. When the system of plank roads came into vogue, about 1845, one was built a few miles south of, but more or less paralleling, the Turnpike. It is known as the Orange and Fredericksburg Plank road, and at the time of the battle was in about the same forlorn state as its old rival, the Pike. If the reader has interest enough in the narrative to consult a map, he will see the relation of these roads to each other at the battle-field, and will be able to locate three other roads, namely the Brock, Germanna Ford and the Flat Run roads, also two runs, Wilderness and Caton's, and the Lacy farm. These are the natural features in the richly crimsoned damask, so to speak, of the battle of the Wilderness.

The Lacy farm is a part of a once large domain

THE BATTLE OF THE WILDERNESS 61

known as Elkwood, and has what in its day was a stately homestead. Its fields, leaning against a ridge, all face the morning sun. The two runs, Wilderness and Caton's, may well be called Warrior Runs, for at their cradles and along their voiceless banks more men lost their lives, and more blood mingled with the leaves that fall around them, than along any two runs in our country, I believe. Caton's is much the smaller and heads among the swales, in the angle between the Germanna Road and the Pike. It loiters down through the woods with many feathery branches till it meets the Germanna Ford road, and then runs alongside of it to within a few rods of the Pike, when it strikes across and falls into Wilderness Run; sometime before they part, the road and the cowslip-gilded stream are in a narrow crease between two ridges. Wilderness Run drains all the trapezoid between the Pike, the Plank and the Brock roads, or, in other words, the battlefield. After leaving its cradle, around which so much youthful blood was shed, it flows noiselessly under willows and alders, gleaming in the sunlight and moonlight past the Lacy house, on to the Rapidan.

The clearings throughout the Wilderness, save the Lacy farm and the openings about Chancellorsville and Parker's store at the time of the war (and it is almost as true now), are few and small. Many of them are deserted, and their old fields preëmpted by briars, sassafras, dwarf young pines and broom, beneath whose dun, lifeless tops the rabbits, and now and then a flock of quail, make their winter homes. There are several of these little clearings in the battlefield, but the lines so ran in reference to them that they did not allow the artillery of either army to play a part. These lonely places are connected with one another and the roads by paths that are very dim and very deceitful to a stranger. Their real destination is known only to the natives, and the lank cattle that roam the woods, getting a blade here and a blade there, oftentimes up to their knees in the swales and swamps for a tuft. The lonely kling-klang-klung of their bells on a May morning is pensively sweet to hear.

This whole mystery-wrapped country is a mineral region, holding pockets of iron ore and streaked with lean insidious veins of gold-bearing quartz. On account of these ores Colonel Spottswood, for whom the County of Spotsylvania is named, became the owner of large tracts of the Wilderness. He uncovered the ore-beds, built iron furnaces, and converted the primeval forest into charcoal to feed them. Some of the pits, and many of the wood roads from them and the ore-beds to the furnaces, are still traceable. All this was at an early day, as far back as the reign of King George II; for the colonel speaks of him in his deeds as his Sovereign Lord. The present timber aspect is due entirely to the iron furnaces and their complete destruction of the first noble growth.

THE BATTLE OF THE WILDERNESS

My mind never turns to those long-since cold furnaces that a mantled figure, mysterious but very real, does not arise before me, and which, like a portentous note, now and again keys the narrative. Lo! there it is, its uplifted hand pointing toward a resurrected procession of dim faces, and as they move in ghostly silence I hear it saying: By the labor of slaves chiefly those iron furnaces were reared; it was they who mined the ore, cut down the woods, and faithfully tended the lonely smouldering pits (in the solemn hours of the night, alone in the woods, what a vocation that was for reflection on the rights and wrongs in life, — some of the pits were not far from where Stonewall Jackson and Longstreet received those fateful volleys from their own men); they who at last tapped the stacks of their molten, red metal, metal that sooner or later found its way, some into the holy uses of bar-iron and utensils, and some, alas! into cruel manacles clasping possibly the wrists of a Spottswood slave who after long days of enforced and unpaid labor had more than once in the dead hours of night sat before the pit, his cheek resting in his broad hand, looking with gentle eyes pleadingly into the face of his hard fate.

Who knows what happened there, what heartbreaking, due to slavery and to slavery alone, and which the Wilderness was witness to or moved by mournings of far distant exiles! Is our fellow mortal robed in green and called Nature nearer to us than we realize? And was there a Spirit of the Wilderness, that, as tears gathered in eyes of fathers and mothers over separation from children and home, recorded an oath to avenge the wrong? Else why did the Wilderness strike twice at the Confederacy in its moments of victory? Who knows!

III

I AM free to confess that the strategy, grand tactics, and military movements of the Civil War, stirring as they were, are not the features which engage my deepest interest, but rather the spirit which animated the armies of North and South. That, *that* is what I see. And while my mind's eye is gazing at it with emotion, on my ear fall the sounds of ringing trowels in the hands of workmen rearing a new wing to the old battlemented Palace of History, an addition not to house the tale of soldiers engaged, soldiers killed and wounded, or to preserve the records of the charge of this regiment upon that, or the slaughter of one division by another. No, no, not the multitude of dead, or the pictures of their glazing eyes and pleading, bloodless hands, shall engage the pen that fills the records of that new wing. We do not know what the genius of history will treasure there, yet we know that on its hearth a fire will burn whose flames will be the symbol of the heroic purpose and spirit that beat in the hearts of the pale, handsome youths who strewed our fields. And where the beams from those flames strike against the walls, new ideals will appear, and up in the twilight of the arches will be faintly heard an anthem, an anthem of joy that new levels have been reached by mankind in gentleness and in love of what is pure and merciful. Wars that will not add material for this extension of the old Palace ought never to be fought.

So then, before the movements begin and our blood mounts, let us in peaceful, thoughtful mood take a view of our enemies, not of their numbers or position, but fix our attention rather on Lee's character and the spirit of his army, two ethereal but immortal elements. True, what we are gazing upon is not so clearly defined as the Army of Northern Virginia in camp on the banks of the Rapidan, but the everlasting things that appeal to us are never quite distinct; and yet how real they are and how they long for expression in Art, Worship, Charity, Honor, and high chivalric deeds.

But be all this as it may, what was it that so animated Lee's army that, although only about one-half as strong in numbers as we were, they came near overthrowing us in the Wilderness, and held their lines at Spotsylvania, although we broke them several times? In all seriousness, what sustained their fortitude as they battled on, month after month, through that summer, showing the same courage day after day, till the times and seasons of the Confederacy were fulfilled?

Well, to answer this, I know no better way than to propose a visit to the Army of Northern Virginia, say on the night of January 18, 1864. But before

THE BATTLE OF THE WILDERNESS 67

setting off on our quest, let us recall that, through either exhaustion, mismanagement, or unavoidable necessity, supplies for man and beast were, and had been, so meagre that there was actual suffering, and not forget that it was an unusually severe winter. The snow from time to time was four and six inches deep, and again and again it was bitter cold. We do not know what the weather was on that particular night of January 18, but in the light of the following letter to the Quartermaster-General of the Confederacy, does it seem unfair to assume that snow covered the ground, and that the wind was blowing fiercely? Or does it seem unfair to fancy that Lee, on hearing it howl through the cedars and pines near his headquarters, thought of his poorly clad, half-fed pickets shuddering at their lonely posts along the Rapidan, and took his pen and wrote to the Confederate Quartermaster-General?

HEADQUARTERS ARMY OF NORTHERN VIRGINIA, *Ja'y* 18th, 1864.

GENERAL: — The want of shoes and blankets in this army continues to cause much suffering and to impair its efficiency. In one regiment I am informed that there are only fifty men with serviceable shoes, and a brigade that recently went on picket was compelled to leave several hundred men in camp who were unable to bear the exposure of duty, being destitute of shoes and blankets.

Lee's correspondence seems to show that this state

of affairs continued, and that repeated pleas were made both for food and for clothing. Whatsoever may have been the response to them throughout the winter, those who saw the contents of the haversacks taken from the dead or wounded in the Wilderness will remember that they contained only a few pieces of corn-bread and slices of inferior bacon or salt pork. Well, in this want do you find any explanation of Southern fortitude? No, but it helps us to appreciate it truly.

With this prelude, let us go on with our visit. And as we breast the fierce wind, and tramp on through the snow from camp to camp, what is it that we hear from those houses built of logs or slabs? Lo, men are preaching and praying earnestly; for during those bleak winter nights, so have the chaplains recorded, a great revival was going on; in every brigade of the sixty odd thousand men, the veterans of Gaines's Mill, Fredericksburg, and Gettysburg were on their knees asking God to forgive their sins, to bless their far-away homes and beloved Southland. One of the officers of a battery tells us in its history that right after retreat they always met for prayer and song, and that when the order came to march for the Wilderness, while the teams stood ready to move, they held the battery long enough to observe their custom of worship.

In those sacred hours when the soldiers of Northern Virginia were supplicating their Creator through

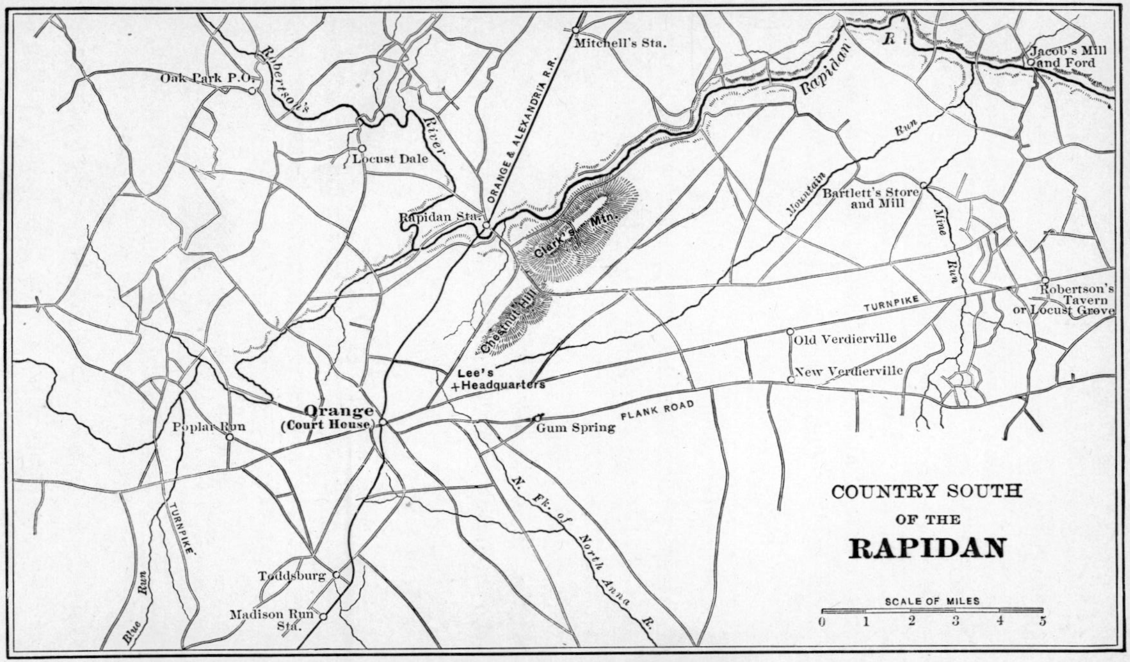
COUNTRY SOUTH
OF THE
RAPIDAN
SCALE OF MILES
0 1 2 3 4 5
Oak Park P.O.
Robertson's
River
Locust Dale
Rapidan Sta.
ORANGE & ALEXANDRIA R.R.
Mitchell's Sta.
Rapidan
R
Jacob's Mill
and Ford
Mountain
Run
Bartlett's Store
and Mill
Mine
Run
Clark's Mtn.
Chestnut Hill
Robertson's
Tavern
or Locust Grove
TURNPIKE
Old Verdierville
New Verdierville
Lee's
+Headquarters
Orange
(Court House)
Gum Spring
FLANK ROAD
Poplar Run
N. Fk. of North Anna R.
TURNPIKE
Blue
Run
Toddsburg
Madison Run
Sta.

his Son to forgive them all their sins, and imploring his hand to guide them on in the paths of righteousness, I think we find at least profoundly suggestive material for the answer to the question: Whence came the spirit that animated and sustained their fortitude through those eleven months of battle? The sense of peace with God is as much a reality as the phenomenon of dawn or the Northern Lights. Moreover, hear what Carlyle says about an idea: "Every society, every polity, has a spiritual principle, the embodiment of an idea. This idea, be it devotion to a man or class of men, to a creed, to an institution, or even, as in more ancient times, to a piece of land, is ever a true loyalty; has in it something of a religious, paramount, quite infinite character; it is properly the soul of the state, its life; mysterious as other forms of life, and, like those, working secretly, and in a depth beyond that of consciousness."

Do not the losses and sufferings of the Southern armies and people tell us that there was an idea, something of a religious, paramount, quite infinite character, possessing the South? If they do not, go stand among the graves in the Confederate cemetery at Spotsylvania, and you certainly will hear from the tufted grass that a principle was embodied in an idea.

In seeking for the answer to our question there is one thing more to be mentioned, — the strength that came to the Army of Northern Virginia through the personality and character of Lee; a strength so spiritual and vital that, although he and most of his army are in their graves, it still lives, preserving and consecrating the memories of the Confederacy. I sincerely believe that with him out of the Rebellion, so-called, its star that hangs detached but glowing softly over those bygone days would long since have set.

Two forces contributed to his ascendency, one fortuitous, of the earth earthy, the other fundamental and celestial, that of ideals. By birth he belonged to one of Virginia's noted families and by marriage he was connected with Washington, Mrs. Lee being the granddaughter of Mrs. Washington. Thus he had the advantage of the regard which prevailed throughout the South for distinguished ancestry supported by wealth, character, and attainments.

Furthermore, nature in one of her radiant moods had made him the balanced sum in manners and looks of that tradition of the well-bred and aristocratic gentleman transmitted and engrafted at an early age through the Cavaliers into Virginia life. Moreover, she had been generous with her intellectual gifts, bestowing abilities upon him of the very highest order.

But for his military prowess he had something vastly more efficacious than ancestry or filling the mould of persistent traditions. He had the generative quality of simple, effective greatness; whereby his

THE BATTLE OF THE WILDERNESS

serenely lofty character and dauntless courage were reactive, reaching every private soldier, and making him unconsciously braver and better as a man. So it is easy to see how the South's ideal of the soldier, the Christian, and the gentleman unfolded, and was realized in him as the war went on. His army was made up chiefly of men of low estate, but the truth is that it takes the poor to see ideals.

Taking into account, then, these mysterious yet real forces, religion, martial skill, and exalted character, we have all the elements, I think, for a complete answer to the question we have raised. But now, let the following extracts from Lee's letters leave their due impression of what kind of a man he was at heart; for it is by these inner depths of our nature that we stand or fall, whether we were born, as he was, in the same room of the palatial mansion of Stratford where two signers of the Declaration of Independence were born, or as Lincoln, in a log cabin in Kentucky. The first was written to his son Custis on the 11th of January, 1863, just about a year before our fancied visit to his camp:—

CAMP, 11th *January*, 1863.

I hope we will be able to do something for the servants. I executed a deed of manumission, embracing all the names sent me by your mother, and some that I recollected, but as I had nothing to refer to but my memory I fear many are omitted. It was my desire to manumit all the people of your grandfather, whether present on the several estates or not.

Later, he sent the following: —

I have written to him [a Mr. Crockford] to request that Harrison [one of the slaves] be sent to Mr. Eacho. Will you have his free papers given him? I see that the Va. Central R. R. is offering $40 a month and board. I would recommend he engage with them, or on some other work at once. . . . As regards Leanthe and Jim, I presume they had better remain with Mrs. D. this year, and at the end of it devote their earnings to their own benefit. But what can be done with poor little Jim? It would be cruel to turn him out on the world. He could not take care of himself. He had better be bound out to some one until he can be got to his grandfather's. His father is unknown, and his mother dead or in unknown parts.

In a letter to his son, W. H. F. Lee, who had just been released from captivity, and whose wife Charlotte had died: —

God knows how I loved your dear, dear wife, how sweet her memory is to me. My grief could not be greater if you had been taken from me; and how I mourn her loss! You were both equally dear to me. My heart is too full to speak on this subject, nor can

I write. But my grief is for ourselves. She is brighter and happier than ever,— safe from all evil and awaiting us in her heavenly abode. May God in His mercy enable us to join her in eternal praise to our Lord and Saviour. Let us humbly bow ourselves before Him, and offer perpetual prayer for pardon and forgiveness. But we cannot indulge in grief, however mournfully pleasing. Our country demands all of our strength, all our energies. . . . If victorious, we have everything to hope for in the future. If defeated, nothing will be left us to live for. This week will in all probability bring us work, and we must strike fast and strong. My whole trust is in God, and I am ready for whatever He may ordain. May He guide, guard, and strengthen us is my constant prayer.

Your devoted father,
R. E. Lee.

In the foregoing reference to Lee, and to the spirit of his army, I trust there is some food for reflection, and somewhat that is informing. For I cannot make myself believe that a true history of the war can be written, fair to the South and fair to the North, that does not try at least to make these spiritual forces real. Surely due measure cannot be given to the gallantry of the soldiers of the North, who won victory for their country at last, if we do not realize what they had to overcome in the almost matchless courage of their adversaries.

But let no one be deceived, — Lee's soldiers were not all saints, nor were ours. In his, as in all armies, there were wretches guilty of most brutal conduct, — wretches who habitually rifled the dead and wounded, — sometimes under desultory firing, as when our lines after assaults were close, — crouching and sneaking in the darkness, from one dead body to another, thrusting their ogreish hands quickly and ruthlessly into pockets, fumbling unbeating breasts for money and watches, and their prowling fingers groping their way expectantly along the pale, dead ones for rings. Thank God! the great mass of the armies, North and South, respected the dead, and turned with aversion from those ghoulish monsters, the barbarous and shameful outcome of bitter and prolonged war. But there are vermin that breed in the darkness of the cellar walls of cathedrals and lonely country churches; and yet a holy spirit breathes around their consecrated altars, and in the voices of the bells and the tops of the spires catch the first gleam of dawn. So, so it is, and so, so it was with both armies that went into the Wilderness.

IV

EVERYTHING being ready, Grant, on Monday, May 2, directed Meade to put the army in motion at midnight of the following day for the lower fords of the Rapidan. Grant at the same time notified Burnside, then along the railroad north of the Rappahannock, to be ready on the 4th to start at a moment's notice for Germanna Ford. The orders to carry this into effect were written by Humphreys, Meade's Chief of Staff, and were sent to the corps commanders the same day, who at once, in compliance with them, placed guards around all the occupied houses on or in the vicinity of their line of march, to prevent information being carried to the enemy that the army was moving.

Early on Tuesday morning the depots at Brandy began to ship back to Washington. It was a very busy day for me and for every one else in charge of stores. Trains were backing in to be loaded with surplus stores; fresh troops, infantry and cavalry, were arriving and had to be supplied at once, whole regiments in some cases, with arms and equipments. Teams stood, waiting, the drivers clamorous for their turn to load with ammunition or delayed supplies; others under the crack of their drivers' whips, quickly taking their chance to unload condemned stores, and all more or less impatient because they could not be served immediately, so as to get back to their commands who were preparing to move.

If, in the midst of the hurly-burly, you had gone out where the condemned stores were received, I believe that you would have seen and heard much to amuse you. These stores were usually sent in charge of a corporal or sergeant, and were tallied by a couple of my men. One of them, Corporal Tessing, it would have delighted you to see, he was such a typical, grim old regular. His drooping moustache and imperial were a rusty sandy, streaked with gray, his cheeks furrowed, his bearing and look like a frowning statue. The other, Harris, his senior, was a mild, quiet, open-eyed, soft-voiced man, with modesty and uprightness camped in his face. Well, if the stores came from a regiment of cavalry, the corporal in charge, booted and spurred, — and such an air! — would pick up a few straps, some of them not longer than a throat-latch, and possibly having attached to one or two of them an old nose-bag, would announce brazenly to Tessing or Harris who would be tallying, "two bridles, three halters, and four nose-bags." If an infantryman, he would throw quickly into a pile an old wrinkled cartridge-box, a belt or two, and a bayonet-scabbard, and sing out, "five sets of infantry equipments complete." If an artilleryman, he might point with dignity to a couple of pieces of carefully folded, dirt-stained, scarlet blankets, and in a voice of commercial deference observe, "three horse-blankets."

And so it was with everything their commanding officers were responsible for: they tried to get receipts for what was worn out, what had been lost, and now and then for what they had traded off to a farmer or sutler. If you could have seen Tessing's face as he turned it on some of those volunteer corporals when they tried to beat him! He rarely said anything to the young rascals; now and then, however, he addressed the very unscrupulous in tones, terms, and looks that could have left but little doubt as to what he thought of them. They never disputed his count, but pocketed their receipts, and off they went as light-hearted as birds. He and the old sergeant lost their lives at the explosion of the depot at City Point: the former was literally blown to atoms; how and where I found the sergeant is told in "The Spirit of Old West Point." Heaven bless their memories, and when I reach the other shore no two hands shall I take with warmer grasp than the hands of these two old soldiers; and, reader, I believe they will be glad to take mine, too.

Count the stores as carefully as they might, there was sure to be a generous allowance, so that by the time we reached City Point I was responsible for a vast amount of stuff that was n't there. But let me confide that, when the depot exploded, all those absent stores had in some mysterious way gotten to the James; and I am free to say that I loaded them, and everything under the heavens that I was charged with and short of, on that boat or into the depot-buildings, and thereby balanced the books to the complete satisfaction of everybody, and I believe with the approval of Honor and Justice.

At last all was done at Brandy, and a little before midnight the train with my ordnance supplies on board was under way for Alexandria; its engine, old Samson, laboring heavily. I waved good-bye to my faithful Regulars and tired colored laborers, and turned in.

That night all the camp-pickets were called in, rations and ammunition issued, and perfect silence maintained after taps sounded.

During the afternoon of Tuesday, the Second Division of cavalry under Gregg, then at Paoli Mills, moved southeastward to the road already described connecting Stevensburg and Fredericksburg. He struck it at Madden's, and followed it eastward till he came to Richardsville, a hamlet about two and a half miles from Ely's Ford. There he went into bivouac, with orders from Sheridan to keep his command out of sight as much as possible. About ten o'clock P. M. a canvas pontoon train that had been brought up from the Rappahannock drew into his sleeping-camp, rested till midnight, and then, preceded by an advanced guard, set out for the river. When daylight broke they were at the ford, and Gregg, after laying

THE BATTLE OF THE WILDERNESS 79

the bridge, one hundred and fifty feet long, moved on up with his cavalry to Chancellorsville.

Meanwhile Hancock at midnight awakened his great Second Corps, and at two A. M. set off with it from Lone Tree Hill, to follow Gregg. His troops kept in the woods and fields till they came to Madden's, so as to leave the road free from Stevensburg to that point for Warren. The Madden's referred to is an old farmhouse on a gentle knoll, with some corn-cribs, log-stables, and huddled fruit trees where chickens and turkeys roost, all overlooking a flat field to the west that is dotted with blackened stumps of primeval oaks. It is about a third of the stretch from Stevensburg to the river.

Dawn had broken, and the morning star was paling, when the head of the Second Corps reached the bluffy bank of the Rapidan at Ely's Ford. There it halted for a moment while the wooden pontoon bridge that accompanied it was laid. The river spanned, the corps filed down and began to cross into the Wilderness. Hour after hour this bridge pulsed with the tread of Hancock's twenty-seven thousand men, veterans of many fields. The swelling bluffs offer more than one point where in fancy the reader might sit alone and overlook the moving scene. I wish for his sake that with one stroke of this pen, as with a magic wand, I might make it real.

The river flowing on in sweet peace, glimmering with the morning sun; accumulating masses of infantry waiting for their turn to join the neverending column in blue blossomed by the colors, colors that had flashed their crimson on many a field; the bridge rumbling under the heavy wheels of the batteries; guns, men, and colors crossing over the river to win glory at last for their country. Yes, there go the men and the guns against whom Pickett made his mighty charge and who hurled him back into immortality. There go the men and guns who within ten days will carry the Bloody Angle at Spotsylvania. Oh, gallant Second Corps, led on by Webb, Birney, and Smyth; Hays, Brooke, and Carroll; Miles, Barlow, and Gibbon, my heart beats as I recall your deeds of valor! Having crossed, they took the sadly quiet country road which makes its way through thickety sombre pines and surly oaks and by ragged forlorn openings, to their old battlefield of Chancellorsville, where so many of their comrades were sleeping their last long, long sleep.

Hancock with his staff reached Chancellorsville by nine-thirty, his last division about three P. M. Some of his troops had marched over twenty-three miles, which, inasmuch as they carried three days' rations, their muskets, and fifty rounds of ammunition, — under a hot sun and with not a leaf stirring, — was a hard tramp. On Hancock's arrival, Gregg moved on several miles to the south, along the old Furnace road which just about a year before Stonewall Jackson had taken to reach the Brock road and from there

THE BATTLE OF THE WILDERNESS

to strike the right of Hooker's army, posted over the identical field where Hancock's corps had now gone into bivouac. A reference to this last, fateful move of Jackson will be made when we come to place the army before the reader's eye as night fell that first day, and after all had reached their allotted camps. Gregg picketed heavily on the roads coming from the direction of Hamilton's Crossing where Sheridan under misinformation had located the bulk of the Confederate cavalry.

And now, leaving Hancock at Chancellorsville, let us turn to Wilson and Warren; the former commanded Sheridan's Third Cavalry Division. At dark on Tuesday, his pontoon train took the road for Germanna Ford. When it got within quick reaching distance, a half-mile or so, of the river, it halted in the thick woods. It was then ten o'clock, a moonless but beautiful starlit night. At three o'clock the Third Indiana Cavalry, under Chapman, cautiously drew near the ford, waited till dawn appeared among the trees, then hurried down, forded the river, and brushed away the startled Confederate pickets of the First North Carolina Cavalry who had their reserve in the old, briery field overlooking the ford.

Meanwhile, the bridge material was brought forward, and Wilson was on hand with the rest of his division, which included Pennington's and Fitzhugh's batteries of light artillery. By half-past five — the sun rose at 4.49 — two bridges, each two hundred and twenty feet long, were thrown, the three thousand horsemen meanwhile fording the river, and by six o'clock all the trains and batteries of the cavalry division had crossed, and the head of Warren's Corps, which had marched from the vicinity of Culpeper at midnight, was drawing near. The infantry in sight, Wilson pushed on, up toward the Lacy farm, and the Fifth Corps, Ayres with his Regulars in the lead, began to cross. The troops, once they gained the bluff, threw themselves down and rested by the roadside while they ate their breakfast, and then followed Wilson up the narrow and deeply over-shadowed road.

The Sixth Corps began its march at four o'clock from beyond Brandy for Stevensburg. There it fell in behind Warren, and followed him to Germanna Ford. Sheridan left the first division of his cavalry, under Torbert, to mask the upper fords of the Rapidan and to look out for the rear of the army as it moved away from its winter-quarters. Later he with his staff threaded the infantry, and after crossing the river at Germanna established his headquarters on Wilderness Run, about midway between the ford and Chancellorsville.

Several hours before Warren and Hancock began their march the enormous supply-train, in bands of from twenty to two hundred wagons, headed eastward on lanes and roads for Richardsville. They were rumbling by my tent at Brandy all through the

THE BATTLE OF THE WILDERNESS 83

night. Grant's, Meade's, and the different corps headquarters-trains, and half of the ammunition and ambulance trains moved with the troops.

The sun had just cleared the tree-tops when Meade with his staff came by, and I mounted my horse, saddled and groomed by my colored boy Stephens, and joined them. The whole army was now in motion, and I cannot convey the beauty and joy of the morning. The glad May air was full of spring. Dogwoods with their open, enwrapped blossoms, that have always seemed to me as though they were hearing music somewhere above them in the spring skies, violets and azaleas, heavenly pale little houstonias, and the richly yellow primroses, which here and there beautify the pastures and roadsides of this part of old Virginia, were all in bloom, and the dew still on them.

Never, I think, did an army set off on a campaign when the fields and the bending morning sky wore fresher or happier looks. Our horses felt it all, too, and, champing their bits, flecking their breasts at times with spattering foam, bore us proudly. When we gained the ridge just beyond Stevensburg, which commands a wide landscape, an inspiring sight broke on our eyes. To be sure, we had been riding by troops all the way from Brandy, but now, as far as you could see in every direction, corps, divisions, and brigades, trains, batteries, and squadrons, were moving on in a waving sea of blue; headquarters and regimental flags were fluttering, the morning sun kissing them all, and shimmering gayly from gun-barrels and on the loud-speaking brass guns, so loved by the cannoneers who marched by their sides. Every once in a while a cheer would break, and on would come floating the notes of a band. As I recall the scene of that old army in motion that morning, its brigade, division, and corps, flags, some blue, some white, and some with red fields, whipping over them, with its background of Pony and Clarke's Mountain, and away in the west the Blue Ridge looming with her remote charm, a solemn spell comes over my heart, and it seems as if, while I look back through the Past at the magical pageant, I hear above me the notes of slowly passing bells.

The troops were very light-hearted, almost as joyous as schoolboys; and over and over again as we rode by them, it was observed by members of the staff that they had never seen them so happy and buoyant. The drummer-boys, those little rapscallions, whose faces were the habitual playground of mischief and impudence, were striding along, caps tilted, and calling for cheers for Grant, or jeering, just as the mood took them; but there was illumination in every soldier's face. Was it the light from the altar of duty that was shining there? No one knows save the Keeper of the key of our higher natures, who some day will open the doors for us all.

Soon after we left Stevensburg, to my surprise,

General Hunt, by whose side I was riding, suggested that we take it easy, and let the rest of the staff go ahead, for it never was comfortable to keep up with that fox-walk of Meade's horse; so we fell to the rear, and I really felt proud to have him ask me to ride with him, for he was so much older, and held such a high place at headquarters and in the army generally. We struck across the country, and while watering our horses at a run of considerable flow, — it rises well up among the oak timber of the old Willis plantation, one with the greatest domain of any along the Rapidan, — Hunt's eye fell on the violets that strewed its banks, and he insisted that we dismount and pick some of them. The violets here, and those in the Wilderness, are large and beautiful, the two upper petals velvety and almost a chestnut brown. As we lounged in the refreshing shade, he manifested so much unaffected love and sentiment for the wild flowers and the quiet of the spot, — the brook was murmuring on to the Rapidan near by, — that the stern old soldier whom I had known was translated into an attractive and really new acquaintance. I do not remember ever to have seen him smile, yet I never read the story of Pickett's charge, or recall him at the Wilderness or Spotsylvania, without having that half-hour's rest on the banks of the run come back to me.

The road we were on, the old Stevensburg plank, and the one from Madden's which had been taken by two of Warren's divisions, meet at Germanna Ford, both roads availing of short narrow ravines to get to the water's cheery edge, for the Rapidan here is flowing right fast. Under the open pines on the bluff we found Warren, Meade, and Grant, with their headquarters colors. They and their staffs, spurred and in top boots, all fine-looking young fellows, were dismounted and standing or lounging around in groups. Grant was a couple of hundred yards back from the ford, and except Babcock, Comstock, and Porter, he and all of his staff were strangers to the officers and the rank and file of the army. His headquarters flag was the national colors; Meade's, a lilac-colored, swallow-tailed flag having in the field a wreath inclosing an eagle in gold; Warren's Fifth Corps, a blue swallow-tail, with a Maltese cross in a white field.

Down each of the roads, to the bridges that were forty or fifty feet apart, the troops, well closed up, were pouring. The batteries, ambulances, and ammunition trains followed their respective divisions. Of course, in the three years of campaigning many officers, of all branches, — and I honestly believe I knew every captain and lieutenant in the artillery with the army, — had become acquaintances and personal friends of my own as well as of members of the various staffs assembled; and warm greetings were constantly exchanged. Hello, Tom! Hello, Bob! Good-morning, Sandy, old fellow, and how did you leave your sweetheart? How are you, John, and you, too, Mack, dear old boy! And on with their radiant smiles they went.

If the reader could take his place by my side, on the bare knoll that lifts immediately above the ford, and we could bring back the scene; the Rapidan swinging boldly around a shouldering point of darkened pines to our right, and on the other side of the river the Wilderness reaching back in mysterious silence; below us the blue moving column, the tattered colors fluttering over it in the hands of faithful-eyed, open-browed youths, I believe that the reader would find an elevated pleasure as his eyes fell on the martial scene. And if we could transport ourselves to the banks of the James, and should see the army as I saw it on that June day, heading on after it had fought its way through the Wilderness and Spotsylvania and by Cold Harbor, leaving behind those young faces whose light now gives such charm to the procession all hidden in the grave, I believe that both of us would hear, coming down from some high ridge in our spiritual nature, the notes of a dirge, and our hearts with muffled beats would be keeping step as the column moved over the James.

But, thank God! that scene of June is not before us now. No, we are on the Rapidan, it is a bright May morning, the river is gurgling around the reef of black projecting boulders at our feet, and youth's confident torches are lit in our eyes, and here comes the small band of Regulars. That solid-looking man, with an untended bushy beard, at their head, is Ayres. The tall slim man with that air of decision, stalking walk, drooping moustache and sunken cheeks, who commands the division, is Griffin, one of my old West Point instructors. At Gettysburg, when Longstreet's men had carried the Peach Orchard and broken Sickles's line, and were coming on flushed with victory, driving everything before them, Griffin's Regulars, then under Sykes and Ayres, were called on and went in. They were only 1985 strong, but they fought their way back, leaving 829 killed or wounded. Out of the 80 officers in one of the small brigades, 40 were among the killed or wounded.

Reader, let me tell you that I never think of the Regulars without a feeling of pride and affection for them all. For the first real soldier I ever saw, the one who conducted me — on reporting at West Point, a light-haired, spare, and rather lonely looking boy — to the barracks that were to be my home for four years, was a Regular; moreover, all of my springtime manhood was spent as an officer among them, and let me assure you that if in the other world there shall be a review of the old Army of the Potomac, I shall certainly fall in with the Regulars.

And here, brigaded with them, comes a regiment, the One Hundred and Fortieth New York, to which,

THE BATTLE OF THE WILDERNESS   89

for the sake of a boyhood's friend who fell at their head, I wish you would uncover. It is Pat O'Rorke's, a cadet and sojourner at West Point with me, to whom this pen has referred on another occasion. That regiment followed him up the east slope of Round Top, and there looking out over the field is a monument which tells with pride the sacrifices it made. Ryan, "Paddy" Ryan, — so Warren called him when some one of the staff asked him who that young officer was that had just tipped his cap to him smiling as he rode by, — Ryan, a graduate of West Point, tawny-haired and soldierly, is leading it now. At the close of the next day, the first of the Wilderness, of the 529 of the One Hundred and Fortieth who went into action up the turnpike, cheering, only 264 reported with the colors. The rest were in the hospital wounded, or lying dead under the stunted, sullen pines; a few were on their way to Southern prisons.

And there, just coming on the upper bridge, is another regiment in the same division, the Twentieth Maine, a worthy companion of the One Hundred and Fortieth and the Regulars. Its record at Round Top, where it was on the left of O'Rorke, under Chamberlain, is thrilling; and it was still under that same scholar, soldier, and gentleman, a son of Bowdoin, at Appomattox, when the overthrown Confederate army came marching along, under Gordon, with heavy hearts, to stack their arms, and say farewell to their dearly loved colors. Chamberlain ordered his line to present arms to their brave foes. Gordon, who was at their head, with becoming chivalry wheeled his horse, and acknowledged duly the unexpected and touching salute. Yes, the guns you see them bearing now were brought to a present, and those old battle-torn colors were dipped. It was a magnanimous and knightly deed, a fit ending for the war, lifting the hour and the occasion into the company of those that minstrels have sung. I feel glad and proud that I served with an army which had men in it with hearts to do deeds like this. The total killed and wounded of this regiment in the war was 528.

That large man, fifty-four years old, with silvered hair and nobly carved features, is Wadsworth who has only about forty-eight hours to live, for he was killed Friday forenoon, and the writer has every reason to believe that he bore the last order Warren ever gave him. But before I reached him, his lines were broken, and our men were falling back in great confusion, and he was lying mortally wounded and unconscious within the Confederate lines. His brigade commanders are Cutler and Rice, the latter a Yale man who, when dying a few days after at Spotsylvania, asked to be turned with his face to the enemy. In Wadsworth's division is the Iron Brigade of the West, made up of Seventh and Nineteenth Indiana, Twenty-Fourth Michigan, First

New York, Second, Sixth, and Seventh Wisconsin. They too were at Gettysburg, — in fact, the fate of that day pivoted on their bravery, — and proudly may they tread those bridges to-day.

Those troops just ahead of the battery that is now coming on to the lower bridge are the rear of the Maryland brigade. Its front is with that headquarters flag you see in the column over the top of willows and trees on the other side of the river. It is known as the Iron Brigade of Maryland, and is made up of the First, Fourth, Seventh, and Eighth Maryland.

If ever you should visit the field of Spotsylvania, you will find standing in the Spindle farm, within reach of the evening shadows of an old wood, and amid tufts of broom-grass, a gray rectangular stone, and on one of its faces you will read "Maryland Brigade," and on another this legend, a copy of an order given by Warren, then in the road about where Sedgwick was killed the following morning: "8th May 1864. Never mind cannon, never mind bullets, press on and clear this road," — meaning the road to Spotsylvania, that lies but a mile and a half beyond. On the south face is, "Nearest approach on this front."

I saw the troops with my own eyes as they tried gallantly to carry out Warren's order, wondering at every step they took how much longer they could stand it under the withering cross-fire of artillery and musketry; and the whole scene came back to me vividly as I stood by the stone the other June day. And I'll confess freely, it came back with a sense of pensiveness such as always attends a revisit to one of the old fields. I got there about the same hour as that of the charge, and the day resembled exactly that of the battle, one brimming with glad sunshine; that kind of a May morning when new-shorn sheep look so white in the fields, the brooks ripple so brightly, and joy is in the blooming hawthorn.

But there, by the stone, all was very still, — silence was at its highest pitch. Huge white clouds with bulging mountain-tops, pinnacled cliffs, and gray ravines were floating lazily in the forenoon sky, and across the doming brow of one of them whose shadow was dragging slowly down the timbered valley of the Po, a buzzard far, far above earth's common sounds, was soaring half-careened with bladed wing. There were no men or herds in sight, the only moving thing was an unexpected roaming wind. Suddenly the leaves in the near-by woods fluttered a moment, and then the broom-grass around waved silently as the wandering wind breathed away. My left hand was resting on the stone, and a voice came from it saying, as I was about to go to other parts of the field, — to where brave, sweet-hearted Sedgwick laid down his life and our batteries had stood, — "Stay, stay a while! I stand for the men you saw marching across the Rapidan, who after facing the volleys of the

Wilderness were called upon to move on at last under the severe order, 'Never mind cannon, never mind bullets, but press on and clear this road.' Here many of them fell. Stay a while, I love to feel the warmth of a hand of one who, as a boy, served with them. Do not go just yet, for, here alone throughout the long days in the silence of the dead broom, I am sometimes lonely."

And so, dear reader, I might call your attention to deeds like theirs which have been done by about every one of the veteran regiments that cross the river this morning, but something tells me that I ought to refrain, and proceed with the narrative.

As soon as the last of his troops were across — it was well on toward noon — Warren mounted his big, heavy, iron-gray horse and, followed by his staff, the writer among them, started up the Germanna Ford Road for the Lacy farm and the opening around the Wilderness Tavern. Warren's adjutant-general was Colonel Fred Locke; his chief surgeon, Dr. Milhau, whose assistant was my friend, Colonel Charles K. Winne of Albany, New York, — and may every day of his declining years be sweet to him. Warren's chief personal aide, and one of the very best in the army, was Washington Roebling, the builder of the Brooklyn Bridge, and a man whose fame is wide. Warren's brother Robert, a boy of my own age, was also an aide. I find, by referring to my book of dispatches, that I sent my camp blankets to him at Culpeper the night before we moved. Besides those mentioned there were eight or ten other officers connected with the staff; so that, when we were under way on the narrow road, followed immediately by headquarters guards, couriers, and servants, we made quite a cavalcade behind the general.

After all these years there are only three distinct memories left of the march. First, its seeming great length, — and yet it was only about four and a half miles. But the eye met nothing to distract it; to be sure now and then there was a field, and on the right-hand side, and not far apart, were two little old houses. When passing over the road last May, the houses were gone, a superannuated cherry tree was trying to bloom, and a feeble old rheumatic apple tree had one of its pain-racked, twisted boughs decked in pink and white. But the most of the way the road's course is through stunted oaks, lean, struggling bushes, pines with moss on them, obviously hopeless of ever seeing better days, the whole scene looking at you with unfathomable eyes. Second, the road was strewn with overcoats which the men had thrown away. The wonder is that they had carried the useless burden so far, for the day was very warm, with not a breath of air; moreover, they had been marching since midnight, and were getting tired. The other memory is almost too trifling to record, but, as it was the only time I burst into a hearty laugh in all the campaign, I shall be loyal to it, and give it a place alongside of the stern and great events.

THE BATTLE OF THE WILDERNESS

About half-way to the Lacy house we come to Flat Run, which steals down out of the woods and heads right up where the battle began. Its tributary branches are like the veins of a beech-leaf, frequent and almost parallel, coming in from both sides, and bordered all the way with swamp or thicket. When we reached it, and while several of us with rein relaxed were letting our horses drink, my friend Winne approached on our right hand. The wagons and batteries ahead of us had ploughed through, deepening and widening the deceitful stream into a mud-hole. Winne's horse, rather thirsty, and undoubtedly looking forward with pleasant anticipations of poking his nose into refreshing water, had barely planted his fore feet in it before he turned almost a complete somersault and landed Winne full length in the water. When, to use the language of the New Testament, he came up out of the water, his cap had disappeared, and he certainly was a sight. Well, heartlessly and instantaneously we youngsters broke into howling delight. Thereupon Winne's lips opened and his language flowed freely, marked with emphatic use of divine and to-hellish terms both for us and his poor brute, which was fully as much surprised as any one at the quick turn of events. The doctor's address soon reduced our loud laughter to suppressed giggles, which brightened our way for a good many rods, and which still ripple along the beach of those bygone years.

When Griffin's division, leading the advance of Warren's corps, reached the Pike, it moved out on it for a mile or more to the west, the road rising steadily, and there in the woods beyond the leaning fields of the Lacy farm it went into bivouac. Griffin pitched his tent alongside the old road and just at the edge of the woods. Little did he or his men dream, as they rested after their long march, — how sweet the fragrance of the boiling coffee, how soft the pine needles under hip and elbow, how refreshing every soft breeze on the forehead, how still the woods and with what lovely serene delight the sunshine sifted down through the intermingled branches of the trees! — yes, little did Griffin or his men dream that Early's Confederate division of Ewell's corps would go into bivouac along the same road and only three miles away.

Crawford's division of Warren's corps, next in the column, on gaining the Pike took the grassy Parker's Store Road, which winds up Wilderness Run through the Lacy plantation. He halted near the mansion and made it his headquarters for the night. The house is about a half mile from the Pike, faces the east, and has some venerable trees in the dooryard.

Wadsworth, next in line, camped opposite Crawford on the east side of the run, picketing toward Chancellorsville. The regiment sent on this duty was the Second Wisconsin, Cutler's brigade, and its adjutant, G. M. Woodward of La Crosse, Wisconsin, says that where he established the line of pickets the ground here and there blazed with wild azaleas, and at first presented no evidence that it had ever been the scene of battle; dismounting he soon found scattered in every direction the débris of war — knapsacks, belts, bayonets, scabbards, etc. Farther on he saw what appeared to be a long trench about eight feet wide, filled up and mounded, its edges sunken and covered with grass, weeds, and wild flowers. This picket-line ran undoubtedly through Stonewall Jackson's field hospital of just a year before, to which he was carried when wounded.

Robinson, who brought up the rear of the corps, camped on the Germanna Road, the middle of his division about where Caton's Run comes down through the woods from the west.

Some of the batteries parked on the Lacy farm, others with the trains in the fields back of the deserted old Wilderness Tavern. This old stage-house, indicated on all the maps and mentioned many times in orders and reports, was a two-storied, hewn-log house in its day, standing on the north side of the Pike, at the top of the ridge about three hundred yards east of Wilderness Run. It overlooked all the Lacy estate, and had the reader stood in its lonely dooryard as the sun was going down and the shadows of the woods were reaching into the fields, the men of Crawford's and Wadsworth's divisions, all preparing their evening meals, the smoke of their little fires lifting softly over them, would have been in full view below him. From the same point, should some one have directed his eye to a banner with a white field and a red Maltese cross in the centre, a mile or so to the west, at the edge of the woods, it would have been Griffin's.

Warren made his headquarters near the Pike, on the bare ridge which separates Wilderness and Caton's runs, and about opposite the knoll that Grant and Meade occupied during the battle. At supper that night he was in fine spirits, cheerier at heart, I believe, than ever afterwards, unless it was on the field of Five Forks just before he met Sheridan, who, in that passionate moment, then and there peremptorily relieved him, just as the veterans of the Fifth Corps, whom he had led so often, were cheering him over the victory he had helped to win. Sheridan's harsh dealing with him, however, was not wholly unstudied; for Warren's relations with Grant, which felt their first strain in the Wilderness and at Spotsylvania, had been at the breaking-point, and Sheridan knew it. Moreover, Grant during the day had sent his trusted aide Babcock to him, with authority to relieve Warren in case he should not come up to the mark. In fact, then, and in extenuation of Sheridan's conduct, who knows all that Babcock said, or his look and tones? But that awful hour of storm for Warren has long since drifted by, and

THE BATTLE OF THE WILDERNESS 99

his saddened mind found the grave's repose. I have no doubt, however, that when they finally met in the other world, the impulsive Irishman asked and received his pardon.

After supper I filled my pipe and sat alone, on an old gray rail-fence near by, till the sun went down and evening deepened into a twilight of great peace. A brigade camped up the run was singing hymns and songs that I had heard at home as a boy; and, probably with feelings deeper than my own, the timber of the Wilderness listened also. Slowly out of the sky bending kindly over us all, — woods, the Lacy fields, the old tavern, and murmuring runs, — the light faded softly away and on came night.

Sedgwick's divisions were in bivouac along the Germanna Ford Road as far as Flat Run; Getty next to Warren, then Wright, in the old Beale plantation fields; and behind him, just this side of the river, Ricketts, who had crossed the Rapidan about a quarter of four.

Sheridan had pitched his headquarters a third of a mile or so east of the Sixth Corps, near the workings of an old gold mine; orderlies, with his cavalry corps flag, were stationed on the Germanna Road to show the way to his camp. Custer, perhaps the lightest-hearted man in the army, with whom as a cadet I whiled away many an hour, was back just this side of Stevensburg, his brigade guarding the rear of the army and especially the trains at Richardsville. Davies, with another brigade of cavalry, was at Madden's; in fact, all of Sheridan's first division was posted from the Rapidan to the Rappahannock at eight o'clock that beautiful May night.

Wilson with the Third Division was at Parker's store, one brigade picketing up the Plank Road to the west and front, the other to the east and south. When I was there last May, a couple of apple trees were in bloom, and on the roadside I met an old Confederate whose tawny beard was streaked with frost. "Can you tell me where General Wilson was camped?" I asked. He replied, "Stranger, he was camped all around over that field and all around yonder," waving his hand sweepingly; "but I was off with Rosser's cavalry. It is very quiet now, sir." And so it was.

The trains were crossing at Ely's and Culpeper Mine fords and going into parks near Chancellorsville.

Grant and Meade, after crossing the river, established their headquarters near a deserted house whose neglected fields overlooked the ford. At 1.15 P. M., Hancock and Warren having met with no opposition in their advance, Grant telegraphed for Burnside to make forced marches until he reached Germanna Ford. There is reason to believe, it seems to me, that it would have been better had Burnside been brought up nearer before the movement began. For, as it was, his men were nearly marched to death to overtake us; and as a result, they were altogether too fagged out for the work they were called on to do the morning of the second day. The same criticism, however, can be made on Lee's failure to bring Longstreet within striking distance. Though, to be sure, in his case, he did not know whether Grant would cross the Rapidan at the fords above or below him; if above, then Longstreet was just where he would have needed him. I have always suspected that Lee feared a move on that flank more than on his right, for there the country was so open that he could not conceal the paucity of his numbers, as in the Wilderness. But, however this may be, while Hancock's, Warren's, and Sedgwick's men on our side, and Hill's and Ewell's on Lee's, were resting around their camp-fires, Burnside's and Longstreet's were still plodding away, long after their comrades in the Wilderness were asleep. Such, then, were the movements and the camping-places of the Army of the Potomac on the 4th of May.

Meanwhile the enemy had been moving also. Ewell reports that, by order of General Lee, his corps and division-commanders met him on Monday, May 2, at the signal station on Clarke's Mountain, and that he then gave it as his opinion that Grant would cross below him. It was the last time that Lee and his valiant subordinates ever visited that charming spot, with its wide, peaceful view. If ever the reader should be in that vicinity, I hope he will not fail to go to the top of the mountain.

At an early hour on Wednesday it had been reported from various sources to Lee that Grant was under way. By eight o'clock this news was fully confirmed and he transmitted it through the proper channels to his corps-commanders, with orders to get ready to move. Sorrel, Longstreet's adjutant-general, at nine o'clock notified General E. P. Alexander — a soldier and a gentleman whose name will last long — as follows: "Many of the enemy's camps have disappeared from the front, and large wagon-trains are reported moving through Stevensburg. The lieutenant-general commanding desires that you will keep your artillery in such condition as to enable it to move whenever called upon." It was the artillery that under Alexander tried to shake our lines at Gettysburg before Pickett's charge. The same despatch was sent to Longstreet's division-commanders, Field and Kershaw. The former was our instructor in cavalry at West Point, and rode at the head of the troop that escorted Edward VII, when as Prince of Wales he came to West Point in the fall of 1860.

It is reasonably clear that by eleven o'clock at the latest Lee was convinced that Wilson's and Gregg's crossings of the Rapidan were not the beginning of a raid, or a feint to cover an advance up the river, but the opening of the campaign. Apparently he

THE BATTLE OF THE WILDERNESS 103

seems not to have hesitated, but set his army of sixty-odd thousand men in motion for the Wilderness, taking the precaution to leave Ramseur with three brigades at Rapidan station, to meet any possible danger behind the mask of our cavalry under Custer. Ewell, who commanded his Second Corps, consisting of Rodes's, Johnson's, and Early's divisions, was to draw back from the river to the Pike and, once there, to march for Locust Grove, some eighteen miles to the eastward and within, as has been related, three miles of where Griffin camped. His Third Corps, A. P. Hill's, at Orange Court House, was to take the Plank Road for Verdierville or beyond. It had about twenty-eight miles to go.

Longstreet at Gordonsville and Mechanicsburg was first ordered to follow Hill, but later, at his suggestion, he took roads south of the Plank leading into the Catharpin, which strike the Brock Road, the key of the campaign, at Todd's Tavern. From his camp to where his men met Hancock the morning of the second day, east of Parker's store, was forty-two miles. None of Lee's corps got well under way before noon; and by that time over half of Hancock's and all of Warren's were across the river. It was after dusk when Ewell passed through Locust Grove; and the bats were wavering through the twilight over the heads of Hill's men as they dropped down to rest at Verdierville. Longstreet's veterans, those who in the previous autumn smashed our lines at Chickamauga and who left so many of their dead at Knoxville, were still on the march.

Sometimes, when alone before my wood-fire, my mind floating over the fields of this narrative, and one after another of its scenes breaking into view, I have been conscious of wishing that with you, reader, at my side, I could have stood near their line of march. I should like to have seen those men, — and so would you, — the heroes of the Peach-Orchard and Round Top at Gettysburg, as well as of Chickamauga. I should like to have seen also the North Carolinians of Hill's corps who, with the Virginians, made Pickett's charge. But above all I should like to have seen the face of the officer who, on the succeeding night, hearing the pitiful cries for water of our wounded in Griffin's front, could stand it no longer and crawled over the breastworks, notwithstanding the persistent fire from our lines, made his way to where one of our wounded men lay, took his canteen, and, groping to a little branch of Wilderness Run, filled it and brought it to his stricken enemy and then went back to his own lines. If ever the spirit of that Good Samaritan should come to my door, he shall have the best chair before my fire; I'll lay on another stick of wood and let its beams kiss his manly face as we talk over those bygone days. Yes, I wish that with a reader who would enjoy such a scene I could have stood under a spreading-limbed tree on the roadside and seen Field and Kershaw,

THE BATTLE OF THE WILDERNESS 105

Ewell and Gordon, Heth and Alexander, march on their way to the Wilderness.

Stuart began to draw in his cavalry toward Verdierville as soon as he knew of our movement. The regiments which had wintered in the vicinity of Hamilton's Crossing and at Milford on the Fredericksburg and Richmond Railroad directed their march by way of Spotsylvania; Rosser set out from Wolf Town in Madison County, passed through Orange Court House, and camped beside Hill. Fitz Lee came in from the neighborhood of Gordonsville and bivouacked on the Catharpin, near enough to go to Rosser's aid the next morning.

Lee encamped in the woods opposite the home of Mrs. Rodes, near Verdierville.

Able critics have blamed him for fighting Grant in the Wilderness. They maintain that he might have avoided all of his losses there by going at once to Spotsylvania, and entrenched, for they assume that Grant would have followed the same system of repeated assaults that he did after the Wilderness, and that he would have met with severer repulses. It will be conceded, knowing Grant as we do, that in all probability he would have gone straight at his adversary, and that no works which Lee could have thrown up at Spotsylvania or elsewhere would have daunted him: the appalling record of that battle-summer would certainly seem to justify such a conclusion. And, by the way, one among the reasons which contributed to make it so deadly may be found possibly in the fact that Grant came to the army with an impression that in many of its big engagements under McClellan, Pope, Hooker, and Meade, it had not been fought to an end. However this may have been, long before we got to the James River the grounds for a like impression, I think, were gone. At any rate, go ask the slopes before the Confederate works at Spotsylvania, Cold Harbor, and Petersburg what they think about it, — if they even dream that the Army of the Potomac was not fought to its limit.

Perhaps there was a better way than Grant's way of handling the gallant old army but I find no fault: I am only sorry so much blood had to flow. We are in the habit of thinking it was a war between North and South; not at all, it was between two mutually antagonistic forces vastly older than our country — it was the final death grapple on this earth of Freedom and Slavery, and the sacrifice of sons North and South had to be made, bringing many tears.

In regard to the wisdom of Lee fighting in the Wilderness, I think we can be sure of one thing, — that his decision was not the result of sudden impulse. For what he should do with his army, little as compared with Grant's, when spring should open, had no doubt been weighed and re-weighed, as night after night he sat before his green-oak fire at the foot of Clarke's Mountain. His critics, moreover, will

THE BATTLE OF THE WILDERNESS 107

agree that he was too good a tactician not to know that, if he should adopt the defensive from the outset and go to Spotsylvania, Grant could flank not only that position but any position he might take between there and Richmond. Again, those who find fault with him for fighting in the Wilderness will have to acknowledge, we believe, that he was too good a general not to realize that any backward steps he might be forced to make, for any reason whatsoever, would have a bad effect on the spirit of his army. Of course, he knew that sooner or later in the campaign he would have to assume the offensive, and take his chances. It is obvious that in case of defeat, the nearer Richmond he should be the more serious might be the results: he had had one experience of that kind at Malvern Hill, which is within ten miles of Richmond, and I am sure he never wanted another like it; for all accounts agree, and are confirmed by what I have heard from Confederates themselves, that his army and Richmond were on the verge of panic.

In justification of the plan that he followed, where is there a field between the Rapidan and Richmond on which his sixty-five thousand men could have hoped to attack Grant's one hundred and twenty thousand under such favorable conditions? where his numbers would be so magnified in effectiveness, and Grant's so neutralized, by the natural difficulties and terror of the woods? — for dense woods do have a terror. Again, where on the march to Richmond would the Army of the Potomac, from the nature of the country and the roads, be more embarrassed in the use of its vastly superior artillery, or in concentrating its strength, if battle were thrust upon it suddenly?

Save right around Chancellorsville, the region was an almost unknown country to our people, while to Lee and his men it was comparatively familiar. He himself was thoroughly acquainted with its wooded character, paths, runs, and roads. Moreover, he knew the military advantages they afforded, for he had tested them in his campaign against Hooker. Taking all this into account, then, it seems to me that in planning his campaign to strike at Grant just when and where he did, he planned wisely. For it presented the one good chance to win a decisive victory, which, as I have said before, was absolutely necessary to save the life of the Confederacy. It is true Lee failed to win the victory he had planned and hoped for. But little had he reckoned upon a second intervention of Fate: that the spirit of the Wilderness would strike Longstreet just as victory was in his grasp as it had struck Stonewall.

Reader, if the Spirit of the Wilderness be unreal to you, not so is it to me. Bear in mind that the native realm of the spirit of man is nature's kingdom, that there he has made all of his discoveries, and yet what a vast region is unexplored, that region along whose misty coast Imagination wings her way bringing one suggestion after another of miraculous transformations, each drawing new light and each proclaiming that nature's heart beats with our own.

A little before sundown, when all were in camp for the night, Grant issued his orders for the next day. Sheridan was to move with Gregg and Torbert against the enemy's cavalry, who at that hour were supposed to be at Hamilton's Crossing, and who, as a matter of fact, were not there at all. Wilson, with his Third Cavalry Division, was to move at 5 A. M. to Craig's Meeting House, on the Catharpin Road, the one that Longstreet had chosen for his approach. Warren was to take Wilson's place at Parker's store; Sedgwick to move up to Old Wilderness Tavern, leaving one division at Germanna Ford till the head of Burnside's corps appeared; in other words, he was to occupy Warren's present position with his whole corps across the Pike. Hancock was to advance by way of Todd's Tavern to Shady Grove Church on the Catharpin Road, and from there, about three and a half miles south of Warren, throw out his right and connect with him at Parker's store. Of the infantry, Hancock had by far the longest march to make, about twelve miles; the others only very short ones, not more than three or four miles. The trains were to be parked at Todd's Tavern.

None of the moves, as we have stated, were

long, or apparently any part of a well-defined series of movements, but, rather, precautionary. They neither seriously threatened Lee's communications with Richmond, nor indicated an active offensive, but were clearly made with a view to allow Burnside to overtake the army, and to get the big, unwieldy supply-trains a bit forward; for there was practically only one narrow road, and not a very good one at that, from where they were then halted to Todd's Tavern. It was for these reasons, I think, that Grant's orders did not push the army on clear through the Wilderness the second day. But whatsoever may have been the reason, there is something very striking in his repetition of Hooker's delay of the year before. All vitality (and bluster, for that matter) was Hooker till he reached the heart of the Wilderness, but no sooner was he there than he became mentally numb and purposeless as though he had breathed some deep, stagnating fumes. A year, almost to a day, the army marched again, briskly and cheerily, to the heart of the Wilderness; and before its bivouac fires had died down, — indeed, before the sun had set, — the orders for the following day seemed to indicate that the lotus in the fateful region's gloom was again at work. While aides are carrying the orders to their respective destinations for the next day's march, the day ends, and twilight comes on.

After night had set in, Meade, having disposed of

THE BATTLE OF THE WILDERNESS 111

all his current official duties for the day, came over from his headquarters — they were only a few steps away — and joined Grant before a large camp-fire made of rails. Grant's staff withdrew to a fire of their own, and left them alone.

Meade was Grant's senior by about ten years, and the paths of their lives had run widely apart; unclouded sunshine had fallen richly on Meade's, adversity's blasts had blown fiercely across Grant's. They were practically strangers to each other as they met at this camp-fire, and we may credit Meade, as he took his seat in its mellow blaze, with a wandering curiosity, a keen interest to fathom the medium sized diffident man with the marvelous career. He would not have been human without it; for as Grant had risen in his mighty flight, there had drifted to him as to every old officer of the army, minute details of the awful eclipse under which he had left it and the hard, honest trials he had met in supporting his family.

Knowing ourselves and our fellow men as we do, it is not unreasonable then to imagine Meade, a man of the world, of cultivation, and at home in society and clubs, following Grant's motions and speech with the unobtrusive yet keen observation of men of his class; or to imagine Grant having to meet from him, as from all his old fellow officers of the army, that searching look which had met him invariably since his emergence from obscurity. But I can easily see Meade's curiosity disarming, and his noble, fiery nature breathing naturally and strengthening in the soothing influence of Grant's deep calm; every utterance of his low vibrating voice gliding modestly from one grasp of a subject to another, every tone simple and un-self-conscious, every thought as distinct and fresh as a coin from the mint.

I have no doubt that Grant's naturally sweet, modest nature, together with the auguries, which were all good, made Meade's first camp-fire with him a pleasant one; and that, before its flames and in the wild charm of the place, was born the spirit of loyal coöperation which he showed to his chief on every field and clear to the end.

Our country owes a great deal to both of these men; justice, but not more than justice, has been done to Grant. Meade has never had his due. As I look back and see his devotion day and night in that last great campaign, his hair growing grayer, and the furrows in his face deeper, under its trying burden, and then, when it is all over and the cause is won, see him relegated to the third or fourth place in official recognition and popular favor, I feel deeply sorry, knowing, as I do, how the country's fate hung in the balance when he was called on to take command of the Army of the Potomac. I hope his last hour was comforted, that there came to him out of the Past the cheers of his countrymen, greeting his victory at Gettysburg.

After his death it was found that his system had

THE BATTLE OF THE WILDERNESS 113

never recovered from the wound he received at Charles City Cross Roads.

From all accounts they were both cheery over having the army across the Rapidan. Anxiety over their first move was all gone. The stubborn resistance that Lee might have offered to their crossing of the river had not been made; and now that they were well established on his flank, he would be forced to decisive action: he would either have to fight it out at once, or fall back and ultimately undergo a siege. In the way they misconceived what Lee would do, there is almost a suggestion of fatality. For although there is no absolute corroborative evidence to support the conclusion, yet the movements show that what they expected was this: that he would hastily withdraw from his works and place his army to receive, but not to give, attack. Hooker had yielded to the same illusion. In forecasting his Chancellorsville campaign, he had imagined that when Lee at Fredericksburg found that he was on his flank at Chancellorsville, he would fall back from Fredericksburg and contest the way to Richmond. The difference between the results in Hooker's case and in Grant's was wide: the former was driven from the field in almost utter disaster; Grant met Lee's attack in the Wilderness, threw him back, and pushed on undaunted.

Had Meade and Grant,—as they sat there, the stars over them and the Rapidan swirling along, now and then breaking into a gurgle, — had they known that Ewell was within three miles of Warren, it would have been, I think, quite another camp-fire, and Meade might never have gained those first fine impressions of Grant which were so honorable to him and so valuable to the country, for whose sake, I sincerely believe, Fortune so turned her wheel that they might be made that night.

It is a matter of singular interest that all this time Lee's position was barely suspected, and his purpose entirely unknown to either of them. And how it all came about is one of the mysterious features of the Battle of the Wilderness. Let me state the circumstances, and I promise to make the account as short and comprehensible as I can.

Wilson, with his third division of cavalry, reached the Lacy farm about half-past eight in the forenoon; halted, and sent patrols westward and southward, that is, out on the Pike toward Locust Grove and along the county road to Parker's store. At noon, when the head of Warren's corps bore in sight, he set off for Parker's, first sending orders to the scouting party on the Pike to push out as far as Robertson's Tavern (now, and by the Confederates during the war, called Locust Grove) and, after driving the enemy away from that place, to ride across country and join the division in the neighborhood of Parker's store. Wilson, with the bulk of his division,

THE BATTLE OF THE WILDERNESS 115

on arriving at the store about two o'clock, sent a strong reconnoissance up the Plank Road, with directions to keep an active lookout for the enemy. In a despatch to Forsythe, Sheridan's chief of staff, dated 2.10 P. M., he said, "I send herewith a civilian, Mr. Sime, a citizen of Great Britain. He says he left Orange yesterday 2 P. M.; Longstreet's corps lies between there and Gordonsville; passed at the latter place; Ewell and Hill about Orange Court House. Troops well down toward Mine Run [about half-way between the Lacy farm and the Court House], on all the roads except this one [the Plank]; none on this nearer than seven miles to this place. I have sent patrols well out in all directions, but as yet hear of nothing except few light parties scattered through the by-roads."

Sheridan sent the following despatch to Meade, — the hour not given, but presumably toward sundown: "I have the honor to report that scout sent out the first road leading to the right from Germanna Ford went as far as Barnett's Mill at or near Mine Run [Barnett's Mill is on Mine Run], found the enemy's pickets. Also the scout sent out on the second road to the right [the Flat Run Road that intersects the Pike where the battle began] went to within one-half mile of Robertson's Tavern, found a small force of the enemy's cavalry on picket. It was also reported that a brigade of rebel infantry was sent down to Barnett's Mill or Mine Run yesterday."

These scouts referred to were probably individuals in Confederate uniform, for Sheridan always kept a group of these quiet, daring men about him on whom he called for hazardous service.

At 7.40 P. M. Wilson again reported to Forsythe: "I have executed all orders so far. My patrols have been to the Catharpin Road. Did not see Gregg, and only two of the enemy; also to within one mile of Mine Run on Orange Pike [Plank?] skirmishing with small detachments of the enemy. Patrol to Robertson's Tavern not yet heard from."

Ten minutes later, or at 7.50 P. M., Wilson sent this despatch to Warren: "My whole division is at this place [Parker's store], patrols and advanced parties well out on the Spotsylvania and Orange roads. No enemy on former, and but small parties on this. Drove them six miles or to within one mile of Mine Road. Patrol from here toward Robertson's not yet reported. Rodes's division reported to be stretched along the road as far as twelve miles this side of Orange. Will notify you of any changes in this direction."

Here we have all the recorded information that Meade could have received of the enemy up to when he joined Grant at his camp-fire.

Probably the reason why Wilson's report as to Rodes's position made no impression on Humphreys or Meade — for it must be assumed that it reached them — was because they interpreted it as meaning

THE BATTLE OF THE WILDERNESS

his winter-quarters, which was nothing new, for prisoners and deserters had given them that information during the winter, and they had so located him on a map kept for the purpose. Their interpretation accounts, too, for neither Warren nor Sheridan making any further suggestion to Wilson as to Rodes's whereabouts. The fact is that at that very hour of 7.50 P. M. he was bivouacked just behind Johnson's and Nelson's battalion of artillery two miles south of Locust Grove, and the head of Hill's corps was east of Verdierville.

There is but one explanation for this mysterious indifference in the presence of an enemy, namely, that Grant and Meade were possessed with the idea that Lee, as soon as he should find that we had crossed the Rapidan, would hasten from his lines to some position beyond the Wilderness. No fog ever drifted in from the sea, wrapping up lighthouses and headlands, that was deeper than this delusion which drifted in over the minds of Grant and Meade, and, so far as I know, over corps and division-commanders as well.

But how about Wilson's patrols? And especially that one he had sent toward Locust Grove? This is probably what happened. It got to Locust Grove before noon, having scattered into the by-roads and paths the videttes of the First North Carolina cavalry whom they had brushed away from the ford at daybreak. From there I assume they went on to

Mine Run, which they found glinting brightly down through the old fields from one clump of willows to another. Beyond the run, and in full sight, rose Lee's breastworks of the year before, not a flag flying on them or a soul in them. All was peaceful at Mine Run. After a while, having scouted up and down the run as far as Barnett's Mill on the north, and off toward the head of the run on the south, they rejoined the main patrol at Locust Grove. No one disturbed them, and there they waited till they saw the sun approaching the tree-tops, and then they obeyed their orders and struck off through the woods for Parker's store. The chances are that their dust had barely settled before on came Ewell. Had they stayed at Locust Grove a few hours longer, what would have happened? Why, the orders issued at 6 o'clock would have been countermanded at once. Warren and Sedgwick would have struck at Ewell early in the morning, and Hancock, instead of going to Todd's Tavern, would have reached Parker's store by sun-up, and probably before noon a great victory would have been won.

Is there nothing mysterious in all this? Knowing the situation as we now do, does it not add interest to that camp-fire of old rails, before which Grant and Meade are sitting smoking? Does it not give a weird echo to the bursts of laughter of their staffs? Laugh on, gay children of fortune! and meanwhile the spirit of the Wilderness is brooding.

THE BATTLE OF THE WILDERNESS 119

Lee's camp-fire was in the woods opposite the house of a Mrs. Rodes near Verdierville; and it must have been a cheery one, for General Long, his military secretary, says that at breakfast the following morning he was in unusually fine spirits, chiefly over the fact that Grant had put himself in the meshes of the Wilderness, just as Hooker before him had done, giving him the one chance to overbalance his one hundred and twenty thousand men.

From Grant's headquarters to Lee's was, as the crow flies, between nine and ten miles; and a circle with its centre where Warren was in camp and a radius of six miles would have taken in the bulk of ours and half of Lee's army. And yet the Army of the Potomac lay down to rest, unconscious that they were almost within gunshot of their old foe!

Happily all of their camps were on less gloomy and fated ground than Hancock's. His were on the old battlefield of Chancellorsville, and some of his regiments found themselves on the identical lines where they had fought in that engagement. The ground around their camp-fires, and for that matter everywhere, was strewn more or less with human bones and the skeletons of horses. In a spot less than ten rods square, fifty skulls with their cavernous eyes were counted, their foreheads doming in silence above the brown leaves that were gathering about them. In sight of a good many of their camp-fires, too, were half-open graves, displaying arms and legs with bits of paling and mildewed clothing still clinging to them: — oh, war's glory, this is your reverse side! — On all hands there were tokens of the battle: shriveling cartridge-boxes, battered and ricketty canteens, rotting caps and hats, broken artillery-carriages, barked and splintered trees, dead, or half-dead, dangling limbs, and groves of saplings, with which the woods abound, topped by volleys as if sheared by a blast. Of course, there was line after line of confronting, settling breastworks, whose shallowing trenches nature was quietly filling with leaves and dead twigs. All these dismal reminders met the eyes of Hancock's men until they were closed in sleep. I do not know how it would have affected others, but I think that if I had been sitting before one of those camp-fires, night having well come on and the whippoorwills, of which there are thousands that make their homes in the Wilderness, repeating their lonely cries, and the fire drawing to its end should have suddenly kindled up as fires do, — and mortals, too, sometimes before they die, — and thrown off a beam into the darkness upon one of those skulls, it seems to me that I should have felt a low, muffling beat in my heart, and heard the rap of life's seriousness at its door.

Hancock's tent was in the old peach-orchard. (What is there about a peach-orchard that war should choose it for the scene of battles? There was the battle of Peach-tree Creek near Atlanta, the

THE BATTLE OF THE WILDERNESS 121

Peach-Orchard at Gettysburg, and now Hancock is in the old peach-orchard at Chancellorsville, where the battle raged fiercest. Does war love the red blossom, or did the blood of some noble-hearted soldier quicken the first peach-bloom of the world?) It is reasonable to believe that the whole disastrous scene of the year before must have passed in review before Hancock. But the feature of the battle that would come back to him, I think, with most vividness, and make the deepest impression on him as a corps-commander, was the flank attack that Stonewall Jackson made. In fact, judging from his own reports of the first two days' fighting at the Wilderness (which took place within less than three miles of where he slept), he not only thought about it, but dreamed about it. For, the entire time he was fighting Hill, he was haunted with the fear, paralyzing a great share of his customary aggressive and magnetic usefulness, that Longstreet would come up on his left by way of Todd's Tavern and give him a blow on his flank such as Jackson had given Howard.

I wonder, Reader, if the ghost of Stonewall did not really come back? You see, it was about the anniversary of the night on which he received his mortal wound, and the old armies that he knew so well were on the eve of meeting again. What should be more natural than that he should come to this side of the river, that river whose beckoning trees offered such sweet shade to the dying soldier? Did

I hear you say that you thought he did? Why lo! here he is on the field of Chancellorsville, looking for his brigade, — for his old legion of the Valley. Let us draw near. "They are not here, Stonewall; these men you see are Hancock's men." And now he goes to the peach-orchard, for no soldier ever took part in a battle who does not have a longing to see the ground the enemy defended. He approaches Hancock's tent, — they had known each other in the old army, — with his right hand — his left arm you remember was amputated two inches below the shoulder — he draws the walls softly, and looks in on the gallant friend of other days. Perhaps it was then that Hancock dreamed Longstreet was on his flank.

Stonewall closes the tent and seems to ponder; is he debating where he shall go next? Shall it be off to where he parted with Lee to make his great flank movement via the old Furnace Road where Gregg's cavalry outposts, saddled and bridled, are now dozing, or shall it be back to where he met the fatal volley? The latter has won. If you will follow him, so will I, for the road, the woods that border it, and the spot to which he is going, I know right well. And now that he has reached there his lips seem to move; is it a prayer he is offering? Or is he addressing some aide, telling Hill as on the night of the battle to come up and Pender to push right on?

Abruptly, and with almost a gasp, he fastens his astonished gaze on a cowled figure that has emerged

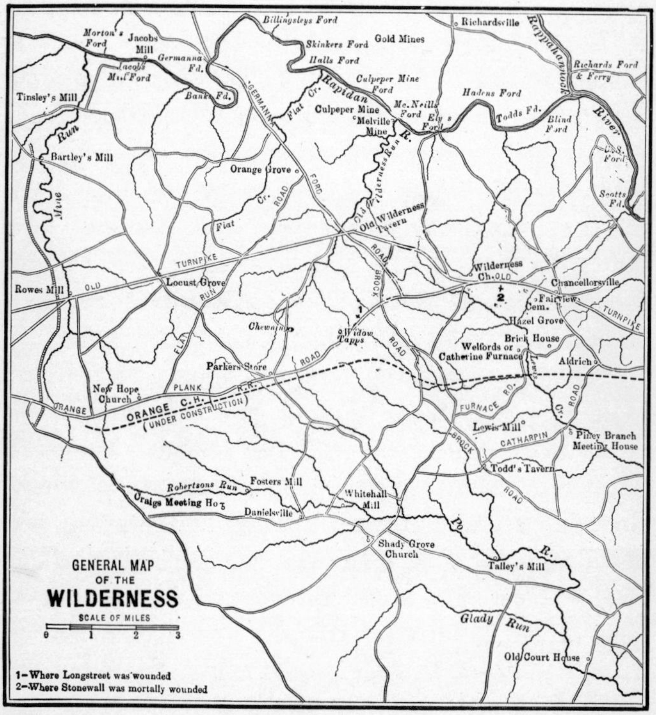

GENERAL MAP OF THE WILDERNESS

SCALE OF MILES

0 1 2 3

1—Where Longstreet was wounded

2—Where Stonewall was mortally wounded

THE BATTLE OF THE WILDERNESS 123

from the trees and is looking at him. Is it the Spirit of the Wilderness, whose relentless eyes met his as he fell, and does he read in their cold depths the doom awaiting Longstreet? Who knows his thoughts as he turns away from the fated spot and sets off up the Orange Plank Road, for his melancholy heart yearns to be with Lee and his valiant corps once more. And now he has reached the junction of the Orange and the Brock roads which is in the midst of woods; the stars, although hazy and dim, light the crossing a little and he halts. Down the latter, up which he rode on his historic march, he looks long and wistfully; is he expecting his old corps again? Deep is the silence in the slumbering woods. A little bird in its dreams utters one strain of its lonely wood-note and then is still; and now instead of oncoming troops across the Brock Road from east to west, the direction Stonewall is going, and with the soft pace of a phantom, flits the cowled figure, turning her face hastily toward him as she enters the sullen oaks. With a sigh he moves on toward Parker's store, and when he draws near where Mahone's men fired on Longstreet, something on his left attracts his attention and he pauses suddenly.

Whose hands are those pulling aside the bushes and overhanging limbs? Lo! there again is the Spirit of the Wilderness, with the same ominous, relentless look. A moment's glance is exchanged. The figure withdraws, the branches swing back into place, and the ghost of Stonewall moves on, with troubled brow.

Hark! he hears something. It draws nearer, and now we can distinguish footsteps; they sound as if they were dragging chains after them through the dead rustling leaves. Presently, off from the roadside where two oaks press back the tangle, admitting a bit of starlight, Stonewall sees a gaunt, hollow-breasted, wicked-eyed, sunken-cheeked being. Behold, she is addressing him! "Stonewall, I am Slavery and sorely wounded. Can you do nothing to stay the Spirit of the Wilderness that, in striking at me, struck you down?"

"No, no," says the ghostly commander, impatiently waving the staring creature away. "Your day, thank God! has come. To-morrow morning Lee will strike, but it will not be for you."

"And is this history?" comes a peevish voice from the general level of those who are as yet only dimly conscious of the essence and final embodiment of History. Yes, it is a little sheaf out of a field lying in one of its high and beautifully remote valleys.

Such then is the chronicle of the first day of the campaign. And now it is midnight; all save the sentinels are asleep, and the whippoorwills are still chanting.

V

AT Warren's headquarters we breakfasted early, and at 5 A. M., just as the sun had cleared the tree-tops, he sent the following despatch to Humphreys: —

"My command is just starting out. As I have but little ways to move, I keep my trains with me instead of sending them around by the plank road, which I fear might interfere with the main trains, which I understand to be those to be assembled at Todd's Tavern."

A half-hour later he notified Getty, camped back at Flat Run on the Germanna Road, that Griffin, in conformity with Meade's orders of the night before, would hold the Pike till he (Getty) got up. At the same time he sent word to the officer in charge of the pickets in Griffin's front not to withdraw till the column got well in the road on the line of march to Parker's store. He then mounted his big, logy dapple-gray, wearing as usual his yellow sash of a major-general, and started to follow Crawford and Wadsworth, who from his camp he could see were already under way, passing the Lacy house. Just as he was reaching the Pike, — we had not left camp three minutes, — a staff officer, riding rapidly, met him and, saluting, said that General Griffin had sent him to tell General Warren that the enemy was advancing in force on his pickets.

I do not believe that Warren ever had a greater surprise in his life, but his thin, solemn, darkly sallow face was nowhere lightened by even a transitory flare — Hancock's open, handsome countenance would have been all ablaze. There was with Warren at this time, as I recall, only Colonel Locke, Dr. Winne, the general's brother Robert, and Lieutenant Higbee, an aide who had been on his staff for a good while, and who was a very brave man. Warren first turned to me and said, "Tell Griffin to get ready to attack at once"; then, for some reason, perhaps because of my youth and inexperience, he told Higbee to take the message, and at once notified Meade as follows: —

"6 A. M. General Griffin has just sent in word that a force of the enemy has been reported to him coming down the turnpike. The foundation of the report is not given. Until it is more definitely ascertained no change will take place in the movements ordered."

(And now he yielded to one of his weaknesses, referred to by Grant in his Memoirs, namely, informing his commanding officer what should be done. He had another and more fatal one, that of commenting at times unfavorably, regardless of who were present, on the orders he received.)

"Such demonstrations are to be expected, and show the necessity for keeping well closed and prepared to face Mine Run and meet an attack at a moment's notice. G. K. WARREN."

Before the above despatch left headquarters another aide came in and Warren added: —

"6.20. Bartlett (Griffin's advanced brigade) sends in word that the enemy has a line of infantry out advancing. We shall soon know more. I have arranged for Griffin to hold the pike till the 6th corps comes up at all events. G. K. W."

He then sent this order to Griffin: —

"Push a force out at once against the enemy, and see what force he has."

Even Warren had not quite thrown off the delusion that Lee was falling back; but within three hours, like a fog, it lifted, not only from his mind but from Meade's and Grant's also.

Griffin, on receipt of these orders, forwarded them to Bartlett, who sent at once the Eighteenth Massachusetts and Eighty-third Pennsylvania, the former on the right, the latter on the left of the Pike. When they reached the pickets, still on their posts of the night before, skirmishers were thrown out, who promptly engaged those of Ewell, driving them back, and quickly ascertaining that the enemy was there in strong force. On this reconnaissance Charles H. Wilson of Wrentham, Company I, Eighteenth Massachusetts, was killed, the first to fall in the campaign. He was only eighteen years old, and the son of a farmer.

In a short time after these orders were sent to

Griffin, Meade with his staff came up hurriedly to Warren, and, hearing what he had to say, exclaimed emphatically, "If there is to be any fighting this side of Mine Run, let us do it right off."

I have seen many statements as to what Meade said, but I was within ten feet of him, and recall with distinctness his face, his language, and its tones. Meade then sent this despatch back to Grant, who was still at his camp waiting for Burnside. It was received at 7.30 A. M.

"The enemy have appeared in force on the pike, and are now reported forming line of battle in front of Griffin's division, 5th Corps. I have directed Gen. Warren to attack them at once with his whole force. Until this movement of the enemy is developed, the march of the corps must be suspended. I have, therefore, sent word to Hancock not to advance beyond Todd's Tavern. I think the enemy is trying to delay our movements and will not give battle, but of this we shall soon see." (General Meade, may I ask when Lee ever declined battle with you? All your doubts on this point will soon be removed, however; for he is right on you and means to deliver a blow, if he can, that will send you reeling, as he sent Hooker, back across the Rapidan.)

Grant, on receipt of this unexpected news from Meade, replied, "If any opportunity presents itself for pitching into a part of Lee's army, do so without giving time for disposition."

Meanwhile Warren, having hurried aides off to Crawford and Wadsworth, the former to halt, the latter to move up on Griffin's left, established his headquarters at the Lacy house. From there he sent this message, dated 7.50 A. M., to Griffin: —

"Have your whole division prepared to move forward and attack the enemy, and await further instructions while the other troops are forming."

He then rode, and I went with him, to Wadsworth, who had halted about a mile beyond the Lacy house. Where we overtook him there was an old chimney that probably marked the home of one of Major Lacy's overseers. I remember it very distinctly, for one of Warren's staff having observed that a bare little knoll near the chimney would be a good place for a battery, he observed coolly that when he wanted advice from his staff he would ask for it. I have always thought that it was an uncalled-for snub on the part of Warren, but a great deal must be excused when a battle is pending; I doubt, however, if Grant or Sedgwick or Thomas under any stress ever spoke to a young officer or soldier in a way or tone that made him uncomfortable.

Wadsworth was just forming his division, to the right of the Parker's Store Road which at that point and for quite a distance runs almost west, following up the main branch of Wilderness Run. Warren said to him, "Find out what is in there," indicating the deep woods. And did they find something? Yes, indeed they did — many their eternal rest. We then went back to the Lacy house, and Warren soon set off to see Griffin.

By the time Warren's aide overtook Crawford (it was just eight o'clock), the head of his division had reached the Chewning farm which lies somewhat beyond where Wadsworth was forming. The ground from the run rises up sharply to its rather high, dipping, and swerving fields, which, when I saw them last, were beginning to clothe themselves in springtime green. The heaving plateau is on swings eastward around the valley of Wilderness Run, like the rim of a great kettle, falling away at last in the angle between the Brock and the Plank roads into many zigzag, swampy ravines, the heads of the easterly branches of the Run.

Two roads connect Chewning's with the Plank, one through the woods to the Store about a mile south; the other follows the rim of the kettle for a while and then breaks away to the Widow Tapp's. Let any one stand on the rolling fields now and he will recognize at once their value to us could we have held them.

In acknowledging the receipt of Warren's orders, Crawford said: —

"There is brisk skirmishing at the store between our own and the enemy's cavalry. I am halted in a good position."

The cavalry he saw were the Fifth New York,

five hundred strong, whom Wilson had left to hold the place till Crawford should arrive. They were not skirmishing, however, with cavalry, but with the head of Heth's division of Hill's corps — the same one that opened the battle of Gettysburg. And here is what had happened. On Wilson's departure for Craig's Meeting House, Colonel Hammond, a very gallant man, in command of the Fifth New York, sent two companies under Captain Barker of Crown Point, New York, to scout the road toward Verdierville. He had not covered more than two miles before he ran up against Heth marching leisurely in column. The Captain, a resolute man as you can readily see on looking into his steady dark eyes, dismounted his men, formed them as skirmishers across the road, and notified Hammond, who at once came up with the rest of the regiment. Of course they were driven back, but not without making a fine stubborn resistance and meeting with heavy losses. By the time Crawford reached Chewning's, Hammond had been pushed to Parker's store. Roebling then with Crawford hastened to the store, and Hammond told him that perhaps he could hold on fifteen minutes longer, whereupon Roebling hurried back to Crawford; but it was too late for him to interpose behind Hammond. Moreover, a heavy skirmish line from Heth's leading brigade was being thrown out toward him. He formed one brigade facing toward the store, the other west, and by that time Hammond had been driven from the store and Heth with his main column was slowly following him, unmindful apparently of Crawford's position on his flank.

When Crawford's despatch, quoted above, reached corps headquarters, Warren was still with Griffin; and it was sent to Meade, who, judging from the indorsement he put upon it, — "I have sent to Wilson, who I hope will himself find out the movement of the enemy," — was not even at that early hour — it was just after nine — in a very good humor.

Had Warren's orders to Crawford been delayed twenty or thirty minutes in delivery, the entire day's operations would have been changed, for his advance would have brought him into immediate contact with the Confederate infantry and Lee's plans would have been disclosed at once. It is all conjecture what would have been the moves Grant would have made in that case, but the chances are, however, that Hancock would have been diverted to the junction of the Brock and Plank roads; that Getty would have been pushed immediately to the Chewning farm, and with Hancock forcing his way to Parker's store, and those open fields firmly in our possession, it would have made Lee's position very critical. If Warren, after giving Wadsworth his orders to find out what was in the woods to the left of Griffin, had continued up the road to Crawford, his quick eye would have

THE BATTLE OF THE WILDERNESS 133

taken in the strength and importance of the Chewning plateau at a glance, and he would have repeated his brilliant coup on Round Top by bringing Wadsworth right up to hold it as he had brought up O'Rorke. But that was not to be; fate had decided that Lee and not Grant was to hold these fields.

Warren, on reaching Griffin, impressed with the seriousness of the situation as he saw it in front of him and practically ignorant of that in front of Crawford, ordered Wadsworth to connect with Griffin's left and Crawford to join Wadsworth's left as quickly as possible. When this order came to Crawford, Roebling, who was then with him, sent in all haste this despatch to Warren: "It is of vital importance to hold the field where General Crawford is. Our whole line of battle is turned if the enemy get possession of it. There is a gap of half a mile between Wadsworth and Crawford. He cannot hold the line against attack." [1]

Warren's only reply was curt. Crawford was to obey the orders he had received. Meanwhile, Warren in a despatch dated 10.30 had directed Wadsworth to "Push forward a heavy line of skirmishers followed by your line of battle, and attack the enemy at once and push him. General Griffin will also attack. Do

---

[1] I beg to acknowledge my obligations to Col. Washington A. Roebling, Warren's chief of staff, for the valuable aid his notes have given me; and to Prof. Theodore Lyman, son of Col. Theodore Lyman, Meade's most confidential staff officer, who has allowed me to consult his gallant father's notes of the battle.

not wait for him, but look out for your left flank." This injunction as to Wadsworth's left flank was obviously due to Warren's fear that, owing to the character of the country, Crawford's division might be delayed in joining him.

This order to Wadsworth is so inconsistent with what actually transpired that it can only be accounted for by the fretful nagging which had begun on Warren from headquarters, and by the fact that Griffin, Ayres, and Bartlett, having visited their skirmish lines and discovered that the enemy were in strong force, were averse to moving unpreparedly, and had so notified him. Colonel Swan of Ayres's staff, whose account is altogether the clearest and most comprehensive yet written of that part of the field, says he went back to Warren at least twice, at Griffin's behest, to report the gravity of the situation, and that Warren used sharp language to him the second time. Colonel Swan says, "I remember my indignation. It was afterwards a common report in the army that Warren had just had unpleasant things said to him by General Meade, and that General Meade had just heard the bravery of his army questioned."

The ground for the latter might have been some heedless remark from one of Grant's aides who had come with him from the West. But however this may be, such was the situation and its feverishness at eleven o'clock on Warren's front. It should be

THE BATTLE OF THE WILDERNESS

said that while Wadsworth and Crawford were trying to get into line Griffin had thrown up some pretty strong breastworks, for he was feeling the weight of the force in his front.

And now let us leave the pestered Warren and see what was going on elsewhere. As soon as Grant could communicate the necessary orders to Burnside as to the disposition of his troops at the ford, he came to the front with all speed: it was then about nine o'clock. On his arrival he found Meade and Sedgwick standing near the Pike, and after a short consultation he and Meade pitched their headquarters near by, on a knoll covered with pines from four to seven inches in diameter, the ground strewn with needles and bits of dead limbs. It is now part of an open leaning field, with here and there an old tree dreaming of the past; and nearly opposite, on the Pike, is a little frame chapel, its bell on Sunday mornings pealing softly over it.

They had barely dismounted before news of importance besides Crawford's first despatch came in. Captain Michler of the engineers, whom Meade had sent to reconnoitre to the right of Griffin, had been suddenly fired on while making his way through the thickety heads of Caton's Run. After satisfying himself that trouble was brewing, he hurried down the Flat Run Road to its junction with that from Germanna, and notified Meade of the situation. Wright, with his division of the Sixth Corps, was moving along unconscious of danger; but as soon as he heard Michler's story he formed his division, facing it west, and soon orders came to move up and join the right of Griffin. He had to advance through about the most broken and confusing district of the Wilderness; his left, under Upton, having to cross all the branches of Caton's Run, which are densely packed with bushes, vines, and low-limbed trees.

Meanwhile, to the wonder of headquarters, no news had come from Wilson; but it is easy of explanation. Not having received counter-instructions and the enemy having made no demonstration, he had set off promptly for Craig's Meeting House on the Catharpin Road. His division got there at eight o'clock; and shortly after its leading brigade engaged Rosser and drove him westward several miles. Rosser was soon reinforced, and pushing Wilson back got possession of the road to Parker's store, thus cutting him off from communicating with Meade.

Every little while, however, as the morning had worn on, wounded men had come down Wilderness Run from the gallant Hammond's command, all telling the same story of the advance of Hill toward the Brock Road. Meade realized his danger; with the junction of the Brock and Plank roads in Lee's possession, Warren's position would be turned and Hancock at Todd's Tavern completely isolated from the other corps. So about half-past ten Getty, who had been lying near headquarters, with the third division of the Sixth Corps,—waiting, shall I say, for the delusion to lift that Lee was retreating? — was ordered to move thither with all haste, and head off Hill. At the same time Hancock, who, dismounted, was resting in a pine grove beyond Todd's Tavern, was told to come up without delay and support Getty.

Meanwhile Winne and the other surgeons were busy locating their hospitals and getting ready for what they knew was coming. And by ten o'clock the yellow flags of the first, second, and third divisions of the Fifth Corps were flying on the ridge east of Wilderness Run; that of the third was first near the Lacy house, but later moved back with the rest; those of Wright's and Rickett's divisions of the Sixth Corps were behind them respectively to the east of the Germanna Road; that of Getty, and later those of Hancock's corps, were pitched near Lewis Run among the fields of the Carpenter farm, which when I saw them last were in blading corn.

Sheridan had made an early start for Hamilton's Crossing, but finding he was on a wild-goose chase, turned back toward Todd's Tavern, and, fortunately, his leading division under Gregg reached there just in time to relieve Wilson, who after severe fighting had been driven rapidly by Rosser and Fitz Lee from the right of Lee's advance.

The absence of any news from Wilson, the threatened danger on the Plank and Brock roads, and the delay of Warren, all added to the intensity of the situation; and impatience at Meade's and Grant's headquarters grew apace as the sun rose higher.

Again and again inquiries were made of Warren when Griffin would move, and each time with more edge, for no one at headquarters shared his conviction that the situation called for a thoroughly organized and formidable attack; why, it was only a rear guard! Moreover, had any one of the eager, self-sufficient headquarters staff tried to put a division or even a regiment in line, he would soon have realized the difficulties and would have had abundant charity for Warren. It is true that the delay that morning was almost inexplicable. But once a division left the roads or fields it disappeared utterly, and its commander could not tell whether it was in line with the others or not. As it turned out, they were almost as disconnected when they struck the enemy as if they had been marching in the dark. Yet it took nearly four hours to get ready to form, and when the orders came to go ahead, divisions were still looking for each others' flanks.

By half-past eleven Meade, with Heth advancing every minute toward the Brock Road, could stand the delay no longer, and, whether or not Wright was abreast with Griffin, "Send him ahead!" was the firm command from headquarters.

The situation, then, on our side, thirty minutes before the battle began, is as follows: Bartlett's

THE BATTLE OF THE WILDERNESS 139

brigade of Griffin's division is forming in two lines of battle on the south of the Pike. The first line is the Eighteenth Massachusetts and Eighty-third Pennsylvania, the latter next the road; the second line, the One Hundred and Eighteenth Pennsylvania and Twentieth Maine, the First Michigan deployed as skirmishers. Ayres is moving up by the flank of regiments in column of fours, through the tangled cedars and pines on the right of the Pike, the One Hundred and Fortieth New York, Pat O'Rorke's old regiment, on the left of the first line, and then the Regulars. In the second line, its left on the Pike, is the One Hundred and Forty-sixth New York, then the Ninety-first and One Hundred and Fifty-fifth Pennsylvania.

Upton's men, the left of Wright's division of the Sixth Corps, are elbowing their way through a tangle like that Ayres is worming his way through, trying to overtake and connect with him. In fact when I was there last spring Upton's ground seemed to me the worse, but both were bad enough. Wright's second brigade, made up entirely of troops from New Jersey, is on Upton's right and across the Flat Run Road (they too were in the network of undergrowth). Wright himself is close behind them on the road and Sedgwick, the best wheel horse, so to speak, in the army team, is in the corner of the old Spottswood field where the Flat Run Road leaves the Germanna Ford.

Wadsworth, mounted on his iron gray, lighter in color than Warren's, is following up his division that is trying to advance in line of battle to join Bartlett's left. Cutler is on the right with the Iron Brigade, the Twenty-fourth Michigan on its left. Stone is in the centre of the division, Rice on the left. Daniel W. Taft, a brave, one-armed Vermont veteran, who was with Rice in the Ninety-fifth New York, tells me that, as they advanced, a wild turkey, the first and only one he ever saw, broke from a thicket ahead of them.

The Maryland brigade of Robinson's division is in reserve behind Stone, Robinson's other division ready to support Griffin.

Getty at the head of his division has reached the junction of the Brock and Plank roads. He was there just in time, for with his staff and escort, although under fire of the tall North Carolinians who had driven Hammond back, he held them off till Wheaton coming up at run formed across the Plank Road, saving the key of the battle-field. There were bodies of Confederate dead within less than two hundred feet of this vital point. Hancock, urged by orders from Meade, is riding rapidly ahead of his corps up the Brock Road to join Getty. His troops are coming on, too, as fast as they can, sometimes at double-quick, but all are greatly delayed by artillery, trains, and horsemen, the road being very narrow and bordered by such thick woods that they cannot draw off into them to clear the way for the infantry.

For three or four miles this side of Todd's Tavern

THE BATTLE OF THE WILDERNESS 141

the road is packed with his sweltering troops, for it is very hot in the still woods. The main heavy supply trains that had followed Hancock's troops to Todd's Tavern have faced about and are making all speed for Chancellorsville, where the artillery reserve is going into park.

Wilson is being roughly handled but his pursuers are suffering too. Sheridan, under a cloud of trailing dust, is returning from his wild-goose chase (and by the way he had the effrontery to claim that it was Meade's fault and not his that the march had been made, — in fact, his orders were based on his own report of the location of the Confederate cavalry, — which if borne in mind, as well as Meade's temper, may account in part for the character of their future relations). At headquarters, anxiety with Meade and Humphreys is increasing over Hill's move toward the Brock Road. The eagle spirit in Meade is up, and a captious wonder pervades his and Grant's staff why Warren does not attack. No one seems to know or care whether Upton is alongside of Griffin or not; even up to that hour a good many of the wise ones among them were pretty sure that there was nothing very serious in front of Warren.

Burnside's corps suffering with heat is marching as fast as it can for Germanna Ford, the rear of the column, Ferrero's colored division, is on the other side of the Rappahannock.

The batteries in the Lacy fields and on the overlooking ridge east of Wilderness Run stand hitched ready to move, the buglers following their captains as they go from section to section of their batteries, the gunners lying down or leaning against their well-loved pieces. There is one battery close behind Griffin. Ammunition-wagons from the various supply-trains have drawn out and taken positions as close as they dare to their respective brigades. The ambulances, too, have come forward and are waiting for their pale passengers.

At last Meade's imperative orders have reached Warren, Griffin's lines are moving, and every one at headquarters is in momentary expectation of hearing the first volley. One who has never been through it cannot realize the tensity of that hour in the Wilderness: we knew it was the beginning of the end, victory for us at last or victory for them.

Grant is sitting with his back against a young pine, whittling and smoking, his modest, almost plaintive, face as calm as though he were sitting on a beach and waves were breaking softly below him. The sun is in the meridian, not a cloud marbles the sky, and Wilderness Run is glistening down through the fields. In the woods not a living leaf is stirring, and the dead ones are waiting to pillow softly the maimed and dying. "The mortally wounded will be so thirsty!" says a spring beauty blooming on the bank of the little run that crosses the Pike in front of

THE BATTLE OF THE WILDERNESS 143

Griffin. "And some of them I *know* will cry for water," observes a violet sadly. "And if they do, I wish I had wings, for I'd fly to every one of them," exclaims the brooklet. "We know you would, sweetheart," reply violet and spring beauty to their light-hearted companion of the solitude. "And if one of them dies under me, I'll toll every bell that hangs in my outstretched, blooming branches," declares a giant huckleberry-bush warmly. "But hush! *hush!*" cries the bush, "here they come!"

VI

AND now let us take a quick survey of what had gone on meanwhile in Lee's lines. Lee himself with a blithe heart had breakfasted early at his camp near Verdierville on the Plank Road. At eight o'clock the night before, he had sent this despatch to Ewell through his Adjutant-General, Taylor: "He wishes you to be ready to move early in the morning. If the enemy moves down the river (that is, toward Fredericksburg) he wishes to push on after him. If he comes this way, we will take our old line [that is, the one of the autumn before at Mine Run]. The general's desire is to bring him to battle as soon now as possible."

The reason for bringing Grant to battle at once may have been strengthened by a despatch that he had received from Longstreet during the forenoon, in response to one he had sent him as to Grant's movements. "I fear," says Longstreet, "that the enemy is trying to draw us down to Fredericksburg, Can't we threaten his rear so as to stop his move? We should keep away from there unless we can put a force to hold every force at West Point in check." Longstreet doubtless had in mind the possibility of Butler's command, then organized at Fort Munroe, being carried to the mouth of the Pamunkey.

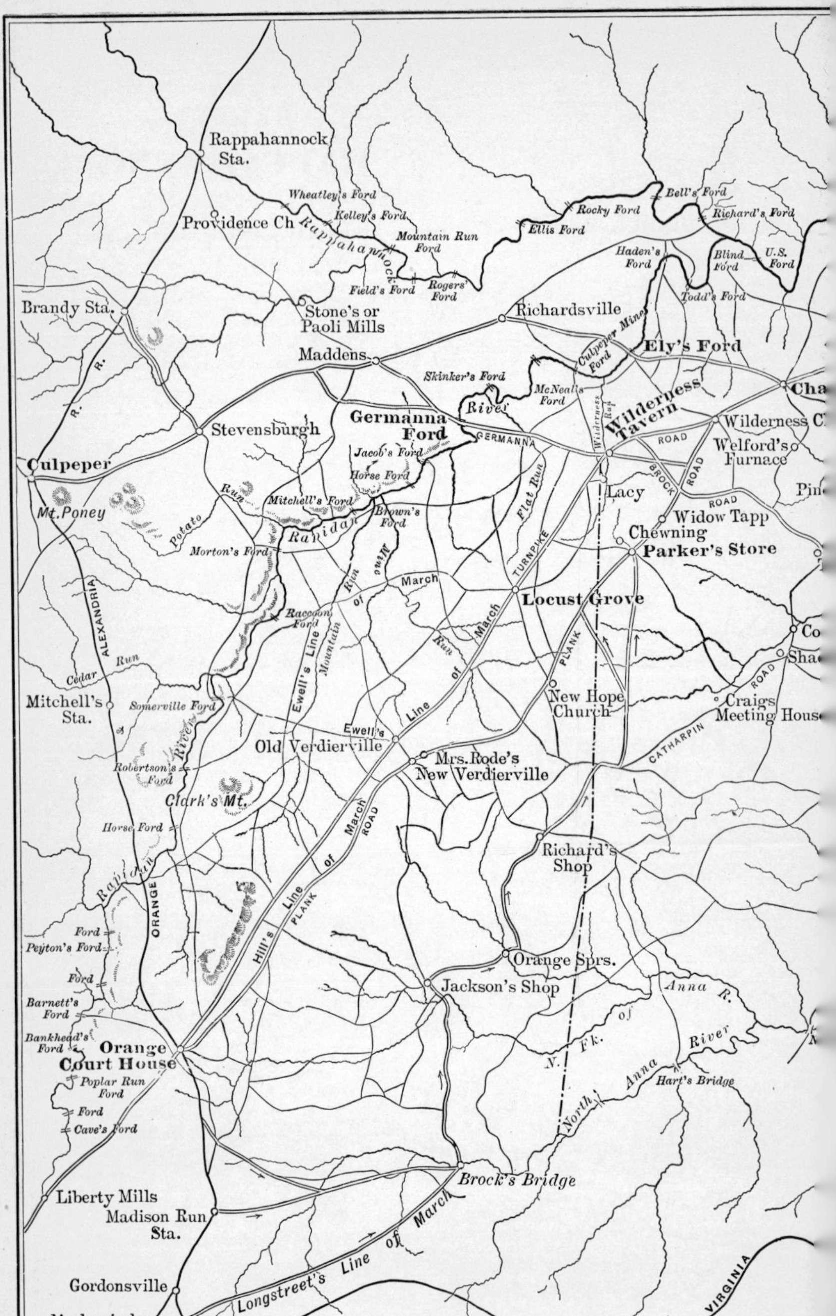
Rappahannock Sta.
Wheatley's Ford
Kelley's Ford
Providence Ch
Rappahannock
Mountain Run Ford
Field's Ford
Rogers' Ford
Rocky Ford
Ellis Ford
Bell's Ford
Richard's Ford
Haden's Ford
Blind Ford
U.S. Ford
Todd's Ford
Brandy Sta.
Stone's or Paoli Mills
Richardsville
Culpeper Mine Ford
Ely's Ford
Maddens
Skinker's Ford
McNeal's Ford
River
Wilderness Tavern
Wilderness Run
Wilderness C
Welford's Furnace
Germanna Ford
Germanna
Road
Brock Road
R. R.
Stevensburgh
Culpeper
Jacob's Ford
Horse Ford
Mt. Poney
Potato Run
Mitchell's Ford
Brown's Ford
Rapidan
Flat Run
Lacy
Widow Tapp
Chewning
Parker's Store
Morton's Ford
Turnpike
Mine Run
March
Locust Grove
Raccoon Ford
Mountain Run
Ewell's Line of March
Run
Line of March
Plank
Alexandria
Cedar Run
Mitchell's Sta.
Somerville Ford
New Hope Church
Craigs Meeting House
Road
Catharpin
Old Verdierville
Ewell's
Mrs. Rode's
New Verdierville
Robertson's Ford
Clark's Mt.
Horse Ford
Richard's Shop
Rapidan
Orange
Hill's Line of March
Plank Road
Ford
Peyton's Ford
Orange Sprs.
Jackson's Shop
Barnett's Ford
Anna R.
Bankhead's Ford
Orange Court House
N. Fk. of
North Anna River
Hart's Bridge
Poplar Run Ford
Cave's Ford
Brock's Bridge
Liberty Mills
Madison Run Sta.
Longstreet's Line of March
Gordonsville
Mechanicsburg
Virginia

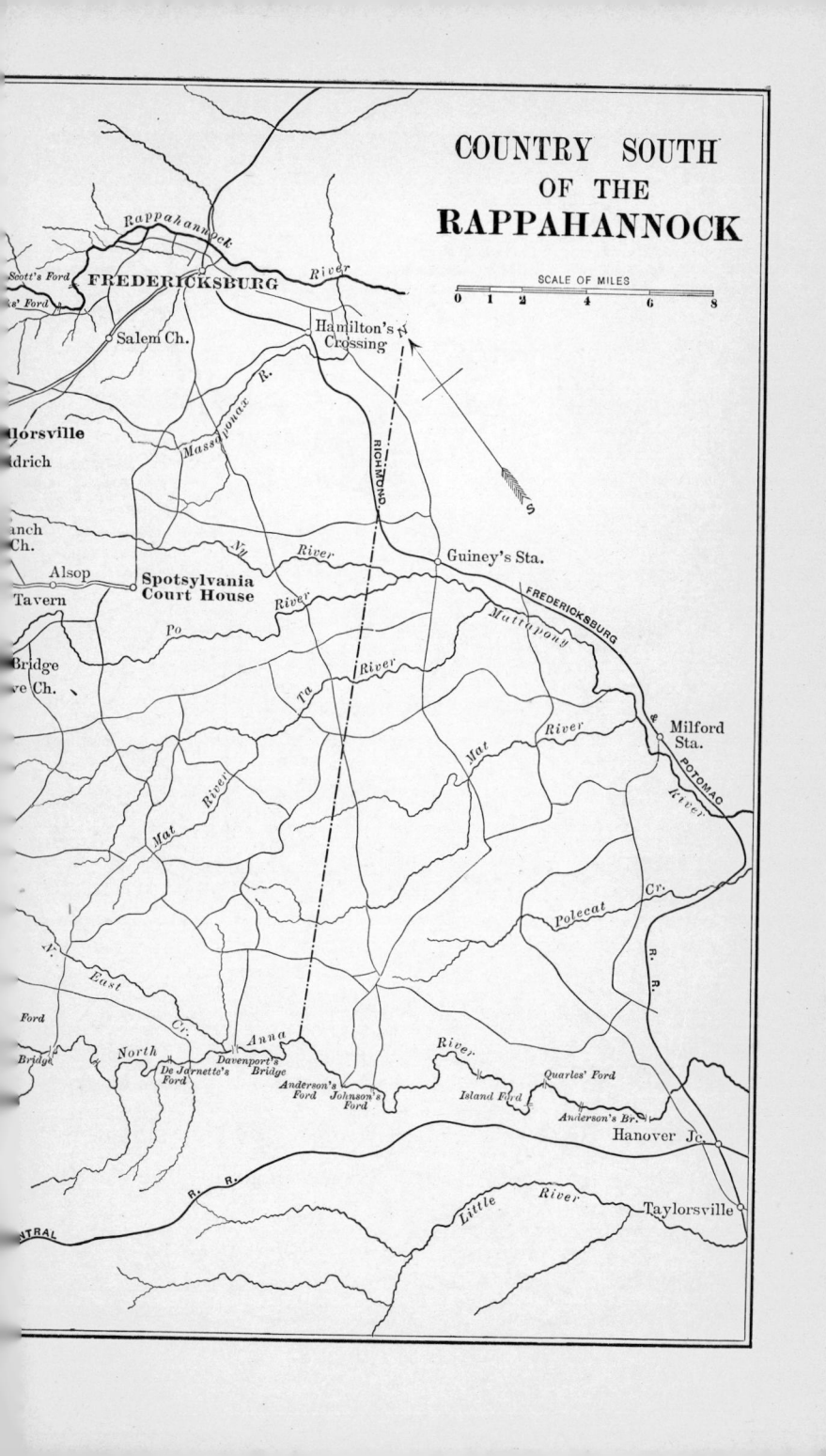
COUNTRY SOUTH OF THE RAPPAHANNOCK
SCALE OF MILES
0 1 2 4 6 8
Rappahannock River
FREDERICKSBURG
Scott's Ford
Salem Ch.
Hamilton's Crossing
N
S
Massaponax R.
RICHMOND
Ny River
Guiney's Sta.
Alsop
Spotsylvania Court House
Tavern
Po River
Ta River
Mattapony
FREDERICKSBURG & POTOMAC
Mat River
Milford Sta.
River
Polecat Cr.
R. R.
East
North Anna River
Cr.
Ford
Bridge
De Jarnette's Ford
Davenport's Bridge
Anderson's Ford
Johnson's Ford
Island Ford
Quarles' Ford
Anderson's Br.
Hanover Jc.
R. R.
Little River
Taylorsville

THE BATTLE OF THE WILDERNESS 145

Heth and Wilcox, who had bivouacked on the Plank Road, the former this side of Lee, the latter beyond, were setting out leisurely for Parker's store. Anderson's, Hill's other division, was still back on the upper side of the Rapidan, the other side of Orange Court House, but under orders to come forward. Ramseur of Rodes's division, Ewell's corps, who with his own brigade and three regiments of Pegram's had been left to resist any crossing between Rapidan station and Mitchell's ford, was making a reconnoissance toward Culpeper, so completely had his old West Point friend Custer bluffed him all through the afternoon while we were moving.

Longstreet, having marched from four o'clock of the previous day and a good share of the night, was now at Brock's Bridge over the North Anna and already under way again. Stuart, Rosser, and Fitz Lee were assembling their cavalry beyond Craig's Meeting House, — at least twenty odd miles from Hamilton's Crossing, where the general orders of the night before had placed them. R. D. Johnston's brigade of Ewell's corps which had lately been sent to guard the bridges over the North and South Anna were on their way back stepping fast: they claim they made the march of 66 miles in 23 hours, but I don't believe it. That kind of time can be made going from a fight but not to it.

When dawn came on, it found Ewell's corps arousing; all of his troops save Rodes and Ramseur were along the Pike, Edward Johnson's division in advance and within a few miles of Griffin. The First North Carolina cavalry, whom Wilson had scattered away from Germanna Ford in the morning, by dusk had re-collected and gone on picket ahead and around Ewell's infantry; and just after sunrise they began feeling their way down the Pike, toward Warren. If they had held back a while, Griffin's pickets would all have been withdrawn to rejoin the moving column, and Ewell could have sprung on Warren most viciously.

Major Stiles, in his "Four Years under Marse Robert," a book of living interest, gives us a glimpse of the early morning up the Pike. He says: "I found him [General Ewell] crouching over a low fire at a cross roads in the forest, no one at the time being nigh except two horses, and a courier who had charge of them, and the two crutches. The old hero, who had lost a leg in battle, could not mount his horse alone. The general was usually very thin and pale, unusually so that morning, but bright-eyed and alert. He was accustomed to ride a flea-bitten gray named Rifle, who was singularly like him, if a horse can be like a man. He asked me to dismount and take a cup of coffee with him." Ewell told the major, while they were drinking their coffee, that his orders were to go right down the road and "strike the enemy wherever I could find him."

About eight A. M., after his corps was moving,

THE BATTLE OF THE WILDERNESS 147

Ewell sent Major Campbell Brown of his staff to report his position to General Lee. Lee sent word back for him to regulate his march down the Pike by that of Hill on the Plank Road, whose progress he could tell by the firing at the head of his column; and that he preferred not to bring on a general engagement before Longstreet came up. Either Colonel Taylor had misunderstood Lee, or Lee for some reason had changed his mind. Had he not done so and tried to put his plans of the night before in execution, another story would certainly have been written of the campaign. Hancock would have been stopped long before he had made Todd's Tavern, and his corps would have been swung over into the Brock Road, which would have effectually stalled off Hill. And although Ewell might at first have staggered Warren and Sedgwick, he never could have driven them from the ridge east of Wilderness Run where they would have been rallied; for Hunt would have had it lined with artillery, and it would have been another Cemetery Ridge for the Confederate infantry. That the chances of war are fickle, I own, but I sincerely believe that if Lee had struck at us early that morning he would have suffered a terrible defeat before sundown, and, instead of the blithe heart at sunrise, when twilight came on he would have carried a heavy one. For Mahone, Anderson, Ramseur, Johnston, and Longstreet would have been beyond reach to give a helping hand to Ewell and

Hill. So I am inclined to think that Colonel Taylor misunderstood Lee: which in a measure is confirmed by his moves that morning, all pointing to a manifest desire not to precipitate a general engagement. For does any one suppose that Hammond's five hundred men could have held Hill's veterans back had they known that Lee wanted them to go ahead? Strangely and interestingly enough, Lee's chances, owing to changing his mind, were growing better and better the farther and farther away Hancock and Wilson were moving from the strategic key of the field. But the truth is that Lee that forenoon knew but little more about Grant's movements than Grant knew about his.

However that may be, Ewell, after hearing from Lee, regulated his march accordingly, slowing up Jones, of Johnson's division, who was in the lead, and who had felt Griffin's and Wadsworth's videttes south of the Pike, having pushed the latter nearly to the western branch of Wilderness Run. When he got to the Flat Run Road which crosses the Pike diagonally, as will be seen by consulting the map, Ewell sent the Stonewall brigade (James A. Walker, who must not be confounded with Henry H. Walker of Hill's corps) down it to the left. Soon, through his field-glasses, from one of the ridges that straggle across the Pike just this side of its intersection by the Flat Run Road, he caught sight of Getty threading his way up across the leaning field east of Wilderness

THE BATTLE OF THE WILDERNESS 149

Run. Thereupon he halted Jones and sent Colonel Pendleton of his staff to report his position to Lee and ask instructions; and no doubt Pendleton told Lee about the column of troops seen moving toward the junction of the Brock and Plank roads. While Pendleton was away, and our people showing more and more activity and earnestness, Johnson, commanding Ewell's leading division, began to arrange his brigades in line as they came up.

Now in those days there was an old field (it has since grown up) about five-eighths of a mile east of the crossing of the Pike by the Flat Run Road. It was narrow, deserted, occupying a depression between two irregular ridges, and extended both sides of the Pike which crossed it a little diagonally nearer its southern end. The east and west sides sloped down to a gully in the middle, the scored-out bed of a once trembling primeval wood-stream; in its palmy days the Pike crossed it on a wooden bridge. The field was known as the Saunders or Palmer field, and was about eight hundred yards long north and south, and four hundred yards wide. It was about the only open, sunshiny spot along the four and a half to seven or eight miles of our battle-line, if we include Hancock's entrenchments down the Brock Road. The last crop of the old field had been corn and among its stubble that day were sown the seeds of glory. The woods were thick all around the field, but the ground east and north of it, in the angle between the Pike and the Flat Run Road was very broken, its low humpy ridges cradling a network of marshy, tangled places, the birthplace of mute lonely branches of Caton's Run, and everywhere crowded with cedars and stunted pines. In truth, I know of no place in the Wilderness where nature seemed more out of humor than right here in the making of it.

Johnson drew Jones back to the west side of the field, his left resting on the Pike, his line of battle stretching off into the woods. He posted Steuart's brigade on the other side of the road, then Walker's and then Stafford's as they came up; their fronts reaching from the Pike northward almost, if not quite, to Flat Run itself.

Millidge's battery was posted at the junction of the roads. Dole and Battle were getting into position on the right of Jones, and coming on behind them was Rodes. J. B. Gordon, the eagle of Ewell's corps, was coming down the old Pike, ready to plunge wherever the smoke of battle rose.

Lee repeated to Pendleton the same instructions as before, not to bring on an engagement until Longstreet was up. Obviously Lee had greatly underestimated the distance Longstreet had to cover. Pendleton got back to Ewell about 11.30. By that time Kirkland's brigade of Heth's division, Hill's corps, followed by Cooke, had driven Hammond almost to the Brock Road. Scales of Wilcox's di-

THE BATTLE OF THE WILDERNESS 151

vision of the same corps was standing off Crawford, while Lane and Thomas were getting into position in front of McCandless, who was trying to connect with Wadsworth. Such was about the situation of both armies at 11.30 A. M.

Griffin's and the right of Wadsworth's division formed about three-quarters of a mile east of the old field. In the formation for the advance, Sweitzer's brigade of Griffin's division had given place on the left of Bartlett to Cutler, of Wadsworth's division, and had formed in reserve behind Bartlett. On Cutler's left was Stone, then Rice. The Maryland brigade of Robinson's division was in reserve behind Stone and Rice. From the Pike to the left of McCandless it must have been fully a mile and three-quarters, and all through thick woods.

Wadsworth's brigades and their supports were ordered by Warren to move by the compass due west. Now a compass is a trusty friend and has guided many a ship steadfastly and truly through darkness and storm on the open sea, but it is out of its element and worse than nothing as a guide for an army fighting in woods like those of the Wilderness. It was natural though for Warren, the skillful engineer, to rely upon it, but under the circumstances, and with the woods as they were, it was utterly impracticable. The first one hundred yards of underbrush, and then one of those briar-tangled ravines, and all reliance on the compass was gone. Self-protection, if nothing else, called on the regiments and brigades to try to keep in touch with each other, whatever the compass might say. As a matter of fact, only one of the commands was guided by it, — McCandless, who had the opening of the Chewning fields on his left to help him. But it ended in taking him away from everybody, and in coming mighty near to causing him to lose his entire brigade. For Wadsworth's people on McCandless's right naturally swung toward the Pike, thus leaving a wide gap between him and Rice.

Well, as already stated, when they began to move, it was almost noon. The troops tried at first to advance in line of battle from the temporary works which had been thrown up while the reconnaissances and preparations had been going on; but owing to the character of the woods, they soon found that was out of the question, and had to break by battalions and wings into columns of fours. So by the time they neared the enemy, all semblance of line of battle was gone and there were gaps everywhere between regiments and brigades. Regiments that had started in the second line facing west found themselves facing north, deploying ahead of the first line. As an example of the confusion, the Sixth Wisconsin had been formed behind the Seventh Indiana, with orders to follow it at a distance of one hundred yards. By running ahead of his regiment, the colonel of the Sixth managed to keep the Seventh in sight till they were close to the front; but when the firing began, the

Seventh set out at double-quick for the enemy and disappeared in a moment; and the next thing was an outburst of musketry and the enemy were coming in front and marching by both flanks.

But there was almost the same state of affairs on the other side, except that the Confederates, being more used to the woods, observed the general direction better and handled themselves with much more confidence and initiative than ours, when detached from their fellows. For instance, the Forty-fifth North Carolina, of Daniels's brigade, having lost all connection with the rest of its brigade, stumbled right on to Stone or Rice, and before they knew it were within a few rods, only a thickety depression between them. Ours were the first to fire, but the aim was too high and scarcely any one hurt; the return volley, however, so says the regiment's historian who was present, was very fatal, and our men broke, leaving a row of dead. Cases of this kind could be repeated and re-repeated of what took place in the Wilderness; and I am free to say that, as I walked through the woods last May, looking for the old lines, more than once I halted with a feeling that some spectral figure, one of those thousands who fell there, would appear suddenly and ask me where he might find his regiment. As a proof of the savage and unexpected encounterings, a line of skeletons was found just after the war, half-covered in the drifting leaves, where some command, Northern or Southern, met with a volley like that of the Forty-fifth North Carolina, from an unseen foe. It is the holding of the secrets of butchering happenings like these, and its air of surprised and wild curiosity in whosoever penetrates the solitude and breaks its grim, immeasurable silence, that gives the Wilderness, I think, its deep and evoking interest.

The woods being somewhat easier for Bartlett's troops to move through than for those in front of Ayres, he gained the eastern edge of the old field quite a little ahead. His first line no sooner came out into the light than Jones, from the woods on the other side of the field, opened on it. Our men dashed down to the gully and then up the sloping side at them, and at once became hotly engaged. As the second line cleared the woods, Bartlett rode galloping from the Pike, flourishing his sword and shouting, "Come on, boys, let us go in and help them."

Meanwhile Cutler, on Bartlett's left, with his Iron Brigade, made up of western regiments, whose members were more at home in the woods than their brothers of the East, had gotten considerably ahead of Bartlett's men, and swinging more and more toward the Pike at every step, struck Jones's and the left of Dole's brigade, and, going at them with a cheer, smashed through, capturing three battle flags and several hundred prisoners. In this attack Battle's brigade directly behind Jones was so severely handled, also by Cutler and Bartlett, that it fell back in

THE BATTLE OF THE WILDERNESS 155

great confusion with Jones's broken regiments for a mile or more. Dole's right held on, and Daniels, moving up and going in on his left, met Stone's and Rice's bewildered commands, some of whom were really firing into each other, and soon stopped all their headway.

When Ewell witnessed Jones's and Battle's overthrow, he hastened back to Gordon, who was just arriving from his bivouac beyond Locust Grove, and implored him to save the day. Gordon moved his strong brigade well to the south of the road; they formed quickly, and at his stirring command dashed at Cutler's and Bartlett's men, who, by this time, were in great disorder, besides having met with severe losses. As showing their jumble, the Seventh Indiana, that started on Cutler's extreme left, had fought its way clear round to the Pike, while the Sixth Wisconsin, that tried to follow it, found itself deep in the woods beyond one of the wandering branches of Wilderness Run, at least a quarter of a mile away from the Seventh. A company of the Twentieth Maine, that had started in Bartlett's second line, came out on the Pike a half-mile west of the field; and, behold, on their return, they were beyond a Confederate line of battle advancing toward their first position. This little command, only seventeen of them, now behaved so well that I think they deserve mention as well as the exploits of brigades and corps. The lieutenant, Melcher, gave the order,

"Every man load his rifle and follow me." Having drawn near the Confederates, intent under fire from our broken men in front, Melcher formed in single rank, he on the right, his first sergeant on the left, and taking deliberate aim, fired, and then with a shout charged. Their attack was a surprise and could only have happened in the Wilderness. With two killed and six wounded they fought their way through, using sword and bayonet, but brought off thirty-two prisoners which were turned over to the provost marshal. Suppose every company in the army had had officers and first sergeants like that!

Such was the state of our lines when Dole's, and those of Battle's and Jones's brigades that had rallied, went in with Gordon, all giving their wildest "rebel yell." And, reader, let me tell you I heard that rebel yell several times; and if you had been there, with the scary feeling one is apt to have in strange, deep woods, the chances are about even, I think, that your legs would have volunteered to carry you to the Lacy farm, or for that matter to the other side of the Rapidan. I mean only that that would have been your first feeling as you heard them coming on; but I dare say you would have faced the enemy right well.

Well, as I have said, what was left of Rice, Stone, and the Maryland brigade, — all somewhat shaky, if not already falling back under the advance of Daniels, — Gordon, Dole, and Battle struck just at

THE BATTLE OF THE WILDERNESS 157

the right time, and practically sent everything flying, but the dead, before them. Bartlett's troops fell back, in great disorder, to the east of the old field and the works they had made in the morning; most of Cutler's and those on the left did not stop till they reached the Lacy farm. There, after great exertion, Wadsworth, who was deeply mortified and in high temper, rallied them. I recall very distinctly their condition, for I was right among them.

Jones and his aide, Captain Early, a nephew of the distinguished Confederate General Early, were killed trying to rally their brigade. I happened to be at Grant's headquarters that afternoon or the next morning, just after the news of his death was received, and overheard some one ask, "What Jones is that?" Ingalls, our chief quartermaster, exclaimed with surprised regret, "Why, that is Jones, J. M.; we called him 'Rum' Jones at West Point." There is a stone on the south side of the Pike, about a mile and a quarter west of the old field, marking the spot where he fell.

Roebling, who was coming back from Crawford, says in his notes: —

"I found the little road (the Parker's store road) crowded with stragglers and large crowds of soldiers pouring out of the woods in great confusion and almost panic-stricken. Some said they were flanked, others said they had suddenly come upon the enemy lying concealed in two lines of battle in the thick underbrush, and that our men had broken at the first volley. Cutler's brigade came back in good order bringing a number of prisoners; the 2nd Division Baxter's brigade came back in much less confusion."

Mr. G. M. Woodward, adjutant of the Second Wisconsin of Cutler's brigade, writes me that just after he had given orders for the regiment to break ranks, and fall back to the Parker's Store Road from which they had moved, all the field officers and two of the captains being either killed or wounded and the regiment outflanked by Gordon's or Dole's counter-charge, he concluded he would stay behind a little and discover, if he could, the enemy's line of advance. While peering around, he suddenly heard a deep bass voice: "Adjutant, what be I going to do with this flag?" Turning, he saw Davidson the color-bearer standing bolt upright in the woods, all alone, grasping the flagstaff. Of course Woodward gave the necessary orders which the brave color-sergeant was waiting for, and together, under a rattling fire, they rejoined the regiment.

And here, reader, let me bring in a word from my friend Dr. Winne, to whom you have already been introduced; and were you to meet him, you would wish that there were more in the world like him. "When Wadsworth's demoralized division was reforming at the Lacy house," says the doctor in his letter to me, "I saw a wonderful example of the triumph of mind over matter which I have never forgotten; and I can almost see the boy's face yet. The shattered division was just moving back to the line when I noticed the youngster in his place going to what may have been his death, with pallid face and trembling lips, yet with his head erect and eyes to the front, going to meet Fate like a gentleman and soldier." I hope, and so do you, reader, that the boy lived through it and on into a good old age, his brave heart ever his cheerful companion, and beating proudly on every fifth of May.

As soon as Wadsworth's men were brought into some kind of order, — and it only took a moment, for once out of the woods and where they could see their colors, all rallied save now and then a man whose heart was not made for war, — I went to the front. And as I reached there Bartlett was reforming, Sweitzer and Robinson having relieved him and stayed the enemy from advancing. He had been wounded in the cheek, and the blood was trickling down on his breast. His complexion was fair and his hair very black, his hat was off, and I can see his bleeding face, as well as Griffin's deeply glum one, across all the years.

So much for the engagement south of the Pike. Ayres, commanding Griffin's right wing on the north side of the road, after overcoming annoying and delaying hindrances, brought his regiments into some sort of line just before they reached the old field, resting his left, the One Hundred and Fortieth New

York, on the road. By this time Bartlett with Cutler had gotten across the south end of the field and had disappeared pursuing Jones; but Steuart's men in the woods on the other side of the field, the continuation of Jones's line, had stood fast, and with their fingers on the triggers were poising among the cedars, scrub-oaks, and young pines, watching Ayres; and as soon as the One Hundred and Fortieth, with their colors flying, came into the field, opened on them with premeditated, withering fire. The regiment, under its gallant yellow-haired leader, "Paddy" Ryan, charged down to the gully and up to the woods, losing heavily at every step. Receiving also a bitter cross-fire from their right, they swerved to the left, the color company astride the Pike, and then at close range grappled with the enemy. The Regulars to their right, under a murderous fire, crossed the upper end of the field in perfect alignment, entered the woods, and began an almost hand-to-hand struggle. But Walker's and Stafford's Confederate brigades, with nothing in the world to hinder, — for the Sixth Corps was not nearly up, — poured deadly vollies into them. The One Hundred and Fifty-fifth and Ninety-first Pennsylvania Volunteers went valiantly to their support. And as the Second, Eleventh, Twelfth, Fourteenth, and Seventeenth Regulars are advancing in the open field under heavy fire, let me say that a steady orderly march like that is what calls for fine courage. It is easy, my friends, to break into a wild

THE BATTLE OF THE WILDERNESS 161

cheer, and at the top of your speed be carried along by excitement's perilous contagion even up to the enemy's works. But to march on and on in the face of withering musketry and canister, as the Regulars are doing now and as Pickett's men did at Gettysburg; or as the Sixth Maine, with uncapped guns, resolutely and silently went up to the works at Marye's Heights, and, by the way, carried them; or as I saw the colored division marching on heroically at the explosion of the mine at Petersburg, their colors falling at almost every step, but lifted again at once, — I say, that is a kind of courage which sets your heart a-beating as your eye follows their fluttering colors.

Meanwhile Griffin, to help the One Hundred and Fortieth to break the enemy's line, sent forward a section of Battery D, First New York, a move of great danger, — and the guns never marched with the Army of the Potomac again. The section, under Lieutenant Shelton riding a spirited chestnut and accompanied by his Captain, Winslow, on a bald-faced brown horse, trotted down the Pike and over the bridge and went into action briskly; the air around them and over the whole field hissing with minie balls. In the edge of the woods, and on both sides of the Pike, at less than two hundred yards away, the One Hundred and Fortieth was fighting almost muzzle to muzzle with the First and Third North Carolina. The first and only round from the section crashed through the woods, ploughing its way among friends and foes, and instead of helping, made it much harder for the brave men. And just then, too,—the One Hundred and Fortieth dreading another round every moment, — on came Battle's and Dole's rallied brigades against their left. Pat O'Rorke's brave men — who helped to save Round Top, the gallant Pat losing his life there — stood the unequal contest for a moment and then broke.

The guns now tried to retire from a position to which many thought they should not have been ordered. But it was too late. Ayres's second line, which had followed the One Hundred and Fortieth and the Regulars with strong hearts, had been suffering at every step by the bitter and continuous cross-fire from their front and unprotected flank; and by the time they had reached the farther side of the field were so mowed down that they could save neither the day nor the guns. The One Hundred and Forty-sixth of this second line reached the gully as the guns tried to withdraw, but was completely repulsed, and many of them made prisoners. Their horses being killed and officers wounded or captured, and the enemy on top of them, the sun-sparkling guns fell into the hands of the enemy. The brave Shelton was wounded and made a prisoner, his proud chestnut was killed.

It was at this juncture that, pursued by Gordon's, Dole's, and Battle's brigades, back came Bartlett's

THE BATTLE OF THE WILDERNESS 163

men, almost in a panic. They rushed into the field and actually ran over the North Carolinians about the guns, many of whom had taken refuge in the gully. The Sixty-first Alabama, of Battle's brigade, was so close behind our people that they hoisted their colors on the pieces and claimed their capture, till the North Carolinians emerged from the gully and said *No!*

By this time Regulars and Volunteers were driven back with heavy loss to the east side of the field.

The victorious Confederates could not pursue beyond the guns, or even stand there, for Sweitzer's of Griffin's, and the First brigade of Robinson's division, under my friend Charles L. Pierson, a gentleman, together with our rallied men, now poured such a fire into them from the east side of the field, that they fled back to their lines on the edge of the woods. Meanwhile the gully was full of their men and ours, most of whom were wounded, and who did not dare to show themselves.

In an attempt to recapture the guns — whose loss Griffin, the commander of our West Point battery in my day, felt deeply — the Ninth Massachusetts, an Irish regiment, and the Ninetieth Pennsylvania suffered frightfully, adding to the thickly lying dead in the old field. Its last year's crop, as already told, was corn; and sweeter by far were the rustling of its swaying blades and tasseling tops than the stinging flights of the bullets and the cries of the wounded.

O! violets, innocent little houstonias, flaming azaleas, broom-grass, struggling pines, cedars, oaks, gums, and sassafras, now dotting the field, when the south wind blows and the stars call out, "This is the fifth of May," do you break into your mellow speech and commemorate the boys I saw lying there beyond the reach of friendly hands? Yes, I know right well you do: and Heaven bless every one of you; and so says every Northern oak and elm, and so says every poplar and Southern pine that borders the old fields of home.

The guns stood there that night and all through the next day, for the fire was so close and deadly from their lines and ours that no one could approach them. When Gordon broke Sedgwick's line at dusk the following night, to the right of the Sixth Corps, the enemy availed themselves of our confusion to draw them off.

On the repulse of Griffin and Wadsworth, Crawford was drawn well down on the Parker's Store Road and began to entrench. Thus by half-past one Warren's corps had been thrown back with heavy loss; and all because the Sixth Corps had not been able to connect with it. Upton's troops did not get abreast of Ayres's bleeding brigade till three o'clock, and the ground where they had fought had burned over. He drove the enemy from an advanced position — for no one in the Army of the Potomac had greater courage or more soldierly abilities than Upton — and

THE BATTLE OF THE WILDERNESS

then entrenched. In front and behind his lines were many scorched and burned bodies of our men and of the Second, Tenth, Fourteenth, and Sixteenth regiments of Stafford's Confederate brigade, who, with James A. Walker's, enveloped the right flank of the Regulars.

Brown's and Russell's brigades of the Sixth Corps, on Upton's right, greatly impeded as he had been in their advance through the scrub-oaks, saplings of all kinds, and intermingling underbrush, came in conflict with Early's division, which, after the repulse of Griffin, had been pushed well out on Johnson's left, and, under Hays, Stafford, and Pegram, was advancing between Flat Run and the road of that name. Russell, on the right, gave them a sudden and severe check, capturing almost entire the Twenty-fifth Virginia of Jones's brigade, which after regaining its hope and courage had been moved to the left. In this engagement, or subsequent ones, for fighting was kept up on and off till dark, Stafford was killed and Pegram severely wounded.

As soon as they had driven us back on Griffin's front, the enemy began to strengthen their entrenchments and brought guns down to their line. Our men did likewise; so, besides musketry, the field was swept with canister, for they were only four hundred yards apart; off on the right, in Sedgwick's front, the lines in some places were within pistol-shot of each other.

The woods on the Confederate side got on fire and

burned widely. "Suddenly, to the horror of the living," wrote a member of the Seventh Indiana who was lying along the Pike, wounded, about where Jones was killed, "fire was seen creeping over the ground, fed by dead leaves which were thick. All who could move tried to get beyond the Pike, which the fire could not cross. Some were overtaken by the flames when they had crawled but a few feet, and some when they had almost reached the road. The ground, which had been strewn with dead and wounded, was in a few hours blackened, with no distinguishable figure upon it."

Some time after his repulse, Griffin, in miserable humor, rode back to Meade's headquarters, and in the course of his interview allowed his feelings to get away with him, exclaiming in the hearing of every one around that he had driven Ewell three-quarters of a mile, but had had no support on his flanks. Then, boiling still higher, he censured Wright of the Sixth Corps for not coming to his aid, and even blurted out something so mutinous about Warren, that Grant asked Meade, "Who is this General Gregg? You ought to arrest him." Meade, however, kept his temper and said soothingly, "It's Griffin, not Gregg, and it's only his way of talking." This flurry of Griffin's was a part of the aftermath of the delusion that Lee would not take the offensive; but in view of all the near and remote consequences of that delusion, the most of which are obvious, it is but a wisp. There is nothing in the campaign which approaches the interest which that delusion has for me. Sometimes as I ponder over it, I think I hear voices near and yet far away, and something within tells me that they are chanting one of Fate's old and weird melodies, — and then all is still.

It seems probable, with what we know now of the situation, that, if Griffin had not been sent forward till Upton had joined him, Ewell would have been driven far away from where Major Stiles found him boiling his coffee. And I wonder where he would have boiled it the next morning: possibly far back on the banks of Mine Run, or, more likely, on the headwaters of one of the streams bearing off to the North Anna, for Lee would have had to fall back in that direction till he met Longstreet. Wherever he may have breakfasted, for me Ewell has always been an interesting character. Major Stiles tells us that he was a great cook. "I remember on one occasion later in the war," says the major, "I met him in the outer defenses of Richmond, and he told me some one had sent him a turkey-leg which he was going to 'devil'; that he was strong in that particular dish; that his staff would be away, and I must come around that evening and share it with him." The major had a part of the deviled turkey-leg and a happy evening with the general. It was this same grim, kind-hearted old Ewell who reported that Stonewall Jackson once told him that he could not eat black pepper because it gave him rheumatism in one of his legs! It would have been well for soldiers in Banks's army if Stonewall had "unbeknownst" eaten some black pepper before he got after them in '62; it might have saved them a part, at least, of that awfully hot chase back to the Potomac.

They say that Ewell looked very sad as he sat before a camp-fire the night he was captured at Sailor's Creek, a few days before Lee surrendered.

And now let us turn from Warren, Griffin, and Sedgwick, to Getty, who reached the junction of the Brock and Plank roads about the very hour when Warren began his attack. That historic point might, not only for the sake of the services they rendered that day, but for services on many other fields, be called Getty's or Hammond's Crossing. Perhaps a descriptive word or two as to its adjacent natural features will aid the reader to see — and I wish he might hear, also — the stirring events that took place there; for I believe that no crossing of country roads on this continent ever heard, or perhaps ever will hear, such volleys.

The roads, the ground of their low banks a dull brick-red, cross each other at a right angle in the midst of dense, silent woods which are chiefly oaks, medium-sized, shaggy and surly, the ground beneath them heavily set with underbrush. The Brock then bears on south some four miles, through whippoor-will-haunted woods, to Todd's Tavern, and thence

THE BATTLE OF THE WILDERNESS 169

on through woods again to Spotsylvania. About half-way between the junction and Todd's Tavern, the Brock is intersected by a narrow-gauge railroad which runs from Orange Court House to Fredericksburg. Having reached Parker's store on its way east from Orange Court House, the railway swings off southerly from the Plank with a long curve, till it comes to the Brock, and then darts across it. When the war came on, its narrow location had just been cleared through the woods, and the roadbed graded. It will be seen in due time what use Longstreet made of this roadbed; how his flanking column under the handsome and gallant Sorrel formed there and swept everything before it to the Plank Road as he charged due northward through the woods, gray and pungent with the smoke of battle and burning leaves. From the junction west to Parker's store is about two and a half miles, and east to where Jackson met his fatal volley on the battle-field of Chancellorsville is less than a half-hour's rapid walk.

The spring-head of the most easterly branch of Wilderness Run crosses the Brock a third or a half mile north of the junction. Over dead leaves and dead limbs and around low tussocks, crowned when I saw them last with blooming cowslips, the darkish water comes stealing out of the gloomy woods on the east side of the road, glints at the sun, and then disappears in those to the west. This branch soon spreads into a zigzagging morass falling in with others like it which head near the Plank Road and creep northward, separated by low, tortuous, broken ridges, the dying-away of the heaving plateau that sweeps around from Chewning's. The waters of all of them unite at last in Wilderness Run. In these shallow depressions bamboo-like vines abound, tangling all the bushes, but here and there is an azalea amongst them, and, when the battle was going on, dogwoods were in bloom along their banks and on the ridges between them. These alternating ridges and swampy interlaced thickets twill the country, that lies inclined like a canted trough in the angle between the Brock Road and the Plank. It was the scene of very, very bitter fighting, and there many men of both armies were lost.

The ground on the south side of the Plank is gently wavy, and about its junction with the Brock may be called dry, level, and firm; but in less than a mile to the west, low ridges are met with like those on the north side, between which are thickety morasses again; but they drain off southward into affluents of Jackson's Run, one of whose branches is a companion of the Brock Road for a while. These waters saunter their way into the Po and Ny and then on at last into the Pamunkey, while those in the morasses on the north side of the Plank flow into the Rapidan and then into the Rappahannock. The land generally, however, is higher on the south than on the north side of the road, and not nearly so broken;

THE BATTLE OF THE WILDERNESS 171

but on either side one can barely see a man thirty yards away.

About a mile and three-quarters west of the junction the Plank emerges from the glooming woods into a clearing of twenty or thirty acres; it is a very quiet spot, and over the most of it the broom-grass is waving. The northern edge of this humble little estate follows the abrupt, bulging descents of the Chewning circular ridge which encloses the basin of Wilderness Run. It is the Widow Tapp's place; her small house, with companion corn-crib and log stable, stand several hundred yards from the road and partly masked by meagre plum and cherry trees. In this old dun clearing Lee made his headquarters during a part of the struggle, and by the roadside just at the border of the woods is the stone with, "Lee to the rear, say the Texans," inscribed upon it.

Getty's leading brigade, Wheaton's, on the run, as already recorded, reached the Plank Road by noon, and with all haste deployed astride it, the Ninety-third Pennsylvania on the left, the One Hundred and Thirty-ninth Pennsylvania on the right, and succeeded, after losing quite a number of men, in checking Heth's advance. As fast as the other brigades of the division came up, they were formed in two lines, Eustis on the right of Wheaton, and the ever-gallant Vermont brigade under Lewis A. Grant on the left. Learning from prisoners that he was confronted by two of Hill's divisions, Heth's and Wilcox's, Getty immediately began to throw up breastworks along the Brock Road, to the right and left of the junction. While thus engaged, his troops skirmishing briskly along their entire front, Hancock, preceding his corps at a fast gallop, reined up before him, looking the soldier through and through, — and I can see his high-headed and high-withered sorrel, with nostrils expanded and pride in his mien that he had brought his gallant rider to the scene of action.

It took but a moment for Getty to make the situation clear to Hancock, whose animated face that morning, and every morning, was handsomely stern with a natural nobility of manner and an atmosphere of magnanimity about him. It was then after one o'clock, and by this time, although unknown to Getty, Warren's repulse was almost complete. Hancock at once sent his staff-officers back, directing division and brigade commanders to hurry the troops forward with all possible speed. His martial and intense spirit so imbued his corps, and his relations with it were of such a personal character, that his fervor in the face of the threatening situation was communicated like a bugle-call to the entire column. But on account of the road being blocked by the trains and artillery, the men were greatly impeded in their march. About half-past two, Birney's, Hancock's leading division, bore in sight, and under orders formed hurriedly on Getty's left, continuing the latter's line of entrenchments so as to be ready if Hill should come on, which was momentarily expected by Getty.

And so, as one after another of his perspiring divisions closed up, each formed on the other's left and entrenched: Birney, Mott, then Gibbon, and last Barlow, whose division was thrown forward of the Brock Road on some high, clear ground which commanded an immediate sweep of country; and there, save two batteries, Dow's and Ricketts's, all the artillery of the corps was massed. Barlow's line then bowed eastward across the Brock Road, not far from where the railway crosses it.

Meanwhile Warren's repulse had made headquarters very anxious, and as early as half-past one, orders suggesting an advance had been sent to Getty. But, believing that Heth and Wilcox were both in front of him, and evidently in no mood to yield, and Hancock's men almost at hand, he used his discretion and waited for their coming, his understanding with Hancock being that, as soon as he was ready, they should go forward. In harmony with this understanding, on Birney's arrival, Getty withdrew Eustis into reserve, moved Wheaton to the north side of the Plank Road, and Lewis H. Grant by flank till his right rested on it. Both brigades, save their heavy skirmish lines, were on the Brock Road behind their temporary works.

Birney's and Mott's divisions, as soon as their tiresome march was over, began, by Hancock's orders, to throw up a continuation of Getty's breastworks along the west side of the road. The old works, now sunk to low, flattened ridges, and covered with bushes and saplings, some of which are quite large, seem almost endless as you travel the lonely road to Todd's Tavern.

The news from Griffin's front growing more and more disturbing, Humphreys, Meade's chief of staff, at a quarter after two reported the serious results to Hancock, who in reply said that two of his divisions, Birney's and Mott's, in conjunction with Getty, would make an attack as soon as they could get ready. This was not the response headquarters had hoped for, but that he would spring to the attack; for the situation demanded it. Minutes followed minutes, worser and worser came the news from Warren, and not a sound from Hancock's and Getty's guns. Meade could stand it no longer and sent Colonel Lyman of his staff with a peremptory order to Getty to attack at once, with or without Hancock. It was the same kind of an order in terms and spirit which had sent Griffin ahead without knowing whether Upton was ready to help him.

Humphreys, in confirming Meade's orders to Hancock to attack, directed him to support Getty with a division on his right and another on his left, "but the attack up the Plank Road must be made at once." Accordingly Hancock ordered Birney to send one of his brigades, Hays's to Getty's right. Hays, that very gallant man, moved as fast as he could up the Brock Road past the junction, but Getty, having caught the spirit of his orders and knowing that he could not wait for any shifting of Hancock's troops, had given the command forward; and before Hays reached his position his men had cleared their works and were desperately engaged. It was then 4.15 P. M.

VII

AND now, having established our forces at the junction, let us go back and establish theirs; let us go to where Lee had bivouacked in the woods near Mrs. Rodes's, and follow the train of events which, as the day progressed, had put Heth ready to plunge at Getty; for, as a matter of fact, he was just about to take the offensive when Getty struck at him. The sun rose that morning at 4.48, — I saw it come up, a deep poppy red, — and by the time it started to clear the tree-tops, Lee was breakfasting and his trusty, heavily-built, iron-gray horse, Traveller, stood saddled, ready for him to mount. Lee was fifty odd years old, about six feet tall, nobly handsome, unmistakably dignified and reserved, his gray trimmed beard darkening as it mounted his subduedly ruddy cheeks, and his enlightened, dauntless eyes, a warm brown hazel. As has been said before, he was very cheerful while he breakfasted with his staff. It may be interesting to know that it was his habit in the field not to loiter at the table, but to leave it early, so that his young and light-hearted friends might enjoy its freedom. He conveyed the impression to all of them that morning — how a reliant spirit in a commander spreads through his staff! —that at heart he was looking forward to a victory over Grant.

THE BATTLE OF THE WILDERNESS 177

The troops of his small, punctilious, courageous, and mysteriously impressive Third Corps commander A. P. Hill, who had been with him on so many fields, were just moving, and "Jeb" Stuart, his buoyant and reliable cavalry leader who had bivouacked that night in rear of the picket-reserve and some distance beyond the infantry, and, according to his biographer, Major McClellan of his staff, was conducting the advance of Hill's corps.

There are no two of the Confederate generals who are more vitally interesting to me than Stuart and Hill, although I never saw either of them that I know of; they may, however, have visited West Point and passed unnoticed in the stream of young and old officers who were coming and going to their Alma Mater when I was there. But, however it may have been, everything I hear or read of Stuart is accompanied with a sense of nearness: I catch sight of his fine features, his manly figure, his dazzling, boyish blue eyes, his flowing, brownly auburn beard, and hear his voice ringing with either command or glee. It is said that rarely was his camp-fire lit that he did not make it joyous, his voice leading in chorus and song. And now the mystic bugles of his troopers are sounding taps from the Rapidan to the James in his old camps, and, hark! as they die away, "Jeb" is still singing on, for woods and fields and running streams all love the memory of a happy heart.

Nature made him a cavalry leader by instinct, and a very sweet character. All of his old army and West Point friends never wearied in testifying to their affection for him. He met his mortal wound just a week after the morning we are dealing with. When told that death was very near he asked that the "Rock of Ages, cleft for me," might be sung, and with his failing breath joined as they sang around his bed. When in the field he always wore a yellow cavalry sash, and a felt hat with a black plume.

Why Hill has been so interesting is perhaps because there is always something very keen to me in the courteous dignity, care of personal appearance, and a certain guarded self-control, of officers who are small in stature, but naturally "military," and whose lives and movements are in harmony with all forms of military etiquette. They say he was quiet in manner, but when aroused and angered, was hard to appease. He wore his coal-black hair rather long, and his face was bearded, his eyes rather sunken, and his voice sharp and stern. But what kindles an enduring, historic light about him is that, when both Stonewall Jackson and Lee were dying, he, this little, punctilious, courteous soldier, was in their misting vision. Stonewall said, as he was fading away, "Tell A. P. Hill to prepare for action"; Lee, like Stonewall, was back on the field and murmured, "Tell A. P. Hill he must come up." Well, well, flowers of Virginia! go on blooming and blooming sweetly, too, by the grave of each of them as this narrative wends its way.

Kirkland's brigade of North Carolinians of Heth's division was in front that morning, and moved leisurely; for Hill had had the same instructions as Ewell, to develop our lines but not to bring on a general battle till Longstreet should overtake them. "Never did a regiment march more proudly and determinedly than the Twenty-sixth North Carolina as it headed the column for the battle of the Wilderness. We passed General Lee and his staff." So says its historian.

It was the same regiment that charged at Gettysburg and lost so heavily on the first day, led by those two fine young men, Burgwyn and "Rip" McCreery, both of whom lost their lives. I wonder if, for the sake of boyhood's memories which I shared with McCreery at West Point, the reader will consent to allow the current of events to eddy for a moment around him and Burgwyn. At Gettysburg their regiment, the Twenty-sixth, waiting for the command, "Forward," was lying down in the edge of the wheat-field that waved up to McPherson's woods.

After a while Burgwyn, spare, refinedly and delicately handsome, gave the long-waited-for command, "Attention!" The lines sprang to their feet, the color-bearer stepped out four paces to the front, and at the command, "Forward!" the regiment, eight hundred strong, moved resolutely across the field toward our men, who were standing partially protected by a stone wall. The engagement soon became desperate, and after the colors of the Twenty-sixth had been cut down ten times, McCreery seized them and, waving them aloft, led on; but within a few paces he was shot through the heart, and his Virginia blood gushed out, drenching the colors. Burgwyn took them from McCreery's flaccid hand, — and again I see that thin, nervous hand sweeping the holy air of the chapel in impassioned gesture as he delivers his Fourth of July oration, — a moment later a minnie ball goes tearing through Burgwyn's lungs, and, as he falls, swirling, the flag wraps about him. The lieutenant-colonel of the regiment kneels by his side and asks, "Are you severely hurt, dear colonel?" He could not speak, but pressed his friend's hand softly and soon passed away.

The Twenty-sixth, with its gallantly commanded Confederate brigade, finally carried the position; and it adds interest and, I am sure, stirs a feeling of pride in every Northern breast, that the Twenty-sixth's worthy opponent that day at Gettysburg was the Twenty-fourth Michigan, now present in the Wilderness, whose exploit of capturing the colors of the Forty-eighth Virginia has already been given. Nine officers and men carried the flag of that Michigan regiment during the action at Gettysburg; four of them and all the color-guard were killed. The Twenty-fourth was from the shores of lakes Erie

THE BATTLE OF THE WILDERNESS 181

and Huron, the Twenty-sixth from the slopes of the mountains of western North Carolina. In one of the North Carolina companies there were three sets of twins, and, when the battle was over, five of the six were lying dead with Burgwyn and "Rip" McCreery.

And now to go on with the narrative, Kirkland's brigade was followed by Cooke's, also made up entirely of North Carolinians, and then came Walker's and Davis's brigades, the latter from Mississippi, the former from Virginia. Wilcox with his division followed Heth. While Ewell was marshaling rather cautiously in front of Griffin, Heth kept on slowly down the Plank Road, and every once in a while from the southwest came the boom of Wilson's guns, who, three or four miles away, on the Catharpin Road, was already engaging Rosser right valiantly. At last Heth was in reach of the Brock Road, but Wheaton's sudden appearance put a new aspect on affairs. Kirkland pushed his skirmish line hard up, and Wheaton not budging, Heth notified Hill that he had reason to believe a strong force was in his front. Before this news could reach headquarters, Lee, his mind being wholly taken up with what had just happened on Ewell's front, namely, the overthrow of Jones's and Battle's brigades and the savage fighting inaugurated on the Pike, had ordered Wilcox to move toward the danger-point. Wilcox left McGowan and Scales to look after Crawford, and pressed northward through the woods with his other brigades, Lane's and Thomas's. Riding ahead of his troops, he found Gordon, and had barely spoken to him when a volley broke from where he had left his men. The musketry he heard was between his people and McCandless, who, having failed to make any connection with Wadsworth, was moving forward by compass, and, as it proved, right into the arms of Wilcox's two brigades, which very soon disposed of him, capturing almost entire the Seventh Pennsylvania. This case illustrates well the chance collisions which marked the fighting in the Wilderness, owing to the density of the woods.

After Warren's repulse, Sedgwick not threatening seriously, Ewell having entrenched himself firmly and apparently safely before both of them, Lee gave attention to the news sent by Heth in regard to our stubborn lines at the junction, and about half-past three he sent this message to him by Colonel Marshall, his chief of staff: "General Lee directs me to say that it is very important for him to have possession of Brock Road, and wishes you to take that position, provided you can do so without bringing on a general engagement."

And here let me make this comment on Lee's message. All authorities agree that his orders in every case to those in front that day were qualified by the caution not to bring on a general engagement. Orders of this kind are embarrassing; for a corps or division commander never knows how far to push his

THE BATTLE OF THE WILDERNESS 183

successes. Their evils had a good illustration at Gettysburg. There Lee used identically the same language on the first day; and when Trimble urged Ewell to take advantage of the complete overthrow of our First Corps and follow up our disordered troops and seize the Cemetery Ridge, he replied that he had orders from Lee not to bring on a general engagement. Lee's indeterminate, and therefore hampering orders, I believe, lost him the battle of Gettysburg.

Heth replied in effect that the only way to find out whether it would bring on a general engagement was to make the attempt; and while Marshall returned for a reply, he formed his division across the Plank Road in line of battle, ready to go ahead if that should be the command. Cooke's brigade was in the centre, the Fifteenth and Forty-sixth on the right, the Twenty-seventh and Forty-eighth North Carolina on the left of the road. Davis's brigade, made up of the Second, Eleventh, and Forty-second Mississippi, and the Fifty-fifth North Carolina, was on Cooke's left. Walker was on the latter's right, Kirkland in reserve. The line on which Heth's troops were formed had not been chosen for the special advantages of defense it offered, but rather by chance, for he expected to be the assailant. A better one, however, as it turned out, could not have been selected. It conformed to the low, waving ridges between the morasses, offering splendid standing ground, and was almost invisible until within forty or fifty yards. Ready to go ahead or ready to hold, there they were when the quick, sharp, cracking fire of the skirmish-line told them that the Union's defenders were coming.

Now let us turn to Getty: it is about half after four, — that hour when the elms in the northern meadows were beginning to lengthen, the cows to feed toward the bars, the thrushes, in the thickets where the dog-tooth violet and the liverwort bloom, to strike their first clear ringing notes, and the benignant serenity of the day's old age to spread over fields and flock-nibbled pastures. It was then that the men from the North, from Pennsylvania, New York, and far-away Vermont, heard the expected order to advance. As they leap over the breastworks, for a moment the scarlet in their colors splash among the fresh green leaves in the edge of the woods, but almost in the twinkling of an eye, the lines of men in blue, the guns, and the rippling flags, disappear. Soon crash after crash is heard, cheers, volleys, and more wild cheers, and in a little while gray smoke begins to sift up through the tree-tops; and in a little while, too, pale, bleeding fellows, limping or holding a shattered arm, some supported by comrades, others borne on litters, begin to stream out of the woods.

Getty, the cool, intellectually broad-based man, moved forward with his men; between him and them and immediately in front of him was a section (two guns) of Ricketts's Pennsylvania battery. Within less than a half-mile his troops had met Heth's almost face to face, and in the lengthening shadows they plunged at each other. Wheaton's men on the north side of the road encountered half of Cooke's and all of Davis's brigade posted on the hither side of the tangled morasses already mentioned, and in some places, at not more than one hundred and fifty feet apart, they poured volley after volley into each other. And so it was on the south side with the gallant Vermonters: they, too, met the enemy face to face; and I have no doubt that the traveling stars and roaming night-winds paused and listened as the peaks in the Green Mountains called to each other that night, in tearful pride of the boys from Vermont who were lying under the sullen oaks of the Wilderness; for never, never had they shown more bravery or met with bloodier losses.

Hays, who had been sent just as the action began to Getty's right, after having double-quicked to his position, rested for a moment and then moved forward, the Seventeenth Maine on his extreme right. As Davis reached far beyond Wheaton's right, Hays soon came up against him and joined battle at once. Owing to the nature of the ground, — the zigzagging morasses were between them, — continuous lines could not be maintained by either side, and the result was that wings of regiments became separated from each other; but, together or apart, the fighting was desperate, and it is claimed that Hays's brigade lost more men than any other of our army in the Wilderness. Hays himself (a classmate of Hancock, both being in the class after Grant's) during a lull rode down the line of battle with his staff, and when he reached his old regiment, the Sixty-third Pennsylvania, that had stood by him so gallantly in repulsing Pickett's charge, he stopped. While he was speaking a kindly word, a bullet struck him just above the cord of his hat, crashing into his brain; he fell from his horse and died within a few hours, and a braver spirit never rose from any field.

When Birney sent Hays to Getty's right, he led his other brigade (Ward's) to Getty's left. As soon as Birney moved, Mott was ordered by Hancock to go directly forward with his two brigades from the Brock Road, which would bring him up on Birney's left. The fighting became so fierce at once and the musketry so deadly, that aide soon followed aide to Hancock, who was posted at the crossing, from Birney, Getty, Hays, and about every brigade commander, calling for help. At 4.30 Carroll was sent for and ordered to support Birney, who, as soon as he came up, advanced him to the right of the Plank Road. Owens's brigade of Gibbon's division followed, and was put in on the left and right. Brooke, who had the rear of Hancock's column as they moved in the morning, and had been halted at Welford's Furnace on the road from Chancellorsville to Todd's Tavern, made his way as fast as he could through the woods, his men quickening their steps as the volleys grew louder; he reached the Brock at 5.30 and at once pushed into the fight, joining Smyth of Barlow's division, who, being nearer, had proceeded with his gallant Irish brigade to the line of battle to take the place of one of Mott's brigades that had barely confronted the enemy, when, receiving a couple of volleys at close range, panic seized it and it broke badly, unsteadying for a moment the troops on its right and left; this brigade did not stop till it crouched behind the breastworks it had left along the road. Miles's and Franks's brigades of Barlow's division had become engaged also.

At an early hour in the afternoon, Williams's North Carolina Confederate battery of Poague's artillery battalion went into position between Widow Tapp's house and the woods, throwing little epaulements in front of their pieces. As soon as Heth became heavily engaged, Lee, who was close by, having established his headquarters in the old field, sent orders to Wilcox to return at once to the Plank Road, — for he could not mistake what the volume of the musketry meant, — and directed Scales and McGowan in person to go to Heth's support, Crawford meanwhile having withdrawn from their front, to within a mile of the Lacy house.

When McGowan received his orders his brigade had just formed in the Widow Tapp field, and the chaplain of the First South Carolina was holding prayer. And there, with the setting sun sweeping them, the roar of Heth's and Getty's musketry breaking on them, the clergyman in front of the ranks, their heads bowed on hands grasped one over the other at the muzzle of their guns, he, with uncovered head, palm to palm, and reverently uplifted face, was praying, as the order came for them to go to Heth's support. The command, "Attention!" rang out, the officers' swords lifted quickly, up went the guns, and away marched the brigade.

Wilcox, on receipt of the urgent orders, set his two brigades, Thomas's and Lane's, in quick motion, filed across the Chewning farm in sight of the signal officers on Crawford's new line, and then took the wood-road — leaf-strewn and shadow-mottled — that joins Chewning's and Widow Tapp's, skirting the abrupt descents to Wilderness Run. Through the timber, and over the tree-tops in the valley, he caught distant views of Grant's headquarters and the old Wilderness Tavern. He caught sight, too, of Wadsworth moving past the Lacy house.

Grant and Meade happened to be at Warren's headquarters at the Lacy house as our signal officers reported the march of Wilcox's column. Grant at once ordered a diversion to be made by Warren against Heth's flank and rear, and inferring from Wilcox's move that Lee was detaching from Ewell, had ordered Warren and Sedgwick to renew the attack on their fronts immediately. Wadsworth, terribly chagrined over the conduct of his division in the attack up the Pike, was anxious to retrieve the reputation of his troops, and asked to be sent against Heth. Accordingly Warren sent him and Baxter's brigade of Robinson's division. It was nearly six o'clock as he filed down across the fields, Roebling leading the way.

When Wilcox reached Lee he reported to him what he had seen through the timber, and Lee sent the following despatch at once to Ewell:—

May 5, 1864, 6 p. m.

LIEUTENANT-GENERAL EWELL,
    Commanding, etc.

GENERAL: The commanding general directs me to repeat a message sent you at 6 P. M. The enemy persist in their attack on General Hill's right. Several efforts have been repulsed, and we hold our own as yet. The general wishes you to hurry up Ramseur, send back and care for your wounded, fill up your ammunition, and be ready to act by light in the morning. General Longstreet and General Anderson are expected up early, and unless you see some means of operating against their right, the general wishes you to be ready to support our right. It is reported that the enemy is massing against General Hill, and if an opportunity presents itself and you can get Wilderness Tavern ridge and cut the enemy off from the river, the general wishes it done. The attack on General Hill is still raging. Be ready to act as early as possible in the morning.

Yours, most respectfully,
C. MARSHALL,
Lieutenant-Colonel
and Aide-de-Camp.

Of all the despatches in the War Records relating to the battle, this one has more intrinsic interest than any other for me. It not only coördinates the movements of Wilcox, Wadsworth, and Sedgwick, but it reveals at a flash the workings of the minds of both Grant and Lee. Let us revert to the situation, illumed by the light it throws.

Grant and Meade, accompanied by several of their staffs, have come over to Warren's headquarters at the Lacy house. Grant is mounted on "Egypt," or "Cincinnati," a black-pointed, velvety-eared, high-bred bay, and Meade with drooping hat, on his old fox-walk, "Baldy." While on the lawn under the same old venerable trees that are dreaming there still, Grant is told that a signal officer on Crawford's line has just seen a column of troops marching rapidly toward Heth, — Locke's despatch to Humphreys confirming the news is dated 5.45 P.M.; with lightning speed, he catches the significance of the news, and moves Wadsworth to fall on Heth's flank, and at the same time orders Warren and Sedgwick to strike at once at Ewell.

THE BATTLE OF THE WILDERNESS 191

Wadsworth is hardly on his way before Wilcox reaches Lee and tells him what he had seen through the timber. Lee's inferences, the converse of Grant's, flood in at once: Grant is weakening his line in front of Ewell, and, as the volleys come rolling up one after another from Heth and Getty, Lee tells Ewell to make a dash if he can for the ridge east of Wilderness Run.

Could we have anything better than these orders to show the clear-sightedness, quick resolution, swift unhesitating grasp, and high mettle of both Grant and Lee? their instinctive discernment of the significance of the shifting phases of battle? Grant's indomitable will to take advantage of them; Lee's warrior blood boiling with the first whiff of the smell of battle, and his tendency to throw his army like a thunderbolt out of a cloud at his adversary? And, by the way, that smell of battle always set Lee ablaze, and with his quick comprehension of the immediate moves to be made, augmented by the warmth of his fiery spirit, I think, was the source of the influence he shed around him as he fought a battle.

Lee had some advantages over Grant that afternoon. Grant was a stranger to his army, Lee knew his, and his army knew him; Lee was where he could see the field, Grant where he could not; Lee knew the country well, Grant had never before entered its fateful labyrinth. Moreover, Lee knew what he wanted to do, what the fate of the Confederacy called on him to do, and the above despatch of

Colonel Marshall's, ringing with its resolute purpose, tells how he hoped to do it.

But, but, Colonel Marshall, allow me your ear for a moment: there is a quiet, modest, blue-eyed, medium-sized man down on that knoll near the Lacy house, — cut a short vista through these pines behind you, and you can see where he is in the distance, — whom at last at Appomattox you and Lee will meet; and, strangely enough, the ink-bottle you are now using will be used then to draw the terms of surrender; down on the knoll is a gentle-voiced man who has an undismayable heart in his breast, and he will meet you to-morrow morning when Longstreet, Anderson, and Ramseur have come, and every morning thereafter, to the end of the Rebellion, with blow for blow.

Wilcox's pregnant interview with Lee ended, he put Thomas's brigade on the left of the Plank Road, and, guided by the continuous roar of musketry, it moved forward toward Heth's battered lines. Lane's brigade was to form on Thomas's left, but just as it reached Hill, Scales, on Heth's right, was smashed, and Colonel Palmer of Hill's staff led it thither.

At ten minutes of six — the sun dropping toward the tree-tops, and twilight, owing to the density of the woods, gathering fast — Lyman, who had stayed at Hancock's side to give Meade timely information as to the progress of events, reported: "We barely hold our own; on the right the pressure is heavy.

General Hancock thinks he can hold the Plank and Brock roads, but he can't advance."

Between half-past five and six o'clock the enemy — McGowan's and Kirkland's brigades having come in to relieve Heth's exhausted troops in front of Getty — charged, and for a moment planted their colors beside one of the guns of Ricketts's section, whose horses had been killed. But Grant's and Wheaton's lines, although thrust back momentarily by the sudden onslaught, braced and drove the Confederates away from the guns. A little later Carroll and Owens, Brooke, Smyth, and Miles came up, and relieved Grant, Wheaton, Hays, and Ward. Carroll then fought his way in the twilight fairly across the now riddled swamp, sent the Eighth Ohio up the south and the Seventh West Virginia up the north side of the road, beyond the disabled section where Captain Butterworth of his staff and Lieutenant McKesson of the Eighth, by the aid of squads from the Eighth Ohio and Fourteenth Indiana, dragged back the guns; Lieutenant McKesson receiving a severe wound.

The battle raged on. Wheaton's men on the north, and the Vermonters on the other or south side of the road, with Ward's brigade, were still standing up to it, although suffering terribly. The Confederates in front of them had the advantage of a slight swell in the ground, and every attempt to dislodge them had met with slaughter. Birney sent a couple of regiments to their support. About sundown the commanding officer of the Fifth Vermont was asked if he thought, with the help of Birney's men, he could break the enemy's line. "I think we can," replied the stout-hearted man. And when Birney's men were asked if they would give their support, they answered, "We will," with a cheer. And again they went at the enemy's line, which partially gave way — it was probably Scales; but so dense were the woods that a break at one point had mighty little moral effect to the right or left, with troops as steady as theirs and ours.

When Palmer got back to the road there he found Stuart and Colonel Venable of Lee's staff sitting on their horses in the dusk, and told them that Lane had become engaged. Venable exclaimed, "Thank God! I'll go back and tell Lee that Lane has gone in, and the lines will be held."

Yes, and here is what he met, so says the report of the Sixty-sixth New York: "The rebels came marching by the flank, distant about ten paces. It being dark, they were at first taken for friends, but the illusion was soon dispelled, and Colonel Hammell gave the order to fire, which was promptly executed, with fatal effect. It proved to be the Seventh North Carolina." The report adds that they advanced again in line of battle, but were repulsed, leaving their dead and wounded. But they did hold the lines.

The sun having gone down, darkness soon settled

around them all, but the struggle did not end. Never was better grit shown by any troops. They could not see each other and their positions were disclosed only by the red, angry flashes of their guns. Their line stretched from about two-thirds of a mile north of the Plank Road to a distance of a mile and a half south of it. And so, shrouded in the smoke, and standing or kneeling among their dead, both sides kept on. All other sounds having died away, the forest now at every discharge roared deeply.

"All during that terrible afternoon," wrote the historian of the Forty-sixth North Carolina, Cooke's brigade, "the regiment held its own, now gaining, now losing, resting at night on the ground over which it had fought, surrounded by the dead and wounded of both sides." The Fifty-fifth North Carolina in Davis's brigade that had fought Hays took into the action 340 men. At the end of the battle it is related in their history that "34 lay dead on the line where we fought, and 167 were wounded. They were on one side of a morass and we on the other." The historian asserts that the sergeant of the Confederate ambulance corps counted 157 dead Federals the following day along their brigade-front. "The record of that day of butchery," says the same authority, "has often been written. A butchery pure and simple, it was unrelieved by any of the arts of war in which the exercise of military skill and tact robs war of some of its horrors."

"At one time during the fighting of the fifth," according to the historian of the Eleventh North Carolina, Kirkland's brigade, "the brigade lay down behind a line of dead Federals so thick as to form partial breastworks, showing how stubbornly they had fought and how severely they had suffered." This statement seems almost incredible, but it will not be forgotten that Kirkland was in reserve when the action began and was not called on till late, so that, as the brigade went in with McGowan, the men had a chance to see the death and destruction that had taken place. This brigade, out of 1753, lost 1080. (The night before Lee's army was forced formally to lay down its arms and give up its colors at Appomattox, the survivors of the Eleventh North Carolina of the above-mentioned brigade took the old flag which they had borne at the Wilderness, into a clump of young pines, and there, collecting some fagots, gathered sadly about it in the darkness and burned it.)

At the close of the battle this regiment and all the other regiments of Heth's and Wilcox's divisions were staggering, and it is highly probable that if the engagement had begun an hour or so earlier, defeat would have overtaken them. Or, had Wadsworth been sent earlier, the chances are that Heth could not have withstood his flank attack.

There was no engagement during the war where the private soldiers of the army showed greater valor

THE BATTLE OF THE WILDERNESS 197

than up the Plank Road that afternoon. Bear in mind that they did all their fighting amid the umbrage and terror of the woods, and not under the eye of a single general officer; not one in twenty could see his colors or his colonel. There was none of the inspiration of an open field with stirring scenes. No, they fought the battle alone, their only companion the sense of Duty who was saying to them, to those obscure boys from the Green Mountains of Vermont, from Connecticut, Pennsylvania, New York, and Ohio: "Stand fast for your country, stand fast for the glory of the old home, for the honor of the gray-haired father and mother." Let garlands be given, too, to Heth's and Wilcox's men, and if I were the son of one who stood there that day under the banner of the Confederacy, I'd feel proud of my blood.

At last, about eight o'clock, the volleys that had been so thundering and dreadful stopped almost suddenly. No one who was with the Army of the Potomac that night will ever forget the immediate silence; Getty's and Birney's scarred and well-tried veterans were led back to the Brock Road, and there, beside its lonely, solemn way, they lay down and rested. And what is this movement of mind and heart? It is imagination lifting the veil from the inner eye, and lo! we see Honor proudly standing guard over them all.

Getty's division on that day and the next met with the heaviest loss experienced by any division during the war, and his Vermont brigade of this division lost more men on that afternoon of the fifth than the entire Second Corps. Of the officers present for duty, three-fourths were killed or wounded.

There is no occurrence of the day that I remember with more distinctness than the setting off of Wadsworth's command that afternoon. I can see the men now moving down the field in column to the road, and then following it up the run for a piece toward Parker's store. They formed in two lines of battle and entered the swampy tangles, guided by Colonel Roebling. Their progress, trammeled by the nature of the woods, was slow; within a half-mile or so they struck the skirmishers of Thomas's brigade of Wilcox's division, who had just been posted on Heth's left. Wadsworth pushed them steadily back, till darkness came on and he had to halt. The extreme right of his line was now nearly at the foot of the abrupt slopes running down from the Widow Tapp's old field, his left perhaps three-quarters of a mile from the Brock Road. His front was parallel to the Plank Road, a half to five-eighths of a mile from it, the ground about him broken and the woods very dense; and there, on the dead leaves and among spice-bushes, spring beauties, violets and dogwoods in bloom, they passed the solemn night through. The men say, however, as well as those on Hancock's lines, that they were restless; their position had been reached practically in the dark, and they were so

THE BATTLE OF THE WILDERNESS 199

close to the enemy that both spoke in whispers, and all realized the inevitable renewal of the struggle in the morning. Roebling got back to the Lacy house, his most valuable notes tell me, about nine o'clock.

When Wadsworth was moving toward Hancock, Russell's and Brown's brigade of the first division of the Sixth Corps, on the extreme right of the line beyond Griffin and Upton, made and received counter and vigorous attacks on Ewell's left, the Confederate brigades commanded by Stafford, Pegram, and Hayes. Stafford was mortally and Pegram very severely wounded, and the Twenty-fifth Virginia of Jones's brigade, which had been transferred to the extreme left along with Gordon's, lost its colors and over two hundred men to the Fifth Wisconsin of Russell's brigade.

And here may I be allowed to say that all the flags save one captured from the enemy in the Wilderness were taken by western regiments. The Twenty-fourth Michigan captured the colors of the Forty-eighth Virginia, the Fifth Wisconsin those of the Twenty-fifth, the Twentieth Indiana those of the Fifty-fifth, the Seventh Indiana those of the Fiftieth Virginia; the Fifth Michigan those of the Thirteenth North Carolina. The Eighth Ohio and the Fourteenth Indiana retook Ricketts's guns. The men from the West were probably no braver, man for man, than those of the East; but I think their success was wholly because so many of the men were woods-wise. From their youth up, both by day and by night, they had roamed through woods under all sorts of sky and in all sorts of weather, and so their depths had no terror for them; like their enemies, they were at home in the timber, and could make their way through it almost as well by night as by day. And I have often thought that perhaps it was this common knowledge of the woods that gave our western armies so many victories. A Confederate line coming on, or rising up suddenly and breaking into their sharp, fierce yells, did not greatly surprise or set them quaking. And yet, although all my boyhood was passed in the grandly deep, primeval forests of Ohio, I am free to own that I never heard that "Rebel" yell in the woods of Virginia that its old fields behind us did not seem at once to become mightily attractive.

Reference should be made, as a part of the day's serious history, to the cavalry engagements under Wilson and Gregg. The former's encounter with Rosser and Fitz Lee has been mentioned; it was severe, and Wilson, overpowered, had to take his way as best he could to Gregg at Todd's Tavern, who bristled up, and with Davies's brigade, the First New Jersey and First Massachusetts Cavalry, met the confident pursuing enemy and drove them back to Corbin's bridge, but only after a loss of ninety-odd killed and wounded.

When night and exhaustion put an end to the fell struggle between Hancock and Hill, it may be said that the first day of the battle of the Wilderness was over. And what a day it had been! Where now were the plans, hopes, and roseate forecasts which the self-reliant natures of both Grant and Lee had made, as they were looking forward to it the night before? All transmuted into solemn, speechful reality. Grant had telegraphed Halleck as soon as he had crossed the Rapidan safely: "Forty-eight hours now will demonstrate whether the enemy intends giving battle this side of Richmond." With his intuitive wisdom, he had predicted truly; yet, as a matter of fact, he did not know or care when or where the battle should begin. He meant to find Lee, clinch, and have it out with him for good and all, wholly undisturbed as usual over possible results. And behold, the day had banished the uncertainties of the night before, and had brought him just where he had wanted to be, in conflict with his famous adversary.

But, imperturbable as he was, I feel sure it had brought some disappointment to him, — not because Lee had obviously the best of it, but because he himself had discovered the Army of the Potomac's one weakness, the lack of springy formation, and audacious, self-reliant initiative. This organic weakness was entirely due to not having had in its youth skillfully agressive leadership. Its early commanders had dissipated war's best elixir by training it into a life of caution, and the evil of that schooling it had shown on more than one occasion, and unmistakably that day, and it had had to suffer for it. But never, on that day or any other, did an army carry its burdens of every kind, and it had many, with a steadier or a more steadfast heart.

But I had better leave the battle's tactics to those who make a special study of military campaigns, venturing the following personal incident for the consideration of those young, cocksure critics who have never been in a big or a little battle, and who are surprised at the mistakes that Grant and Lee made, and contemplate with supreme satisfaction what would have happened had they been there and in command of either army. One night, some time in the winter before we started for the Wilderness, when I was dining with Duane, Turnbull, Michler, and Mackenzie of the engineers, in their spacious pine-bough-decorated mess room, they discussed Burnside's hesitation when Mr. Lincoln, having finally made up his mind to relieve McClellan, offered him the command of the Army of the Potomac. I listened a while, and then piped up that Burnside should not have had any such doubts of himself, that he had been educated for that business and kind of emergency, that it was n't very much of a job, etc., and wound up — the bottle had moved faithfully, yet with genteel moderation — that if I were offered the command I'd take it. Whereupon my astounded listeners flung themselves back in their chairs and there was something between a howl and a roar of laughter as they

THE BATTLE OF THE WILDERNESS 203

threw their eyes, filled with pity and humor, across and down the table at a mere snip of a thin-faced boy. Well, of course, I stuck to it — I should have taken command of the Army of the Potomac.

Now if, at the end of that first night, say at nine o'clock, Mr. Grant should have sent for me and said, "I'm thinking of assigning you to the independent command of one of the empty ambulances," — let alone turning the command of the Army of the Potomac over to me, — "and want you to get it safely out of this," I think I should have said, "Mr. Grant, I'm not very experienced in handling ambulances, and if you can get anybody else I'll not object," so dark was the outlook and so deeply had I been impressed by the responsibilities that encompassed him.

Dear military critics, however vast may be your knowledge of the art of war, and however boldly your youthful confidence may buckle on its sword and parade to the imaginary music of battle, let me tell you that if you are ever on a field where your country's life is hanging as ours hung on Grant's, or as the cause of the South hung on Lee's shoulders, I'll guarantee that you will not volunteer to take the command of anything, but will wonder that more mistakes are not made.

And here answer might be given to the inquiry which is often raised, coming sometimes from those who have been carried away by delving in the tactics of battle, and sometimes from those who have become warmly interested in its history: namely, what did the officers at corps and army headquarters have to say about it among themselves during its progress, and especially at the close of that first day in the Wilderness. In the sense in which the question is asked, nothing, absolutely nothing. For who could possibly have penetrated the rapidly evolving events and seen what the critic sees now so clearly? Who could have told us where the gaps lay between Ewell and Hill, where Longstreet was, and the importance of bringing Burnside's two divisions up to the Lacy farm that afternoon so as to be ready for the next morning?

It is hardly necessary to say that for officers or men to discuss or pass judgment upon the events and conduct of a battle would be death to discipline, and instead of an army, the country would be relying for its life upon a mob. In all my service with the Army of the Potomac, from Chancellorsville to Petersburg, sometimes in the eclipse of defeat, sometimes in the very verge of yawning disaster, never did I hear discussion, or more than barely a word of criticism or protest, over any feature of a campaign, except after Cold Harbor, and then only for a day. Soldiers and officers see so little of the field that they do not give weight to their immediate surroundings or experience.

The question of what the officers at headquarters

said to each other about the battle in its progress, and how they felt, is a very natural one, and its answer may be a minor but essential part of the story itself. I do not know what Grant, Meade, Rawlins, and Seth Williams may have said to each other, or what they may have talked about, but whenever an aide came back from the front and had reported to the General or chief of staff, he would take his place among his fellows, and their first question would be, "Where have you been, Bob, or Tom, or Mack," " how is it going up there, old fellow?" For every one, from the time the battle began, was keen to learn its progress. "Been up [or over] to —— lines. They are holding their own mighty well — Colonel So-and-So [or our dear little 'Dad,' or Bill] has just been killed — old General ——'s command is catching perfect h—l, say, fellers, where can I get something to eat [or drink], I'm hungry [or dry] as the dickens." That is about a fair sample of the conversation at headquarters while a battle is going on, so far as my experience goes.

For the information of those who have followed the paths of peace, let me say, without seeming didactic, that the commanding general and his corps commanders are rarely where the artists have depicted them, on rearing horses, leading or directing amid a sheet of fire. There are times, however, when the artist is true to life: as when Sheridan, seeing Ayres and his Regulars recoiling for a moment under terrific fire at Five Forks, dashed in; and there and then with those flashing eyes, amid the smoke of battle, he might have been painted. And so too, Warren, for that same day he seized the colors on another part of the field, and led on. But, as a rule, the corps commander chooses a position where he can best see his troops as they engage. The test of his genius is in choosing the critical moment when he will join them, and I'd suggest to my old Alma Mater, West Point, that it should impress upon its future generals the importance of catching the crisis in a battle and showing them the weight of their presence with their troops. In that glowing characteristic Sheridan rose above about all of our commanders. Suppose McClellan had shown himself and ridden his lines at Gaines's Mill, or Bragg at Chickamauga, might not the outcome have been different? Owing to the nature of the Wilderness, Grant had few chances to seize opportunities of that kind. At Spottsylvania, the night Upton was making his assault and breaking their lines temporarily, he was close up, and I sat my horse not far from him. There were two or three lines of battle within thirty or forty paces of each other and of him. The fire that reached us was considerable; an orderly carrying the headquarters standard was killed, and a solid shot struck an oak five or six inches through, squarely, not thirty feet from us, shivering it into broom slivers; but through it all Grant wore the same unperturbed, quiet, but somewhat pleading face.

But, to return to the Wilderness and the impressions it made, it goes without saying that the first day was a disappointing one, and that the desperate character of the fighting and the attendant losses had stamped themselves deeply. There was no dejection, however, the army from top to bottom was looking forward to the coming day's trial with resolution and hope.

Notwithstanding that Lee had repulsed Warren and had badly shaken the morale of his entire corps, and also that of Mott's division of Hancock's corps, had held Sedgwick in check, fought Hancock and Getty to a standstill, thrown Wilson back, and brought the formidable movement up with a sudden jarring stop, yet seemingly Grant at the close of the day — and I saw him once or twice — was not troubled, and he issued orders with the same even, softly warm voice, to attack Lee impetuously early the next morning all along his line.

If the day had brought some disappointments and anxious foreshadowings to Grant, it must have brought some to Lee also. For he had hoped that when Grant should find him on his flank ready to take the offensive, that he, like Hooker, would become confused and undecided, thereby giving Longstreet and the rest of his forces time to come up, and to repeat Chancellorsville. The results of the day had put another face on his hopes. Grant was neither undecided nor confused; he had made a savage drive at him, and when, at eleven o'clock that night, all the news had come in, Lee undoubtedly was duly thankful that he had held his own, as his despatch to the Confederate Secretary of War dated at that hour shows. He said in reporting the day's doings: —

"By the blessing of God, we maintained our position against every effort until night, when the contest closed. We have to mourn the loss of many brave officers and men. The gallant Brigadier-General J. M. Jones was killed, and Brig.-Gen. L. A. Stafford I fear mortally wounded while leading his command with conspicuous valor."

His greatest blessings, however, were that Warren was not allowed to wait till Wright came up, that Getty had not attacked an hour earlier, and that we had not seized and held the Chewning farm.

When the firing ceased on Hancock's front, to those of us around the Lacy house and at Grant's headquarters the silence was heavy and awesome. But soon the stars were shining softly and the merciful quiet of night came on; and wheresoever a mortally wounded man could be reached who was crying for water and help, — some of them in high, wild delirious screams of despair and agony, others with just enough breath left to be heard, alas! too often, only by the bushes around them, — surgeons and friendly comrades, and sometimes their foes, stole to them and did all they could for them.

I wonder what was going on in the breast of the Spirit of the Wilderness as the woods darkened. I wonder, too, as the spirits of those youths rose above the tree-tops all through that night, I wonder if they asked which was right and which was wrong as they bore on, a great flight of them, toward Heaven's gate. On and on they go, following the road Christ made for us all, past moon and stars,—the air is growing balmy, landscapes of eternal heavenly beauty are appearing; in the soft breezes that kiss their faces there is the faint odor of wild grapes in bloom, and lo! they hear a choir singing, "Peace on earth, good will toward men!" And two by two they lock arms like college boys and pass in together; and so may it be for all of us at last.

After supper, which did not take place until the day's commotion had well quieted down, I happened to go into the Lacy house, and in the large, high-ceiled room on the left of the hall was Warren, seated on one side of a small table, with Locke, his adjutant general, and Milhau, his chief surgeon, on the other, making up a report of his losses of the day. Warren was still wearing his yellow sash, his hat rested on the table, and his long, coal-black hair was streaming away from his finely expressive forehead, the only feature rising unclouded above the habitual gloom of his duskily sallow face. A couple of tallow candles were burning on the table, and on the high mantel a globe lantern. Locke and Milhau were both small men: the former unpretentious, much reflecting, and taciturn; the latter a modest man, and a great friend of McClellan's, with a naturally rippling, joyous nature.

Just as I passed them, I heard Milhau give a figure, his aggregate from data which he had gathered at the hospitals. "It will never do, Locke, to make a showing of such heavy losses," quickly observed Warren. It was the first time I had ever been present when an official report of this kind was being made, and in my unsophisticated state of West Point truthfulness it drew my eyes to Warren's face with wonder, and I can see its earnest, mournfully solemn lines yet. It is needless to say that after that I always doubted reports of casualties until officially certified.

Shortly after, Warren, accompanied by Roebling, went to a conference of the corps commanders which Meade had called to arrange for the attack which Grant had already ordered to be made at 4.30 the next morning.

I passed through the house, and out to the place where the horses were, in charge of the orderlies. I found mine among others in the semi-darkness of one of the open sheds of the old plantation's clustering barns, gave him the usual friendly pat, and stroked his silky neck as he daintily selected from the remaining wisps of his ration of hay.

All the space between the garden, the back of the house, and the barns, was loosely occupied by the bivouacs of the headquarters orderlies, clerks, teamsters, officers' servants, cooks and waiters of the various messes, provost-guards, etc., who on a campaign form quite a colony about corps and army headquarters. The soldiers, in groups of two or three, were sitting around their little dying fires, smoking; some with overcoat and hat for a pillow, already asleep. The black cooks, coatless and bareheaded, were puttering around their pot and kettle fires, with the usual attendant circle of waiters sitting on their haunches, some with their long, sinewy arms embracing languidly their uplifted knees, eyes of some on the fire, chins of some on their breasts and eyes closed, all drowsily listening to some one's childlike chatter; others on their backs, feet towards the fire, and snoring loudly. And around them all, and scattered about, are the baggage and supply-wagons, their bowed white canvas tops, although mildewed and dirty, dimly looming, outlined by being the resting-place for stray beams wandering through the night. The mule teams, unhitched but still harnessed, stand facing each other across the wagon-pole where their deep feed-box is still resting. Some are nosing in it for an overlooked kernel of oats or corn, or a taste of salt, some among the bits of forage that have fallen to the ground, some nodding. Their driver is asleep in or under the wagon, and his rest unbroken by the every-once-in-a-while quick rattling of the looped-up trace-chains, as one of his mules lets drive a vicious kick right or left at its army mate.

All up and down Wilderness Run, all over the once tilled fields of the Lacy farm and the old, gullied, pine and brier-tufted ones uplifting east of the run, little fires are blinking as they burn low. Some are those of batteries, some of trains, and some, at the top of the ridge, those of the hospitals of the Fifth Corps, where the surgeons, with rolled-up sleeves, are at their humane tasks in the operating tents, instruments by them which they handle with skill and mercy, as one after another the mutilated and perforated bodies of the boys who have been willing to risk their lives for the country are brought in and laid on the table before them, their anxious eyes scrutinizing the surgeon's face for a sign of hope as he examines their wounds and feels their fluttering pulses. Heaven bless their memory, all of them, and wherever the dust of one of them lies, I know the feeling mother earth holds it tenderly.

And now, reader, it is drawing late. Great, majestic, and magnanimous Night has come down, covering the Wilderness and us all in mysterious silence. Let us take a couple of these folding camp-chairs and go out and sit in the starlight on the lawn of the old Lacy house. Here is my tobacco-pouch; fill your pipe, and I'll try to convey to you the situation at this hour on the field, and then we will turn in. There

THE BATTLE OF THE WILDERNESS 213

are one or two incidents that I'd like to tell you also, and if I forget to mention them as I go along, I wish, before I get through, that you would jog my memory.

Meade's commodious living tents are pitched on the east side of the Germanna Road, directly opposite the knoll which he and Grant have occupied all day. Grant's are at the foot of the knoll, and a big, balloon-topped cottonwood or poplar waves over the spot still. Their tents are about two hundred yards apart, and Caton's little warrior Run is between them. Their headquarters tents, flaps thrown back, are indicated by colored lanterns on poles in front of them; and in them a candle or lamp is burning, and on a camp-chair before them, or writing at a table within, is an adjutant-general on duty for the night. Couriers are standing about with their horses saddled, and out where the Germanna Road meets the Pike, is a mounted orderly to point the way to aides coming in from the lines, who have occasion to visit headquarters. And let us hope that blessed sleep on her noiseless wings has found her way without the aid of the sentinel at the Pike to the tents of both Meade and Grant.

There is no moon, the stars are dim, and all is hushed. The night air is permeated with the odor of freshly-burnt-over woods, for the fire spread widely and is still slumbering and smoking in chunks and fallen trees. Here and there it has climbed up the grape-vines or the loose bark of a dead trunk, and aloft throws out little tremulous torch-like flames from their scraggly-limbed tops, pulsing beacons over the dark woods. Single ambulances are still coming and going, and now and then one is picking its way slowly and carefully with its suffering load across the fields.

Up the Pike, barely visible by the light that falls from the starry maze, from those lamps that are hung to show our minds the way to Another's headquarters far, far above Grant's and Meade's, both armies are lying behind their newly-thrown-up breastworks, which stretch from Flat Run well across the Pike toward Chewning's, and are more or less parallel and close. On Sedgwick's and some of Warren's front they are within pistol-shot of one another, and all along between them are many dead and wounded, whose cries and moans can be heard, but cannot be relieved, so persistent is the firing. Sedgwick's headquarters are on the Flat Run Road not far from where it joins the Germanna. Upton, Brown, Russell, Shaler, Morris, and Seymour of his corps, like Griffin, Ayres, Robinson, and Bartlett of Warren's, are up in the woods close behind their troops, blessed, I hope, with refreshing sleep.

Ewell has his headquarters bivouac on the Pike, and I suppose his flea-bitten gray, Rifle, that Major Stiles claimed resembled him, — if so, Rifle must have been a lank, serious-looking horse, with a high broad forehead, rather bony eye-sockets, and lean, scooped-out cheeks, for such were the prominent features of Ewell's face, — Rifle, more or less visible on account of his chalky color, is not far away, tied to a sapling; and, as his rider has lost a leg, he, out of sympathy or weariness, is probably resting one hind leg on its toe and dreaming. Ewell's general hospital, his surgeons as busy as our own, is back near Locust Grove, whence at an early hour in the evening a batch of our prisoners, about twelve hundred in number, most of them from Warren's corps, had set out for Orange Court House. In the middle of the night they met Ramseur and Mahone hurrying toward the front.

Had I been one of the unfortunate prisoners I know that I should have wished over and over again, as I trudged along that night, that I was lying dead back on the field with my fellows, rather than about to face a long term in Confederate prisons, so greatly did I dread them after seeing the wrecks that came down the James from Richmond when I first went to Fort Monroe.

Hancock is bivouacked on the Plank Road a short way east (within a hundred yards) of the Junction, and he may or may not be asleep, for, at his interview with Meade, the latter cautioned him to keep a strict lookout for his left in the morning — hinting at the possibility of Longstreet striking him in the Stonewall Jackson way. Birney has been told that he is to lead in the morning, and the various brigade commanders of his division and Getty's have had their positions assigned them. Sheridan is at Chancellorsville; Wilson and Gregg are so encamped as to cover the roads that come in at Todd's Tavern.

On the Widow Tapp field, dimly lit by the faint starlight, and silent, save that now and then a traveling cry from the wounded in the woods passes over it, Lee, Hill, and Wilcox are camped close up to their well-fought, tired troops, and their headquarters are not far apart. Hill is described as sitting alone at a late hour before a small, languishing fire, made of a few round, crossed-over sticks, near one of the guns of Williams's battery whose right wheel is just on the edge of the road, facing Birney. Wilcox has been to see Hill and asked for permission to withdraw his lines so as to reform them, and the little, punctilious man, who is not very well, has told him to let the men rest.

The reason why Wilcox made this request is explained by the adjutant of the Eighteenth North Carolina in his account of the Wilderness. It seems that when Brooke struck Lane's brigade, the Eighteenth was badly shattered, and, breaking, disappeared in the darkness. The adjutant, while seeking it, got lost, suddenly found himself within our lines, and after cautiously making his way to avoid this body of men and then another in the woods, all at once struck the Plank Road, knew where he was, followed it up to our pickets, and then, staking his life against captivity, dashed ahead through them. On reaching the edge of the woods he saw a white horse standing out in the Tapp field and, going closer, recognized it as General Wilcox's. He sought the general and told him that there was nothing, absolutely nothing, between his lines and ours. Wilcox was cross, and would not listen to him, dismissing him sharply with an aside that there was a brigade in front of his line. The adjutant at last found his regiment, told his fellow officers his story, and they, in view of the danger, went to Wilcox and assured him of their adjutant's truthfulness and good judgment. Thereupon Wilcox made his visit to Hill. Later he tells us that he went to see Lee, whose tent was within less than two hundred yards, in reference to the same matter. On his entering, Lee remarked that he had made a complimentary report on the conduct of his and Heth's division and, holding up a note, that he had just heard from Anderson, that he was going into bivouac at Verdierville, and that he had sent word to him and to Longstreet to move forward so as to relieve the divisions which had been so actively engaged.

Longstreet at that hour was bivouacking at Richard's shop on the Catharpin Road. When we first entered Richmond the following April, the diary of an officer of his corps was picked up in the street by some one of our men, and in it is this entry: —

"Thursday, May 5th. Marched at three o'clock

this morning. Rested after marching thirteen miles, and cooked some rations. After resting a while resumed march, marched 20 miles and camped at dark five miles from the battle-field."

That made a total of thirty-three miles, and as the day was exceedingly hot, especially in the woods, the men must have been very tired.

Lee's orders to Longstreet, carried by that crystal aide, Venable, were to move at 2 A. M., the same hour as that Grant had set for Burnside. Longstreet had a mile or two farther to march, but, unfortunately for us, he had not, on this occasion at least, "a genius for slowness," and was on the very nick of time.

The troops on the move then are Ramseur and Mahone on their way to reinforce Lee's lines, and Ferrero, my old West Point dancing-master, tip-toeing along with his colored division to reach Germanna Ford and swell Burnside's corps.

And that now is the story of the night.

"But you have not told me," exclaims my friend, knocking the ashes out of his pipe, "of the personal incidents you asked to be reminded of." Well, do not fill your pipe again, I'll promise not to be long. There is the body of a young officer lying alone in the woods pretty well south of the Plank Road. It is that of Colonel Alford B. Chapman, aged twenty-eight years, of the Fifty-seventh New York. There is a little pocket note-book beside his lifeless hand, and on one of the open leaves he has written his father's name and address and these words: "Dear Father: I am mortally wounded. Do not grieve for me. My dearest love to all. Alford." I do not know, but I doubt if Death anywhere in the Wilderness has met more steady eyes than those of this dying, family-remembering young man. He was brigade officer of the day, and his duties had called him into the engagement very early; and when, toward dusk, his regiment advanced to fill a gap on account of the lines being extended southward to meet the overlapping of Lane's big North Carolina brigade, it came across Chapman's body, the first it knew of his fate.

And while we are on Hancock's front let me refer to Hays, and, if ever you go along the Brock Road, you will come to a cast-iron gun standing upright on a granite base surrounded by an iron picket fence. It marks the near-by spot where he fell, and is on the right-hand side of the road about where the easterly branch of Wilderness Run crosses it, a little this side of the Junction. He was a very gallant officer, and his lonely monument will appeal to you. There is something illustrative of the man, and mysteriously prophetic, in a letter he wrote to his wife the morning of the day he was killed: "This morning was beautiful," said the letter, "for

> 'Lightly and brightly shone the sun,
> As if the morn was a jocund one.'

Although we were anticipating to march at 8 o'clock, it might have been an appropriate harbinger of the day of regeneration of mankind; but it only brought to remembrance, through the throats of bugles, that duty enjoined upon each one, perhaps before the setting sun, to lay down a life for his country."

It was a translation worthy of the prophets of old that he gave to the notes of the bugles; and the reverential, kindly mood — and to think it was his last! — hailing the sun as the harbinger of the day of regeneration of mankind! Oh! the sanity and spread of the primary emotions!

The other incidents are these, one of which was referred to early in the narrative, namely, the relief of one of our men on Griffin's front by a Confederate officer. The circumstances were as follows: the Confederate, touched by the cries of our men, — he had been trying to sleep, — crawled over the works on hands and knees in the darkness, till he reached a wounded man, who turned out to be a lieutenant of a western regiment, if I remember right, and asked what he could do for him. "I am very, very thirsty, and I am shot so that I cannot move." The good Samaritan crawled to the little brook, — it wimples still across the old Pike, — filled a canteen and came back with it, and, after propping the wounded man's head, went his way. A little while afterwards another Confederate came prowling toward the wounded man and, thinking he was dead, began to feel for his watch. The lieutenant remonstrated, but the hard-hearted creature took the watch, saying, "You will be dead before long, and will not need it." Here we have the extremes of our natures, and how they stand out! the manly and angelic, the brutish and satanic! I know the name of the prowler; but of the other, the noble fellow, I do not. If I did, it should appear on this page and live as long as I could make it live. This story I got from my friend, Mr. Jennings of the Wilderness, who had it from the lips of the western lieutenant himself, who, a few years ago, came back to the old battle-field, and the first place he visited was the little brook; and I have no doubt it murmured sweetly all through that night, full of a native happiness at seeing once more its acquaintance of other days.[1]

The other incident is found in the diary of Captain Robert E. Park, Company F, Twelfth Alabama, Battle's brigade, Rodes's division. "Crawled over the works with two canteens of water to relieve some of the wounded, groaning and calling aloud in front of the line. Night dark, no moon and few stars, and as I crawled to the first man and offered him a drink of water, he declined; and, in reply to my inquiries, told me that he was shot through the leg and body and was sure he was bleeding internally. I told him that I feared he would not live till morning, and

[1] I am indebted to Mrs. and Mr. Jennings for opening their door to me as the day was ending on my last visit to the Wilderness; I was tired, hungry, and chilled, and no stranger ever met a more hospitable welcome. Their house stands nearly opposite where Grant had his headquarters, and while I sat before the crackling fire my eye rested on the spot, over which a cold gray mist was drifting.

asked him whether he was making any preparation for leaving this world. His reply was that he had not given it a thought, as his life had not been one of sin, and that he was content. He was about twenty years of age, and from a northwestern state." Guides of the upper world! I have only one request to make, that you point out to me that boy; for I should like these earthly eyes to rest upon the calm depths of his heroic and innocent face; and I have no doubt his kind benefactor, Captain Park, will be there too.

And now it is near midnight, and all is very, very still. "Hark, what is that I hear?" you ask. It is some staff officer's horse at a brigade headquarters up in the woods, neighing for a mate which will probably never march with him again. Let us turn in.

VIII

MEADE, in transmitting to his corps commanders Grant's orders for the renewal of the battle, directed them to send their train-guards, as well as every man who could shoulder a musket, to join the ranks by daylight; adding that staff officers should be sent at once to his headquarters to learn from the chiefs of departments the location of their special trains and conduct the guards to the front. This order took a deal of hard night-riding to fulfill, and some of those who carried it did not get back to their respective headquarters till long after midnight; for the main trains were scattered about Chancellorsville and along the Ely's Ford Road wherever they could haul off into an opening, and on account of the darkness were hard to find.

Meade, as already told, asked his corps commanders to come and see him in reference to the movement in the morning; and, having had quite a conference with them, sent Lyman over with this message to Grant: "After conversing with my corps commanders, I am led to believe that it will be difficult, owing to the dense thicket in which their commands are located, the fatigued condition of the men rendering it difficult to rouse them early enough, and the necessity of some daylight, to properly put in reinforcements. All these considerations induce me to suggest the attack should not be made till six o'clock instead of 4.30." It was then half-past ten and Grant had retired; he was aroused, and changed it to five; and says in his Memoirs that he was sorry he made the change, and I am sure he was right. In view of the fact that the sun rose in a clear sky at 4.47, and, as every one knows, dawn at that season begins at latest by four o'clock, — I remember its coming on, scattering light like the sower it is, at every step; for we breakfasted early that morning; the mist that had gathered during the night was lifting and all but a few of the stars had faded and gone, — I say, until I saw Colonel Lyman's notes, I always wondered why Meade made this request of Grant to postpone the attack an hour and a half, till the sun had risen above the trees; but I think the notes disclose the reason.

It will be recalled that two of Burnside's divisions were in bivouac just this side of the Rapidan, and that his was a separate command independent of Meade, hence all his orders had to emanate from Grant. Accordingly for the morning's attack Grant sent them to him direct through Colonel Comstock of the engineers, one of my instructors at West Point, a tall, sedate man, and Grant's most modest, able, and confidential aide. They were in these terms: —

THE BATTLE OF THE WILDERNESS 225

HEAD QUARTERS ARMIES OF THE UNITED STATES,
Near Wilderness Tavern,
May 5, 1864, 8 P. M.

Lieutenant-General Grant desires that you start your two divisions at 2 A M. to-morrow, punctually, for this place. You will put them in position between the Germanna Plank Road and the road leading from this place to Parker's Store, so as to close the gap between Warren and Hancock, connecting both. You will move from this position on the enemy beyond at 4.30 A. M., the time at which the Army of the Potomac moves.

C. B. COMSTOCK,
Lt.-Col. & Aide-de-camp.

It seems that Burnside came to Grant's headquarters after the receipt of this order, and then joined Meade. At the close of his interview with Meade and the other corps commanders gathered there, he said, as he rose, — he had a very grand and oracular air, — "Well, then, my troops shall break camp by half-past two!" and with shoulders thrown back and measured step disappeared in the darkness.

After he was out of hearing, Duane, Meade's Chief of Engineers, who had been with the Army of the Potomac since its formation, said: "*He* won't be up — I know him well!" — I can see Duane's face, hear his quiet voice, see his hands slowly stroking his full, long, rusty beard, as he says, "*He* won't be up — I know him well!" — And apparently that was the opinion of them all, that he would n't be up by 4.30 — for they knew him well, too, and recognized what Lyman says of him, that he "had a genius for slowness." But each one felt the importance of his joining them before they tackled Lee again, for they had had about all they could do to hold their own that afternoon. So, fresh troops being very desirable, and knowing him as they did, they wanted to make sure of them by allowing him an extra hour and a half to get them up.

And I suspect that Meade, convinced that they were right, that Burnside would not be up in time, made use of thickets and want of daylight rather than the real reason, to ask for the postponement of the attack. As we shall see, it turned out just as Duane predicted.

Burnside represented a well-recognized type in all armies, the California-peach class of men, handsome, ingratiating manners, and noted for a soldierly bearing,— that is, square shoulders, full breast, and the capacity on duty to wear a grim countenance, while off duty all smiles and a keen eye to please, — who, in times of peace, not only in our country but everywhere, invariably land in high places, and who almost as invariably make utter failures when they are given commands on the breaking out of war. And are not their failures accounted for by the fact that their minds have been entirely devoted to looking out for the main chance, to being agreeable and well-groomed, rather than to the deep serious phases of life? — I am satisfied that reflection is the pole star of genius, — hence, when they are confronted by the inexorable demands of war, they hesitate, appalled and imbecile. Moreover, there is nothing reactive about this type, as in the case of Grant and Lee, Sherman and Sheridan. And yet twice did Congress vote its thanks to Burnside, and old "Burn," as he was affectionately called, died with hosts and hosts of friends.

Knowing that at five o'clock battle was to be renewed by vigorous attack all along the lines, the little colony of orderlies, cooks, and teamsters about Warren's headquarters were astir before daylight. When I aroused, some of the stars were still glowing and belated detachments from the train guards were still coming on to the field on their way to their respective commands, moving through the disappearing mist that had stolen into the Wilderness, and, as we would fain believe, to moisten the cheeks and eyelashes of its living and dead as they slept, and to wrap the latter in its cool gray shrouds. Up near the woods, dimly visible, were a couple of brigades — the Marylanders among them — which Warren had had assembled there during the night as a reserve behind Griffin, to whom, as on the day before, the initiative of the serious work was intrusted. The places of these troops in line had been made good by closing Crawford to the right and abreast of

Griffin, on the assumption that Burnside would be up and take the ground he had occupied, that is, across the Parker's Store Road, near where it leaves Wilderness Run for the rolling plateau of the Chewning farm.

Kitching's brigade of heavy artillery had just arrived from Chancellorsville, and the men were resting near the Lacy house, most of them between the run and the road. It was a big, fresh brigade, over twenty-two hundred strong; and while its regiments were preparing for the night march, — their orders were to move at 1 A. M., — the Colonel and a score or two of his men held a service, and, all kneeling, he led them in prayer. Around the kneeling group were the shallow graves of those who had been killed the year before; and the one who narrates the circumstance says that solitude's dreariest choir, the whippoorwills, of which there were hundreds, and maybe thousands, were repeating their night-long mournful chant. Possibly the earnest student of the battle would prefer to be told why they were serving as infantry, — they were three battalion regiments, — their order of march, and exactly the distance they had had to make; but I wonder which is the more enduring and significant fact, the young colonel with palm to palm pouring out his heart to God under the starlight, or whether Blank's battalion moved first right or left in front.

How all mere military detail of battle fades away

as we lift on the tides of great affairs! Student of war, let me suggest that once in a while as you study battles that you take Imagination's offered hand; she will lead you through simple height-gaining paths till at last fife and drum die away and lo! you are in a blessed company charged to convert what is earthly into what is spiritual.

But to return to the morning: day was coming on fast; bodies of woods, solitary trees on the ridges, and vacant sky-arched distances, were stealing into view as we hastily breakfasted. Our horses were saddled and ready, and those of us who had had a kind word for the colored cooks and waiters found in our saddle-bags a snack of one kind or other wrapped up in bits of paper. Nowhere in this world does it pay better to show consideration for the low in estate, and above all for those of the colored race, than on a campaign. They will look after you faithfully, and, if you should be sick or wounded, will stand by you to the last.

Although a great many years lie between now and then, yet across them all I can see Warren mounting his heavy dappled iron-gray, and wearing his yellow sash. His saddle-blanket was scarlet, and a few days afterward at Spotsylvania, when this horse was shot, I waited near him while saddle and blanket were stripped from him[1] by an orderly.

[1] The shot that hit Warren's horse was aimed at Warren, and possibly fired by the same sharpshooter who the next morning at almost the identical spot killed Sedgwick. Warren was watching Robinson's men,

The first duty I had after breakfast was to go to the intersection of the Pike and Germanna Ford roads and wait there till Burnside should arrive, and then show him the way up the Parker's Store Road to his position. My assignment happened in this way: Roebling had gone to Grant's headquarters at 11.30 the previous night to confer with Comstock as to the position Burnside's corps should take; and in his notes he says: "Two opinions presented themselves, either to go and join Wadsworth by daylight, or else obtain possession of the heights at Chewning's and fall upon the enemy's rear by that route. If successful in carrying the heights, the latter plan promised the greatest results; if not, it would fail altogether. Then again it was thought that when Wadsworth joined the Second Corps, the two together would be sufficient to drive the enemy. General Grant then decided that the Ninth Corps should go to Chewning's, and I prepared to accompany them at four o'clock in the morning." Accordingly, at that hour, he and Cope went to the Pike and waited for Burnside. I suspect that Warren, as the hour for attack

who were briskly engaged along and to the right of the Spotsylvania Road, trying to carry the enemy's position at the old scattered orchard of the Spindle farm. I was directly behind him. We had been there but a short time before I heard the ping of a passing shot. From the same direction, another went directly over our heads, and, in a little while, as soon as the man could reload, another, and this time so much nearer that I said, "General, that man is getting the range on you." The sharpshooter was in the woods beyond the rather wide and deep ravine that makes northeastward from the Sedgwick monument. Warren said nothing but shortly started to move to the right, when down went the horse.

THE BATTLE OF THE WILDERNESS

came on, and Burnside did not appear, feeling the need of both Roebling and Cope, who really were his right-hand men, sent me to take their places and wait for Burnside. They both hurried off Cope to join Wadsworth.

On my way to the Pike I passed the engineer battalion marching in column of fours to report to Griffin. It was the first time in all their history when, as a body, this aristocracy of the rank and file of the army was called on to take a hand as infantry, as common "dough-boys," in the actual fighting. I knew all the officers well: they were the ones I had dined with when I announced my readiness to take command of the Army of the Potomac. Their duties hitherto had been confined to the dangerous business of laying the pontoon bridges, and at other times to repairing roads or to selecting and laying out fieldworks — the officers meanwhile familiarizing themselves with the lines and all the natural features of the scene of operations. But we all recognized the grind of fighting as infantry, and broad grins were exchanged as I rode by them. Fortunately, they were not called on to assault, but were put to throwing a new line of entrenchments across the Pike in rear of Griffin.

The head of Burnside's leading division, Potter's, came on the field to the tune of Hancock's musketry about half-past five. It should have been there at least an hour and a half earlier to move to the attack with Hancock and Wadsworth. Duane's oracular observation of the night before, "He won't be up, I know him well," had been verified. Meade and the corps commanders had reckoned just about right in allowing him till six to be on hand. As a matter of fact, Burnside himself did n't get up to the Pike, let alone to the ground Crawford had occupied, till after six. When he came, accompanied by a large staff, I rode up to him and told him my instructions. He was mounted on a bobtailed horse and wore a drooping army hat with a large gold cord around it. Like the Sphinx, he made no reply, halted, and began to look with a most leaden countenance in the direction he was to go.

It was the first time I had ever seen him, — he had commanded our old Army of the Potomac, he was a famous man, I was young, — and my eyes rested on his face with natural interest. After a while he started off calmly toward the Lacy house, not indicating that my services were needed, — he probably was thinking of something that was of vastly more importance. I concluded that I was n't wanted, and was about to go my own way, when I caught sight of Babcock of Grant's staff coming at great speed down the hill just the other side of the run. He had been out with Hancock, and as he approached, I called, "What's the news, Babcock?" Without halting he replied, his kindly, open face gleaming, "Hancock has driven them a mile and we are going to have a great victory,"

THE BATTLE OF THE WILDERNESS 233

or words to that effect. I do not believe my heart was ever more suddenly relieved, for from my youth forebodings of the very worst that can happen have always thrown its shadow. And now to know we were gaining a victory! I went back to the Lacy house happy, very happy indeed.

Shortly after arriving there, Meade's instruction through Warren for Wadsworth to report for orders to Hancock while detached from the Fifth Corps, was given me to deliver, and with an orderly I started up the Parker's Store Road, encumbered with Burnside's troops moving sluggishly into position, the ground being very difficult to form on speedily. By this time it was about 8 o'clock. The general had passed through them to the front, where Potter was deploying, but he had no sooner arrived there than his big staff caught the eye of a Confederate battery somewhere on the right of Ewell's line, and it opened on them, making it so uncomfortable that they had to edge away. I left the road about where the uppermost eastern branch comes in, and struck off through the woods in the direction Wadsworth had taken the night before. I had not gone a great way when my orderly, a German, riding behind me, said, "Lieutenant, you are bearing too much to the right, you will run into the rebel lines." I sheered to the left; here and there were stragglers and wounded, and at a point alongside the run, propped against a beech tree, his head resting on his right shoulder, his cap on the ground beside him, was a dead fair-faced boy, eighteen or nineteen years old, holding in his bloodless hand a few violets which he had picked. A shot had struck him in the arm, or the leg, I have forgotten which, and he had slowly bled to death. I fancy that, as he held the little familiar wild-flowers in his hand, his unsullied eyes glazed as he looked down into them, and his mind was way off at home. After passing him, the orderly again cautioned me, but this time I paid no attention to him and went on, guided by the firing.

The woods were very thick, and unknowingly we were approaching quite a little rise, when suddenly came the command, "Get off that horse and come in." I lowered my head to the left, and there stood a heavy skirmish line with uplifted guns. It did not take me one second to decide. I suspect that as usual I did not think at all, but gave my horse a sudden jerk to the right, then the spur, and as he bounded they let drive at us. A shot, — I suppose it was one from their 58-calibre Enfields, — grazing my sabre-belt, struck the brass "D" buckle on my left side and tore the belt apart. My Colt's pistol in its holster began to fall and I grabbed it with my left hand. Just then a limb knocked off my hat and with my right hand I caught it as it was passing my right boot-top. Meanwhile the horse was tearing his way along the course we had come. The orderly disappeared instantly, and that was the last I saw of him till the next morning, just after I had returned Grant's despatches that will be mentioned later. When I met him, with unfeigned surprise he exclaimed, "Why, my God! lieutenant, I thought sure you were killed up there yesterday." I hardly know why he should have thought so unless he concluded I was falling when I was reaching for my hat. His judgment was better than mine, however, and had I followed it neither of us would have had such a close call.

Well, as soon as I could get control of my horse and both of us could breathe a bit easier, for the dear old fellow was no more anxious to go to Richmond that way than I, apparently, I struck off more to the left, and in a little while ran into swarms of stragglers, and pretty soon met a group falling back under some discipline. Upon inquiring, I found that they belonged to Cutler's brigade of Wadsworth's division, and they told me that the division had been driven with heavy losses. I gave to the officer who said he was going back to the open ground, that is, to the Parker's Store Road or the Lacy fields, the despatch, which will be found in the War Records, dated May 5th by mistake; the hour given is 8.30. In this despatch to Warren I reported the enemy's skirmish-line as being about a mile from the field, that they had tried Wadsworth's left, and that I would go on till I found him. The person to whom this despatch was handed **either** delivered it in person or sent it by some one to

Warren's headquarters, and it was forwarded from there to Humphreys in a despatch dated 9.05. Soon I fell in with Cutler himself, leading back fragments of his broken command. There may have been seven or eight hundred of them, and possibly twice that number, for they were scattered all through the woods. He was rather an oldish, thin, earnest-looking Roundhead sort of a man, his light stubby beard and hair turning gray. He was bleeding from a wound across his upper lip, and looked ghastly, and I have no doubt felt worse; for he was a gallant man, and to lead his men back, hearing every little while the volleys of their comrades still facing the enemy, must have been hard. On my asking him where Wadsworth was, he said, "I think he is dead"; and one or two of his officers said, "Yes, we saw him fall."

Relying on what they told me, I started back for Meade's headquarters. When I reached there and reported the serious break in Wadsworth's lines, no one could believe it; but just then Cutler's men began to pour out of the woods in full view on the ridge east of the Lacy house, and the seriousness of the situation at once appeared to all. As to Wadsworth's death, Cutler and his officers were mistaken; he was not mortally wounded until about two hours later, but just before they broke the general's horse was killed and that led them to believe. I think, that he was killed also.

THE BATTLE OF THE WILDERNESS

My report, and Cutler's appearance verifying it, brought alarm which found expression in the following despatch sent at once to Warren: —

The Major General commanding directs that you suspend your operations on the right, and send some force to prevent the enemy from pushing past your left, near your headquarters. They have driven in Cutler in disorder and are following him.

A. A. HUMPHREYS,
Major General & Chief of Staff.

But, as a matter of fact, the enemy had not broken our lines seriously, and were not following Cutler.

The batteries in the fields around the Lacy house, and along the Pike, where the little chapel now stands, came at once into "action front," the cannoneers stepping blithely to their places, and, boldly expectant, men and guns stood facing toward where his men came straggling out of the woods.

Before I left Meade's headquarters word was sent in from Hancock that a column was reported coming up the Brock Road deploying skirmishers. This lowering news on the heels of Cutler's appearance was translated by Grant in the light of its premonitory look. He called for his horse and set out to join Hancock where, if at all, the crisis would break.

So much then for the chronicles of the early morning, my attempt to reach Wadsworth, and the events with which it had more or less connection.

IX

Lee's plans for the use he should make of his forces on the renewal of the conflict, in that he aimed a crushing blow at his adversary's most vital point, were indicative, I am inclined to think, of a clearer if not a higher range of soldierly genius than those of Grant ordering a general assault all along his lines. For Grant's plan to have matched Lee's, he should have struck at Lee's most vital point, namely, the Chewning farm; but in that case troops would have been drawn for the assault from Sedgwick and Warren, to support Burnside's two divisions, and with him in chief command ask the fields of Fredericksburg, the bridge at Antietam and the mine at Petersburg, what would probably have happened. Besides, he would have come plump against Longstreet, Anderson, and Mahone on their way to Hill and Ramseur to the right of Ewell's line.

But let all this be as it may, Lee ordered Ewell to attack at 4.30, — the very hour Grant had first set for resuming the offensive, — his object being to divert attention from the Plank Road where he meant to make his supreme effort, assuming that Longstreet, Anderson, and Mahone would certainly be up by that time, or shortly after.

Ewell, accordingly, a little before five o'clock, threw

his left brigade against Sedgwick's right; but Sedgwick flung him back with a vengeance, and then by determined assault forced him to his very utmost to hold his lines. The loss of life on both sides was heavy.

Griffin in his front drove the enemy's weighty skirmish line into their breastworks, which, during the night, had been made exceedingly strong, and was assembling batteries to shake them before he assaulted.

At five o'clock the signal gun at Hancock's headquarters boomed, and his troops and those of Wadsworth, who had been waiting for it, moved promptly, the latter through the dense, trammeling woods, with Baxter in his centre, Rice on his right, and Cutler on his left, all facing south for the Plank Road. To Birney, an erect, thoughtful-looking man, wearing a moustache and chin-beard, — the steady light of his eyes would have made him notable in any company, — Hancock assigned the command of his right. It included Birney's own, Mott's and Getty's divisions, together with Owen's and Carroll's brigades of Gibbon's division. He moved with Hays's old brigade on the right of the road, its front when deployed, owing to its losses of the day before, barely equal to that of an average regiment. On the left was Ward's of his own division and part of Owen's brigade. Mott's second brigade was on the left of Ward and completed Birney's front line. In the second line was Getty, formed with Wheaton across the road, the valiant Vermonters on his left; and in rear of their fellow brigades was Eustis. Carroll was in two lines of battle behind all the foregoing that were north of the road; and there, too, in line but not moving with him, was the Nineteenth Maine of Webb's brigade, which had reported to Carroll when the battle was raging, in the twilight of the previous evening. It was under the command of Selden Connor, late Governor of Maine, and rendered great service that day, as it had on many a field. When Carroll moved, he told Connor to wait for Webb.

Birney soon struck his foes of the night before, and, after some quick, sharp fighting, drove them from their hastily-thrown-together defenses, consisting of logs, chunks, and brush which they had collected during the night, Ward's and Hays's brigades capturing colors and prisoners. Birney, followed by Getty, now pushed on, covering ground very rapidly, allowing the enemy no rest, and gathering in prisoners by the score. By this time Hays's brigade had obliqued to the left, and was wholly on the south side of the road, abreast with its companion brigade. Soon Wadsworth, sweeping everything before him, emerged from the north, and, wheeling to the right, the colors of some of Baxter's brigade mingling with those of Hays, Owen, and Ward on the south side of the road, joined in the pursuit of the now almost routed men of Heth's and Wilcox's divisions, who had experienced such heavy losses the night before.

THE BATTLE OF THE WILDERNESS 241

Birney, finding Wadsworth on the north, drew Getty to the south side of the road. Meanwhile Cutler was advancing in two or three lines of battle, behind the right of Baxter's brigade and the left of Rice's, the former's left was across the road, the latter's right reaching and curving to the northeastern slopes of the Tapp field. The momentum of the advance had not yet been checked.

About this time Lyman reached Hancock at the junction of the Plank and Brock roads, under orders from Meade to report by orderlies the progress of events during the day. On making his mission known, Hancock cried, "Tell General Meade we are driving them most beautifully. Birney has gone in and he is just clearing them out beautifully." On Lyman reporting that only one of Burnside's divisions was up when he left headquarters, which, as will be recalled, were within a few hundred yards of the Pike, "I knew it! Just what I expected!" exclaimed Hancock. "If he could attack *now*, we could smash A. P. Hill all to pieces!"

Learning of Birney's success, Hancock ordered Gibbon to move with Barlow's big, fresh division and attack Hill's right. Unfortunately this order was not carried out: Gibbon said he never got it — two staff officers say they delivered it to him. We cannot resist the vain regret that Barlow was not moved as Hancock wanted him moved, for another story would certainly have had to be written; and I have no doubt that to Hancock's dying day this failure kept repeating itself out of the fogging coast of the Past like a mournful bell on a swinging buoy.

Ward, Owen, and Hays's old brigade, all that is left of it, keeping step to that trumpet of Duty which ever spoke to their dead leader, has crushed or brushed away Lane, Scales, Walker, and Cooke, and is now crowding Thomas back and on to McGowan, who at last, under withering fire from Wadsworth, is staggering into the field behind the guns.

In line behind Birney is Wheaton, and then the iron-hearted Vermonters. Coming up on the north side of the road is Carroll, his brigade in two lines, the crash of the musketry, the battle-field's hottest breath, only bringing new fire into his face. Yes, he is coming up with that brigade, which, when the Confederates in the twilight of the second day at Gettysburg broke our lines and were spiking the pieces, Hancock called on to regain them. As one of those gallant regiments, the Fourth Ohio, had boys in it from my old home, with some of whom I played in my childhood, there comes back from the past a feeling of pride, and tenderness too, for one of them, Nelson Conine, was killed that day and his body never found. Yes, with pride and tenderness I see them following the heroic Carroll.

At some distance behind Carroll, Webb, Alexander S. Webb, my old West Point instructor, — Heaven bless him! his hair, once so dark, now almost as white

THE BATTLE OF THE WILDERNESS 243

as snow, — is leading up his starry brigade, starry for its leader and starry for men like Abbott of the Twentieth Massachusetts and Connor of the Nineteenth Maine that are behind him. Yes, he is leading them up, and nowhere on that field is blood with more native chivalry. Hancock, scenting danger, suggested to Humphreys that he might need help, and Stevenson's division of Burnside's corps which Grant had intended to hold at the Pike as a reserve was sent to him. It arrived at the junction at 8 A. M.

Meantime Wadsworth has crossed the last morass on his side, which, on account of its tortuous course, irregular and in places almost declivitous banks, and densely matted thickets, made a line of strong defense. And now his advance is within two or three hundred yards of the Widow Tapp field, and Baxter and Birney are within a like or less distance of the easterly line of the field prolonged. Rice, on the right, who asked to be turned toward the enemy when he was dying at Spotsylvania a few days later,[1] has caught sight through the trees of the old field's pearly light, and is preparing to charge a battery planted among its starting broom-grass. According to General Pendleton, Lee's chief of artillery, Poague's battalion of four batteries had all taken positions in the field.

[1] Rice's leg had just been amputated high up on the thigh, and he was lying under a fly on some pine boughs. From his moving lips it was seen that he wished to say something, and as the aide leaned over him he sighed, "Turn me." "Which way?" asked the aide. "Towards the enemy," was the faint reply. They turned him and in a little while he died.

Birney's sharpshooters south of the road preceding his troops and Baxter's are already abreast of the east line of the field, and can get glimpses of the meagre, huddled buildings, with their splayed peach and knotted plum trees, — whose leaves and the sashes in the windows tremble at every discharge of the guns, — and are beginning to place their shots among the cannoneers of Williams's North Carolina battery, belching shell and shrapnel, firing over McGowan and Thomas of Wilcox's division, who, the former on the north, the latter on the south, side of the road, are still contesting, but on the verge of disrupting completely. The field and the day are almost ours.

The Plank Road back to the junction is packed, wounded men making their way alone, trying as best they can to stanch their wounds, some more seriously hurt resting their arms on the shoulders of their fellows, many on stretchers, with appealing eyes, and not a few of them breathing their last. In the throng are scores on scores of lank, wildly staring prisoners, trailing one another, quickening their step to get beyond the range of their own men's fire; and, breasting them all, mounted staff officers coming and going with all possible speed. Edging alongside the road are patient little mules with boxes of ammunition strapped to them; and off in the woods on both sides of the road the dead are scattered, some not yet cold; and off, too, among them is many a poor coward who

THE BATTLE OF THE WILDERNESS

at heart despises himself but cannot face danger. And yet I have not a bit of doubt that here and there among them is one who, before yielding a moral conviction, would face the fires of the stake with calm equanimity.

And, all the while, over the motley, fast-breathing, torn shreds and tatters of war, a section of our artillery, with elevations too low and time-fuses cut entirely too short, bursts its shells, shells that are intended for the enemy's line, where our men are beginning to feel a new pressure, and are fighting with increasing desperation, but owing to the character of the woods and the ground they have covered, they are, so far as organization is concerned, in bad shape. At the front there is scarcely the semblance of continuous and effective formation; regiments and brigades that started in the rear are now in the front and on different flanks; their commanders scattered through the woods in little detached, anxious groups, a staff officer or two, an orderly with the headquarters guidon. Every one is filled with a desire to go ahead, but each one is helpless to remedy the disorganization that is growing greater and more distracting at every moment. Wadsworth and Getty — a determined spare-faced man with a brown moustache and hazel eye, and who never got all the praise he deserved for what he did at critical times on so many fields — are in or near the road, the former ablaze and looking for a chance to lead a regiment at the first sight of the enemy, — that was his prevailing weakness as a commander: he had already had a horse killed under him, — the latter cool as usual, although each moment tells him that a crisis is near. For what is that screaming war-cry they hear through the increasing roar of the musketry? We need not tell *them*, they know it well: it is the wild fierce yell of Gregg's Texans as they greet Lee, and come on to meet almost their extermination.

When the narrative parted with Lee about eleven o'clock the night before, he was in his tent on the western border of the Widow Tapp's field. Whether his night was one of care or sleep we know not, but we do know that in the course of the evening he sent his accomplished aide, Colonel Venable, with an order to Longstreet, in bivouac at Richards's shops, to leave the Catharpin Road and strike over to the Plank and join Hill at an early hour. About eleven o'clock a guide reported to Longstreet; at two A. M. he started, following the guide through wood-paths. The guide lost the way, but his divisions reached the Plank Road at daylight, and then, doubling up, quickened their pace, and came down the road abreast. Before them the sun was rising very red, bronzing the tree-tops; behind them was Richard H. Anderson's division of Hill's corps, who had bivouacked at Verdierville. In all, fourteen fresh brigades were coming on to strike the hard-fought, torn, and wearied divisions of Birney, Wadsworth, and

THE BATTLE OF THE WILDERNESS 247

Getty, and to struggle with them and Webb, Carroll, and Owen, for the mastery of the field. And all this time Barlow, Brooke, and Miles, as well as Smyth with his gallant Irishmen, are held by Gibbon, expecting a part if not all of Longstreet's ten brigades to appear on the Brock Road from the direction of Todd's Tavern! Does any one who knows Gregg's record as a soldier think for a moment that he would not have unmasked at a very early hour the first steps of a movement of this kind from his position at Todd's Tavern? It is true that word had been sent in to Hancock during the night that Longstreet's corps was passing up the Catharpin Road to attack his left; but, as a matter of fact, his tired troops, as we have seen, having covered twenty-eight miles or more, had gone into bivouac at dark some eight or ten miles west of the tavern, and were in deep, well-earned sleep.

The record seems to show that Meade, Hancock, as well as Gibbon and presumably Humphreys in a measure, all harbored a fear that Longstreet, on the left, would suddenly appear a portentous spectre, forever casting its image on their minds. There is no evidence, however, that any such notion had stolen into Grant's mind, for, neither at that time, nor ever after, was there magic in the name of Longstreet, Lee, or any other Confederate, for him. (Warren always, when Lee's movements were uncertain and a matter of discussion, referred to him as "Bobbie"

Lee, with an air and tone that said he is not a man to be fooled with.) And so, let Longstreet be on the road to strike him at whatsoever point, Grant wanted Hill and Ewell to be beaten before help could reach them; hence his sound conclusion of the night before, to attack at daylight.

Meanwhile, the sun is mounting and Longstreet's men are coming on, — not long ago I traveled the same road and the limbs of the trees almost mingled over it, and the woods on each side were still and deep, — can now hear the battle, and are meeting the faint-hearted who always fringe the rear at the first signs of disaster. They are passing the crowded field-hospitals, and encountering ambulances, horsemen, stragglers, and the ever-increasing stream of wounded; and swerving off through the woods on both sides of the road are the limp fragments of Heth's division, heedless of their officers, who were shouting to gain their attention. And now comes one of Lee's aides, making his way urgently to Parker's store to tell the trains to get ready to withdraw, and another to Longstreet to hurry up, for, unless he comes quickly, the day is lost. At this appeal the men break into the double-quick, and Kershaw, whose division is perhaps a hundred yards ahead of that of Field, rides forward with a staff officer of General Wilcox who has been sent to show him his position. But before they reach Wilcox's line, it breaks, and Kershaw, seeing it coming, hurries back to meet his division.

THE BATTLE OF THE WILDERNESS 249

Out in the old field Lee, Hill, and their staffs are throwing themselves in front of the fleeing troops, imploring them to rally. From all accounts, Lee's face was a sky of storm and anxiety, and well it might be, for Catastrophe was knocking at the door. When McGowan passed him Lee exclaimed, "My God! General McGowan! is this splendid brigade of yours running like a flock of geese?"

It is now a question of minutes. The rolling musketry is at its height, one roar after another breaking, sheets of bullets are thridding the air, and a half-dozen cannon are firing rapidly blasting-charges of double canister, for our men are close up.

Kershaw throws all of Henagan's brigade, save the Second South Carolina, well to the left of the road; that he deploys on the right under the fire of Birney's troops, who are penetrating the woods to the left of the Confederate batteries. His next brigade, Humphreys's, is rushing up, its left on the south side of the road, Henagan having swung off, making room for him in the immediate front of our most advanced line. Field throws his first brigade, G. T. Anderson's, to the right of the road; but before this movement could be followed, Longstreet, who was on hand, with his usual imperturbable coolness, so says Venable, tells Field to form and charge with any front he can make. Accordingly in an instant he puts his second brigade, the Texans, in line of battle under Gregg. There were three General Greggs on the field, this one the Confederate, and on our side David and Irvin, brothers from Pennsylvania.

Just as they start, Lee catches sight of them and gallops up and asks sharply, "What brigade is this?" "The Texas brigade," is the resolute response. "General Lee raised himself in his stirrups," — so said a courier, in "The Land We Love," only a few years after the war, — "uncovered his gray hairs, and with an earnest yet anxious voice exclaimed above the din, 'My Texas boys, you must charge.' A yell rent the air," and the men dashed forward through the wreckage of Hill's corps and under a stinging fire from our sharpshooters. On they go, and now they have passed through Williams's guns, their muzzles still smoking, when suddenly they hear, "Charge, charge, men!" from a new, full voice, and there behind them is Lee himself, his warm brown eyes aflame. "Come back, come back, General Lee!" cry out the cannoneers earnestly; he does not heed and rides on; but a sergeant now takes hold of Traveller's rein. — It is a great pity that we have not a picture of that sergeant's face as he turns the big gray horse around and exchanges a firm, kindly glance with his rider. — Lee yields to his better judgment and joins Longstreet who, on the knoll near by, is throwing his brigades in as he did at Gettysburg, with the calmness of a man who is wielding a sledge.

Field, the large, handsome "Charley" Field of our West Point days, he who rode so proudly at the head

THE BATTLE OF THE WILDERNESS 251

of the escort for the late King of England when he came as a boy to visit the Point, — I wonder, if Field in the reveries of his old age, while basking in the memories of departed days, whether it was Benning's Georgians or the battalion of West Point cadets he saw himself leading, — oh, what children of Destiny we are! — But on he comes with Benning, who is following the track of the Texans, who are alone, and after smashing through Wadsworth's lines find themselves enfiladed by a terrible fire from the south side of the road against which the Fourth Texas was sent but could not stop it, and was only saved from annihilation by Kershaw's advance. Perry, commanding Law's brigade of Field's division, is turning from the Plank Road into the Widow Tapp field at double-quick, and beginning to form spryly. His Fifteenth Alabama passes within a few feet of Lee, behind whom, on their horses, are a group of his staff. His face is still flushed — he has just returned from trying to lead the Texans — and his blazing eyes are fixed intently on Kershaw's leading regiment that is forming line of battle and through whose ranks the retreating masses of Heth's and Wilcox's divisions are breaking. Aroused by this jeopardous disorder, he turns suddenly in his saddle toward his staff, and, pointing his gloved hand across the road, says in vigorous tones, "Send an active young staff officer down there." Then, casting his eyes on the ragged men filing by him, he asks kindly, "What men are these?"

A private answers proudly, "Law's Alabama brigade." Lee bares his gray hairs once more and replies, "God bless the Alabamians!" They, with colors slanting forward, grasp their arms tightly and swing on, the left obliquing till it brushes the young pines along the northern side of the old opening. Already from the smoke-turbaned woods ahead of them come bleeding and mangled Texans and Georgians, their blood striping across the garden, the dooryard, and the path to the well of the Widow Tapp's humble abode; but on with increasing speed toward the dead-strewn front march the brave Alabamians.

And who is this officer on the litter? Benning; Gregg has already been borne to the rear. And now what organization is that we see coming into line, there on the western edge of the field beyond Lee and Longstreet, obstructed by Hill's retreating fragments? That is "Charley" Field's largest brigade, made up entirely of South Carolinians. And the colors over them? The Palmetto Flag, the ensign and pride of their contumacious, insubordinate state, the first to nurse the spirit which has led the dear Old Dominion and her sister states into their woe. As usual, it is fluttering mutinously, hankering to engage the Stars and Stripes, which has not forgotten that this Palmetto ensign flaunted over the first guns to fire on it, as it flew, the emblem of Union and Peace, flew warm with the hopes of the obscure of all civilized lands, and dreaming of the day when every flag

THE BATTLE OF THE WILDERNESS 253

of the world shall do it homage. And at its very sight the nation's colors blaze up with righteous hostility; and as where or whensoever seen, in the Wilderness or at Gettysburg or Chickamauga, the old banner of Washington's day with a voice like an eagle's shriek, cries "Come on, Palmetto Flag!" And lo! to-day, to the credit of our common natures, the two banners are reconciled.

The onset of Gregg's Texans was savage, — it could not have been less after asking Lee to go back. They dashed at Wadsworth's riddled front, through which the battery had been cutting swaths; and besides that, two 12-pound guns and one 24-pound howitzer had run forward into the Plank Road and were pouring their canister into his huddled and crumbling flanks. Fatigue and want of coherence were breaking down the fighting power of his men, yet they met this shock with great fortitude. Cope, and he was right there, said in a despatch to Warren, "Wadsworth has been slowly pushed back, but is contesting every inch of the ground"; and it was not until Benning and Perry struck them that they began to waver, then break, and finally disrupt in great confusion. About half of them, under Rice and Wadsworth, fled back across the morass to the last line of logs and chunks from which they had driven the enemy; the other half with Cutler took the course they had come the previous evening. The narrative has already told where they were met.

While these troops were breaking, Carroll, not yet engaged, was ordered by Birney in person to send some of his brigade back to the north side, he having moved by flank across to the south of the road, having heard heavy firing in that direction. He sent the Eighth Ohio, Fourteenth Indiana, and Seventh West Virginia. Thus, apparently, at that moment the north side of the road was clear for Field; but he could not push his advantage, for Birney, Ward, and Coulter, who had taken Baxter's place after he was wounded, held Kershaw stubbornly. Moreover, Owen, followed by the Nineteenth Maine of Webb's brigade, who had reported to Carroll the night before, had gained a position on the immediate south side of the road, and was firing into Benning's and Perry's right, causing them to suffer severely.

"The enemy held my three brigades so obstinately," says Kershaw, "that, urged forward by Longstreet, I placed myself at the head of the troops and led in person a charge of the whole command, which drove the enemy to and beyond their original lines."

This position was just about opposite to where Wadsworth was now collecting the fragments of his command on the north side of the road, and was held by Carroll and the Vermonters, and these men Kershaw could not budge. Grimes and Wofford, who had advanced on Kershaw's right, had not made material headway against McAlister on Mott's left, but they had discovered what finally almost gave them

THE BATTLE OF THE WILDERNESS 255

the day, that our lines did not extend to the unfinished railroad, in fact they did not reach over a half-mile, if that, from the Plank Road.

In the midst of Kershaw's onslaught Getty was wounded, and Lyman in his notes says, "Getty rode past me looking pale; to my inquiry he said, 'I am shot through the shoulder, I don't know how badly.' A man [goes on Lyman] of indomitable courage and coolness. One of his aides (the fair-haired one) shot through the arm, the other, his horse shot. Immortal fighting did that Second Division, Sixth Corps, on those two bloody days."

While Carroll, the Vermont brigade, and the stout-hearted of all the broken commands that had rallied behind them, were standing off Kershaw, up the road comes Webb at the head of his gallant brigade. Wadsworth and Birney are there, trying to form troops for an advance. "There were several commands and no orderly arrangement as to lines, front, etc.," says Governor Connor. On reporting to Birney, Webb is directed to deploy on the right of the road and move forward and join Getty, whom Birney had asked to send some strength to the north side of the road. Webb deploys, and on he comes; the Nineteenth Maine have gladly reunited with their comrades and been put on the extreme right. On the left is the Twentieth Massachusetts under Abbott. "Waved my hand to Abbott," says Lyman, "as he rode past at the head of the Twentieth, smiling gayly." Smile on, dear heroic young fellow! Your smile will play on many a page, and the Wilderness holds it dear; for her heart is with you, and in years to come, when the dogwood and the wild roses are blooming, she will softly breathe your name through the tree-tops as she recalls that smile. Oh, how close we are to woods and streams, the traveling winds, the banded evening clouds, and, yes, even the distant stars!

On comes Webb, his line strung out through the woods, no skirmishers ahead, for he is expecting momentarily to come up with Getty, when suddenly there is a terrific crash, causing a fearful loss. But, standing among the wounded and the dying, his brigade holds fast and returns the fire; the enemy are just across the morass, in places not more than twenty or thirty yards away. He has come squarely up against what is left of Gregg's, Benning's, and about all of Perry's fresh brigade. Woolsey of Meade's staff sends back word: "7.27 A. M. Webb, who went in a short time since, is doing very well. The fire is very heavy, but not gaining. Wounded returning on Plank Road. 7.35. The fire is slackening and our men cheer. 7.40. The firing is heaviest on the right of the Plank Road [Webb's]; our men are cheering again." And there they battle back and forward amid a continuous roar of musketry; not they alone, for Kershaw, knowing that Lee's and Longstreet's eyes are on him, is crowding his men desperately against Carroll's and Birney's and Mott's iron-

THE BATTLE OF THE WILDERNESS 257

hearted veterans, and those ever steadfast sons of the Green Mountain State. The bark-scored and bullet-pitted trees around them are wreathed in smoke, and, like sheaves of wheat, bodies are lying on the leaf-strewn ground, unconscious now of the deafening crashes with which the gloomy Wilderness jars far and wide, and roars to the over-arching, listening sky.

There can be no doubt that Webb's desperate fighting saved the north side of the Plank Road at this crisis by checking Field's three brigades — Gregg's, Benning's, and Law's, the latter under General William F. Perry, to whom the credit may be given of saving the north side of the Widow Tapp field from Kitching's grasp who had come up from the Lacy house to help Wadsworth. This Perry accomplished by throwing against Kitching his left regiment, the Fifteenth Alabama, Colonel Oates, as he advanced on his way to support Benning and Gregg. Oates having rejoined his fellow regiments after repulsing Kitching, and Perrin's Alabama and the Florida brigade of Anderson's division having reported, and all taking a hand at Webb's line, he found his right overlapped and changed front to rear at double-quick on his left regiment, the Twentieth Massachusetts resting on the road, and stood them off.

Meanwhile Hancock, having been notified by Meade that Burnside was about to attack Field's flank, sent for Wadsworth and told him that he had ordered three brigades, Webb's, Ward's, and Carruth's, of Stevenson's division, to report to him, and wished that he with these additional troops would carry, if possible, the enemy's position on the right-hand side of the road. In Carruth's brigade was my friend Frank Bartlett's regiment, the Fifty-seventh of Massachusetts and the Fifty-sixth under Colonel Griswold. On their way to the front a member of Griswold's regiment — commanded by S. M. Weld of Boston after Griswold's death that morning — gave drink like a good Samaritan to a wounded Confederate, who, as soon as the line passed him, seized a musket and began to fire on the very men who had been kind to him. With righteous indignation they turned and exterminated the varmint; and then on with renewed determination to have it out with their country's enemies.

The intrepid Wadsworth, returning to the front, and seeing the Twentieth Massachusetts athwart the road where Webb had left it, his vehement spirit set on fire by Hancock's ardent and communicative aggressiveness, asked in pungent, challenging tones, "Cannot you do something here?" Abbott hesitating, mindful of Webb's order to hold that point at all hazards, the high-spirited Wadsworth, who by nature was more an individual combatant than the cool and trained commander, leaped the little barrier of rotten planks torn from the decaying road-bed,

THE BATTLE OF THE WILDERNESS

and of course Abbott and the Twentieth followed him. Wadsworth's second horse was killed, and the regiment was met immediately with a withering volley. After striving in vain to drive the enemy, Abbott had to desist from further efforts. He then ordered the men to lie down so as to escape a wicked, sputtering fire; but he himself, young and handsome, coolly and without bravado walked back and forth before his line, his eyes and face lit by the finest candle that glows in the hand of Duty. "My God, Schaff," said to me the brave Captain Magnitsky of the Twentieth, with moistened eyes, "I was proud of him as back and forth he slowly walked before us." A shot soon struck him and he fell. They tenderly picked up the mortally wounded, gallant gentleman and carried him to the rear. Bartlett reached Webb about the time he had changed front forward onto the sorely stricken Twentieth and formed in rear of his left centre. It was now about 9.30. Wadsworth, catching sight of Bartlett's colors flying defiantly in the face of Field's oncoming veterans, called on him in person to charge over some troops weakened by repulses, who were hesitating — and he and his men responded well. I can hear Bartlett's voice ringing, "Forward," and see his spare, well-bred face lit up dauntlessly by those intense blue eyes; eyes I have seen glint more than once with pleasant humor, for he had, besides courage, the spirit of comradeship, that pleasant, cloud-reflecting stream, rippling and green banked, that flows through our natures. But in a little while a shot struck him in the temple, and he followed his college friend, Abbott, to the field hospital; — he had already lost his left leg at Yorktown, and been seriously wounded in two places leading an assault at Port Hudson. The regiment lost 252 killed and wounded.

Wadsworth, after the charge, exclaimed, "Glorious!" but, like all the gains, theirs was temporary. For Field's fresh veterans coming up from where Burnside should have held them, he attacked fiercely; yet, try as he might, Webb finally fought him to a standstill. And so was it on the other side of the road: Carroll, Grant, and Birney's remnants, and McAlister of Mott's division, had thrown Kershaw and Wofford back till they, too, were glad to stop for a while.

At the mention of McAlister's name my sense of humor asks, "Can't you stop the narrative long enough to tell about General ——?" This general represented Gibbon's lone response to Hancock's order to attack at seven o'clock up the bed of the unfinished railroad with Barlow's division. He was a whiskey-pickled, lately-arrived, blusterous German, and when he reached McAlister on the left of the line, he wanted to burst right through, saying his orders were, "To find the enemy wherever he could find him and *whip him ! ! !*" Having blown this trombone Germanic blast, he spurred his nag and dashed at the "rebels." Pretty soon he sent to McAlister to

THE BATTLE OF THE WILDERNESS

come up and relieve him, which McAlister refused to do, when back came part of the brigade running, and Blank with them. "I want to get ammunition," he exclaimed. "Where?" asked McAlister. "Away back in the rear," he shouted as off he went. "That was the last I saw of him or his command," says McAlister. Notwithstanding there is a considerable strain of German blood in my veins, there is something about the swelling assertive military airs of that nationality which is very humorous and at the same time very nauseating. But I suppose really that McAlister ought to have given the poor fellow a little aid, if, for no other reason, than that his land sent so many Hessians here during the Revolution.

X

When the narrative was halted it was saying that the Confederates and ourselves were glad to stop for a while. It was now going on ten o'clock, and there was a lull all along the lines. And while it lasts, let us turn to Hancock, not forgetting that while Birney and Wadsworth and Webb were engaging so fiercely, he was beset with distracting and untoward happenings "in good measure, pressed down and shaken together and running over." At nine o'clock, while his attention is strained on the renewed offensive up the Plank Road, this despatch from Humphreys is handed to him: "Sheridan has been ordered to attack Longstreet's flank and rear by the Brock Road." "Longstreet's flank and rear by the Brock Road!" he repeats to himself; "Humphreys must have located him definitely; and yet we have prisoners from his corps." Just then to help confirm Humphreys's news the distant boom of Custer's guns comes through the smothering timber; and the footsteps of the haunting peril that has been dogging Hancock all the morning are closer than ever.

To clear up the reference to Custer's guns it should be told that under Sheridan's orders he had left Chancellorsville at 2 A. M. for the intersection of the Furnace and Brock roads, which, as the map will show,

THE BATTLE OF THE WILDERNESS 263

is about a mile beyond where Hancock's return line of breastworks crossed the latter. He reached there just in time to head off Rosser and Fitz Lee from laying hold of this important point.

Gregg, one of the best and most reliable of our cavalry commanders, was at Todd's Tavern looking out for Stuart, Merritt, commanding the Regular Cavalry brigade, within reach. Wilson who had been drawn back to Chancellorsville during the night, after renewal of ammunition and supplies, had posted one of his brigades at Piney Branch Church and the other at Aldrich's.

I cannot mention the names of Wilson and Custer and Merritt without seeing their faces again as cadets, and feeling a wave of warm memories. God bless the living; and Trumpets, peal once more for me, if you will, over Custer's grave.

So much then for the guns which Hancock heard as he read Humphreys's despatch that Sheridan was about to attack Longstreet. Humphreys's aide had just gone when here came Hancock's own trusted aide, the one to whom he always turned for final decision of any fact, Colonel Morgan, who reported that the enemy were actually advancing on the Brock Road. I think I can see Hancock, for I was near him during one of the charges at Spottsylvania and know that kind of news was received. He orders Birney to send a brigade at once to Gibbon (bear in mind that it is a little after nine, and that we have seen that Birney has need of every man along his bullet-sheeted front). Birney detaches Eustis's brigade of the Sixth Corps, and starts it toward the junction. A few minutes elapse, and Hancock tells Carroll to send a regiment; and, probably hearing another of Custer's guns, he sets the resolute Brooke in motion, and with him Coulter, who has gathered the remains of Baxter's brigade — the one which the light-haired and light-moustached, medium-sized and trim Kershaw first struck, and which had drifted back out of action. Before Eustis reaches the junction, along comes Leasure's delayed brigade of Stevenson's division, and Hancock tells them to keep right on down the road and help Gibbon; — Eustis, approaching the Brock, and seeing Leasure's column hurrying by, knows he must not break through, and halts. Hancock, having a moment to think, concludes that Gibbon, aided by Tidball with practically all the artillery of the corps, and the troops already on the way to him, can take care of Longstreet, directs Eustis to countermarch and go back to his fellows under Wadsworth and Birney.

Hancock has a moment's respite, but here comes ill-faced Trouble again. What is it, Creature? "Humphreys orders you to take immediate steps to repair the break the enemy has made through Warren's left" (referring to Cutler). "Great God! What's happened there?" I can hear him say, and off he propels an aide to Birney to send two brigades to his

THE BATTLE OF THE WILDERNESS 265

right to fill Cutler's gap. And that order is no sooner sent than here comes a message from Meade, saying that he hopes that nothing will delay or prevent his attacking simultaneously with Burnside!

Fight Longstreet as he comes up the Brock Road! attack simultaneously with Burnside! detach two brigades from Birney to fill a gap! Surely Hancock's measure of trials was pressed down and running over; and lo! Longstreet was not on the Brock Road at all, there was no gap in Warren's lines, and Burnside was nowhere near attacking, simultaneously or otherwise. — Meade ought to have remembered how long it took "Old Burn" to get ready at Antietam.

But cheer up, gallant Hancock! The hour-glass of your tormenting perplexities is about run out. Gibbon has discovered at last (10.10 A. M.) that the enemy he had seen looming up on the Brock Road are several hundred hospital-bleached convalescents, who, by some stupid provost-marshal at Chancellorsville, have been allowed to follow the corps' march of the day before around by way of Todd's Tavern.

Upon discovering that the dreaded infantry were these limp convalescents, and not Longstreet's veterans, I have no doubt that the wrinkled-browed, closely-cropped, reddish-bearded Gibbon breathed a long sigh of relief, and at once flew with the news to Hancock. Well, of course I do not know just what happened, but I have no doubt that the oaks about the junction remember Hancock's explosion well, or that the recording angel suddenly found himself busy, and, when his pen could n't keep up, looked downward, — apparently there was no end to the emphatic procession in sight, — and, feeling kindly toward Hancock, knowing he was a brave, warm-hearted fellow who would reach his hand compassionately to a stricken enemy, and that he had been badly pestered, closed the books and deliberately turned on an electrical buzzer, and cut off all communication with the Wilderness. And behold, when the books were opened again, some great hand — on the plea of the Centurion, I have no doubt — had written "Excused" after every one of the entries.

I cannot recall an instance during the war when any corps commander had such a badgering hour as Hancock that second morning in the Wilderness. He was naturally impulsive, and when he could not see his enemy, or, in other words, when he was in the woods, he was like an eagle with drenched wings and very restless.

Meanwhile the lull that has heretofore been referred to is going on, in places the woods are afire, and Wadsworth has dismounted and is alone with Monteith of his staff, who says: "He [Wadsworth] told me that he felt completely exhausted and worn out, that he was unfit (physically) to command, and felt that he ought in justice to himself and his men to turn the command over to Cutler. He asked me to get him a cracker, which I did."

THE BATTLE OF THE WILDERNESS 267

And while this gray-haired patriot and gentleman and the North's nearest aristocrat and nobleman is resting for the few minutes that are left of his heroic life, let us see what advantage Longstreet was taking of this ominous lull.

General M. L. Smith, a New Yorker and a distinguished graduate of West Point, doing engineer duty with Lee's army, had examined our left, and, finding it inviting attack, so reported to Longstreet. Now there is on Longstreet's staff a tall, trim, graceful young Georgian, with keen dark eyes and engaging face, whose courage and ability to command, Longstreet knows well, for he has been with him on many a field. His name is Sorrel, and his gallant clay is lying in the cemetery at Savannah, the long, pendulant Southern moss swaying softly over it. His "Recollections of a Confederate Staff Officer" has for me, like all the books I love, a low, natural, wild music; and, as sure as I live, the spirits who dwell in that self-sown grove called Literature were by his side when he wrote the last page of his Recollections, his pen keeping step with his beating heart. Longstreet, on hearing Smith's report, called Sorrel to him, and told him to collect some scattered brigades, form them in a good line on our left, and then, with his right pushed forward, to hit hard. "But don't start till you have everything ready. I shall be waiting for your gun-fire, and be on hand with fresh troops for further advance," said Longstreet.

Sorrel picked up G. T. Anderson's, Wofford's, Davis's of Heth's, and Mahone's brigades, and led them to the old unfinished railroad bed; and, having stretched them out on it, formed them, facing north, for advance. Of course, had Gibbon obeyed Hancock's order, this movement of Sorrel's could not have been made; as it was, the coast was clear. On Birney's left, as everywhere along the front, our forces were in several broken lines, and those of the first had changed places with the second, to take advantage of the little fires at which they had boiled their coffee to boil some for themselves; for many of the troops had not had a bite since half-past three in the morning, and it was now past eleven. Save the skirmish line, the men were lying down, and not expecting any danger, when suddenly, from the heavy undergrowth, Sorrel's three widely-winged brigades burst on their flank with the customary yell, and before our people could change front, or, in some cases, even form, they were on them. Fighting McAlister tried his best to stay the tempest, and so did others, many little groups of their men selling their lives dearly; for the color-bearers planted their banners on nearly every knoll, and brave young fellows would rally around them; but being overpowered, panic set in, and the lines melted away.

As soon as Carroll, Lewis A. Grant, Birney, Webb, and Wadsworth heard Sorrel's quick volleys, they were all on their feet at once, for the character of the firing and the cheers told them that Peril had snapped its chain and was loose. In a few minutes fleeing individuals, then squads, and then broken regiments, began to pour through the woods from the left.

Kershaw and Field, being notified by Longstreet to resume the offensive as soon as they should hear Sorrel, now pressed forward, seriously and exultingly active. Wadsworth, to stay the threatening disaster (for that lunatic, Panic, travels fast, and every officer of experience dreads its first breath), flew to the Thirty-seventh Massachusetts at the head of Eustis's brigade, which was just getting back from the junction, and ordered Edwards, a resolute man, to throw his regiment across the front of Field, who, with several pieces of artillery raking the road, was advancing. The Thirty-seventh moved quickly by flank into the woods, and then, undismayed, heard the command, "Forward." And with it went my friends, Lieutenants Casey and Chalmers, and that pleasant and true one of many a day, Captain "Tom" Colt of Pittsfield, whose mother was a saint. "You have made a splendid charge!" exclaimed Wadsworth, and so they had — the ground behind them showed it; they thrust Field back, gaining a little respite for all hands before disaster; and very valuable it proved to be, for some of the broken commands thereby escaped utter destruction.

While Field and Kershaw assailed Carroll, Birney, and Wadsworth fiercely, fire was racing through the woods, adding its horrors to Sorrel's advance; and with the wind driving the smoke before him, he came on, sweeping everything. Seeing his lines falter, Sorrel dashed up to the color-bearer of the Twelfth Virginia, "Ben" May, and asked for the colors to lead the charge. "We will follow you," said the smiling youth spiritedly, refusing to give them up; and so they did. In the midst of the raging havoc, Webb, under instructions from Wadsworth, now in an almost frantic state of mind, tried to align some troops beyond the road so as to meet Sorrel, whose fire was scourging the flanks of Carroll and the Green Mountain men, through whom and around whom crowds of fugitives, deaf to all appeals to rally, were forcing their way to the rear. But the organizations, so severely battered in the morning, were crumbling so fast, and the tumult was so high, that Webb saw it was idle to expect they could hold together in any attempted change of position; he therefore returned to his command, and quickly brought the Fifty-sixth Massachusetts, Griswold's regiment, alongside the road. Fortunately his Nineteenth Maine, withdrawn during the lull to replenish its ammunition, had been wheeled up by the gallant Connor at the first ominous volley from the South. They had barely braced themselves on the road before Carroll, and then the old Vermont brigade, had to go; and now Connor and Griswold open on Sorrel, checking him up roundly.

THE BATTLE OF THE WILDERNESS 271

Wadsworth undertook to wheel the remnants of Rice's regiments who had stood by him, so as to fire into the enemy on the other side of the road. In trying to make this movement he ran squarely onto Perrin's Alabama brigade, of Anderson's division, which had relieved a part of Field's, who rose and fired a volley with fatal effect, breaking Wadsworth's formation, the men fleeing in wild confusion. In this Alabama brigade was the Eighth Regiment, commanded that morning by Hilary A. Herbert who lost his arm. This gallant man, soldier, member of Congress, and distinguished lawyer was Mr. Cleveland's Secretary of the Navy.

The heroic Wadsworth did not or could not check his horse till within twenty odd feet of the Confederate line. Then, turning, a shot struck him in the back of the head, his brain spattering the coat of Earl M. Rogers, his aide at his side. The rein of Wadsworth's horse, after the general fell, caught in a snag, and, Rogers's horse having been killed by the volley, he vaulted into the saddle, and escaped through the flying balls. Wadsworth lies unconscious within the enemy's lines; his heart, that has always beaten so warmly for his country, is still beating, but hears no response now from the generous, manly, truth-viewing brain. I believe that morning, noon, and night the bounteous valley of the Genesee, with its rolling fields and tented shocks of bearded grain, holds Wadsworth in dear remembrance.

Everything on the right of the Nineteenth Maine, Fifty-sixth and Thirty-seventh Massachusetts is gone, and they, with fragments of other gallant regiments, will soon have to go, too, for Sorrel comes on again with a rush. Griswold, pistol in hand, advances the colors to meet him, and is killed almost instantly; Connor, on foot and in the road, is struck and, as he falls, Webb calls out, "Connor, are you hit?" "Yes, I've got it this time." And his men sling him in a blanket and carry him to the rear. Webb, seeing the day is lost, tells the bitterly-tried regiments to scatter, and the wreckage begins to drift sullenly far and wide, some in Cutler's tracks, and some toward where Burnside is still pottering; but naturally the main stream is back on both sides of the Plank to the Brock Road, and there it straggles across it hopelessly toward Chancellorsville. Chaplain Washiell, Fifty-seventh Massachusetts, says, "I well remember the route as the men streamed by in panic, some of them breaking their guns to render them useless in the hands of the rebels. Nothing could stop them until they came to the cross-roads."

Where now is the morning's vision of victory which Babcock raised? All of Hancock's right wing, together with Wadsworth's division of the Fifth Corps, Getty's of the Sixth, and one brigade of the Ninth all smashed to pieces! The Plank Road is Lee's, — and the Brock, the strategic key, is almost within his grasp too! For Longstreet, followed by fresh brigades at

THE BATTLE OF THE WILDERNESS 273

double-quick, is coming down determined to clinch the victory!! His spirits are high, and Field's hand still tingles with his hearty grasp congratulating him on the valor of his troops. Jenkins, a sensitive, enthusiastic South Carolinian, "abreast with the foremost in battle and withal an humble Christian," says Longstreet, has just thrown his arms around Sorrel's shoulder, — for the graceful hero has ridden to meet his chief, and tell him the road is clear, — and says, "Sorrel, it was splendid, we shall smash them now." And then, after conferring with Kershaw, who had already been directed to follow on and complete Hancock's overthrow, Jenkins rides up to Longstreet's side and with overflowing heart says, "I am happy. I have felt despair of the cause for some months, but am relieved and feel assured that we shall put the enemy back across the Rapidan before night." Put the enemy back across the Rapidan! That means the Army of the Potomac defeated again, and Grant's prestige gone!!

Yes! It is a great moment for Jenkins and for them all. The overcast sky that has been so dark has rifted open, and the spire of the Confederacy's steeple dazzles once more in sunshine. And while it dazzles and youth comes again into the wan cheek of the Confederacy, gaunt Slavery, frenzied with delight over her prospective reprieve, snatches a cap from a dead, fair-browed Confederate soldier, and clapping it on her coarse, rusty, gray-streaked mane, begins to dance in hideous glee out on the broom-grass of the Widow Tapp's old field.

Dance on, repugnant and doomed creature! The inexorable eye of the Spirit of the Wilderness is on you! Dance on! For in a moment Longstreet, like "Stonewall," will be struck down by the same mysterious hand, by the fire of his own men, and the clock in the steeple of the Confederacy will strike twelve. And, as its last stroke peals, knelling sadly away, a tall spare figure, — where are the tints in her cheeks now? — clad in a costly shroud, and holding a dead rose in her hand, will enter the door of History, and you, *you*, Slavery, will be dying, gasping, your glazing eyes wide open, staring into the immensity of your wrongs. And when your last weary pulse has stopped, and your pallid lips are apart and set for good and all, no friendly hand will be there to close them, — oh, the face you will wear! — the eye of the Spirit of the Wilderness will turn from you with a strange, impenetrable gleam. For White and Black, bond and free, rich and poor; the waving trees, the leaning fields with their nibbling flocks, the mist-cradling little valleys with their grassy-banked runs, gleaming and murmuring in the moonlight; the tasseling corn and the patient, neglected, blooming weed by the dusty roadside, — all, all are the children of the same great, plastic, loving hand which Language, Nature's first and deepest interpreter, her widely listening ear catching waves of sound from the immeasurable depths of the Firma-

THE BATTLE OF THE WILDERNESS 275

ment, has reverently called God; all, all through him are bound by common ties.

Hancock's first warning that something serious had happened was the sight of Frank's brigade, and the left of Mott's division, tearing through to the Brock Road. But now the full stream of wreckage begins to float by him at the junction, and he realizes that disaster has come to his entire right front. "A large part of the whole line came back," says Lyman. "They have no craven terror, but for the moment will not fight, nor even rally. Drew my sword and tried to stop them, but with small success."

Colonel Lyman, a tall, lean man with a gracious, naturally cordial manner, an energetic and careful observer, and far and away the best educated officer connected with any staff in the army, rode in and reported the state of affairs to Meade, who at once, realizing the appalling possibilities, directed Hunt to place batteries on the ridge east of the run, the trains at Chancellorsville to fall back to the river, and Sheridan to draw in his cavalry to protect them. "Grant, who was smoking stoically under a pine," says Lyman, "expressed himself annoyed and surprised that Burnside did not attack — especially as Comstock was with him as engineer and staff officer to show him the way."

Meanwhile men were pouring from the woods like frightened birds from a roost. The tide across the Brock Road was at its height, and it was only when

Hancock appealed to Carroll, who had halted his brigade on arriving at the road, to give him a point for rallying, that he and his staff met with any encouragement. "Troops to the right and left of the brigade," states the historian of the Fourth Ohio, "were falling rapidly back beyond it." Carroll (like all the Carrolls of Carrollton that I have known, he had reddish hair and his classmates at West Point dubbed him "Brick") rode among the dispirited, retreating groups, shouting, "For God's sake, don't leave my men to fight the whole rebel army. Stand your ground!" for he expected Lee to strike at any moment. But how strange! Why do his fresh troops not come on and burst through, while Hancock, Carroll, Lyman, and Rice, and scores of officers, are trying to rally the men?

An hour goes by and Leasure, who, it will be remembered, had been sent to Gibbon on the false alarm, was directed, no one having approached the line of breastworks, to deploy his brigade, his right one hundred yards from the road (the Brock), and sweep up the front, which he did, encountering but a single detached body of the enemy. What does the continuing silence mean? Certainly something mysterious has happened. Why do they lose the one great chance to complete the victory?

A few words will explain it all. The Sixty-first Virginia of Mahone's brigade — Mahone, a small, sallow, keen-eyed, and fleshless man — had approached

THE BATTLE OF THE WILDERNESS 277

within forty or fifty yards of the road, and, through the smoke and intervening underbrush, seeing objects emerging on it from the bushes on the opposite side, mistook them for enemies and let drive a scattering volley. What they saw was a part of their fellow regiment, the Twelfth Virginia, who with the colors had crossed the road in pursuit of Wadsworth's men and were returning. The volley intended for them cut right through Longstreet, Kershaw, Jenkins, Sorrel, and quite a number of staff and orderlies, who just then came riding by, killing instantly General Jenkins, Captain Foley, several orderlies, and two of the Twelfth's color-guard. But of all the bullets in this Wilderness doomsday volley the most fated was that which struck Longstreet, passing through his right shoulder and throat, and almost lifting him from his saddle. As the unfortunate man was reeling, about to fall, his friends took him down from his horse and propped him against a pine tree. Field, who was close by, came to his side, and Longstreet, although faint, bleeding profusely and blowing bloody foam from his mouth, told him to go straight on; and then despatched Sorrel with this message to Lee: "Urge him to continue the movement he [Longstreet] was engaged on; the troops being all ready, success would surely follow, and Grant, he firmly believed, be driven back across the Rapidan."

They carried Longstreet — thought at the time by all to be mortally wounded — to the rear, and just as they were putting him into an ambulance, Major Stiles, from whom I have already quoted, came up; and, not being able to get definite information as to the character of his wound, only that it was serious, — some saying he was dead, — turned and rode with one of the staff who in tears accompanied his chief.

"I rode up to the ambulance and looked in," says the Major. "They had taken off Longstreet's hat and coat and boots. I noticed how white and domelike his great forehead looked, how spotless white his socks and his fine gauze undervest save where the black-red gore from his throat and shoulder had stained it. While I gazed at his massive frame, lying so still except when it rocked inertly with the lurch of the vehicle, his eyelids frayed apart till I could see a delicate line of blue between them, and then he very quietly moved his unwounded arm and, with his thumb and two fingers, carefully lifted the saturated undershirt from his chest, holding it up a moment, and heaved a deep sigh. 'He is not dead,' I said to myself."

Longstreet was taken to the home of his friend, Erasmus Taylor, not far from Orange Court House, and, as soon as he could stand the journey, to a hospital in Lynchburg. Although not fully recovered from his wounds, he rejoined the army about the last of October, after it had taken what proved to be its final stand before Richmond.

Field, it appears from one of his letters, when Lee and Longstreet, on their way to the front, reached

THE BATTLE OF THE WILDERNESS 279

him, joined them and rode beside Lee. Coming to an obstruction of logs that had been thrown across the road by their troops in the early morning, or later by ours, Lee stopped, while Field, at his suggestion, gave the necessary orders for the removal of the logs so that the two guns which were following them could pass. Meanwhile Longstreet with his party rode on, and within fifty yards met with the fate already chronicled. Had the road been clear, Lee would have been with them and received the fire of that fateful volley. But fortunately, not there, not in the gloom of the Wilderness, but at his home in Lexington and after his example had done so much to guide the Southern people into the paths of resignation and peace, was his life to end.

A moment's reflection upon the situation into which the wounding of Longstreet plunged Lee, will, I think, leave the impress of its serious gravity. There amid the tangle of the Wilderness, just at the hour when advantage is to be taken, if at all, of our defeat and utter disorder, the directing head on whom he relies for handling his exulting men to clinch the victory is stricken down under shocking circumstances, almost in his immediate presence, and the responsibility of leadership is thrown on him in a twinkling. Put yourself in his place and do not forget its distracting circumstances or the nature of his surroundings, — Hill too sick to command his corps, Longstreet bleeding terribly and propped up against a small pine tree waiting for an ambulance, bloody foam pouring from his mouth when he tries to speak; the road clogged with prisoners, squads trying to regain their commands, dead bodies, limping, wounded, stretcher-bearers with their pale-faced and appealing-eyed burdens, Poague's guns and Jenkins's big brigade trying to make their way through them, Field's and Kershaw's divisions advancing in two or more lines of battle, at right angles to the road, Sorrel's flanking brigades parallel to it, all in more or less disorder, moving by flank to the rear for the time being, preparatory to the execution of Longstreet's order for a second attack on Hancock's left, every step they take bringing them and the advancing organizations nearer utter confusion, and the woods enveloped in heavy, obscuring smoke!

Such were the circumstances into which Lee was suddenly thrown at that hour of momentous importance. It was a chafing trial, one that took him out of his sphere of general command and imposed upon him the burden of details which ordinarily falls on subordinates who, as a rule, from their intimate relations with officers and troops, can more readily deal with them than the commander himself. No doubt Longstreet's plans were told to Lee by Sorrel and Field, but, whatsoever they were and whomsoever he should designate to carry them out, obviously nothing could be done till the lines were untangled; and so he directed Field to reform them, with a view to carry-

THE BATTLE OF THE WILDERNESS 281

ing the Brock Road, on which his heart was resolutely set.

Field at once began his difficult, troublesome task, and, while he is getting his troops ready for the ordeal, Lee giving him verbal orders from time to time, let us turn to the operations of our cavalry, which, for the first time in the history of the Federal army, was on the immediate field with the infantry in a well-organized and compact body and under an impetuous leader.

Sheridan, in his relentlessness, boisterous jollity in camp, and in a certain wild, natural intrepidity and brilliancy in action, came nearer the old type of the Middle Ages than any of the distinguished officers of our day. I need not give details as to his appearance, for his portrait is very familiar. The dominating features of his square fleshy face with its subdued ruddiness were prominent, full, black, flashing eyes, which at once caught your attention and held it. His forehead was well developed, a splendid front for his round, cannon-ball head. Custer insisted on introducing me to him at City Point after his Trevilian Raid — Sheridan was in his tent, bareheaded, and writing, when we entered. He gave me his usual spontaneous, cordial greeting and searching look, and soon thereafter was off for the Valley, where he won great honors, breaking the clouds that were hanging so heavily over our cause, lifting the North from a state of despondency and doubt into one of confidence in its final success, and giving Grant a relief from his burden which he never forgot. But my impression is that, great as Sheridan was, he never could have permanently maintained pleasant official relations with his fellow commanders on any field: he had to be in chief control, tolerating no restraint from equals. Grant alone he bowed to, and the reason Grant admired him and allowed him free rein was that Sheridan did not hesitate to take a bold initiative.

Sheridan early in the morning of the 6th put the cavalry in motion, and Custer's successful fight with Rosser of Fitz Lee's division in the forenoon on Hancock's left has already been mentioned. I wish my readers could have known Custer, felt the grasp of his hand, seen his warm smile, and heard his boyish laugh. And then, too, if they could have seen him lead a charge! his men following him rollickingly with their long red neckties (they wore them because it was a part of his fantastic dress) and as reckless of their lives as he himself of his own. Really, it seemed at times as if the horses caught his spirit and joined in the charge with glee, the band playing and the bugles sounding. There never was but one Custer in this world, and at West Point how many hours I whiled idly away with him which both of us ought to have given to our studies. But what were the attractions of Mechanics, Optics, or Tactics, Strategy or Ordnance, to those of the subjects we talked about: our life in Ohio, its coon-hunts, fox-chases, fishing-holes, muskrat and partridge-traps, — in fact, about all that stream of persons and little events at home which, when a boy is far away from it for the first time, come flowing back so dearly.

It was his like, I have often thought, which inspired that lovable man and soldier, "Dick" Steele, to say in the "Spectator," when descanting in his own sweet way on the conversation and characters of military men, "But the fine gentleman in that band of men is such a one as I have now in my eye, who is foremost in all danger to which he is ordered. His officers are his friends and companions, as they are men of honour and gentlemen; the private men are his brethren, as they are of his species. He is beloved of all that behold him. Go on, brave man, immortal glory is thy fortune, and immortal happiness thy reward."

Reader, let me confide! there are two authors in the next world whom I have a real longing to see: one is Steele, — poor fellow, so often in his cups, — and the other, he who wrote the Gospel of Saint John and saw the Tree of Life.

Well, Custer, after throwing his old West Point friends, Young and Rosser, back from the Brock Road and Hancock's left, made connection with the ever-trusted Gregg, then at Todd's Tavern confronting Stuart, who studiously kept his force under cover, protected everywhere by hastily constructed defenses. That Stuart at this time had some plan in hand is revealed by a despatch to him from Lee's chief of staff, dated 10 A. M., to the effect that Lee directed him (Marshall) to say that he approved of Stuart's designs and wished him success. Probably what he had in mind was one of his usual startling raids around our flanks; but whatever it was, Gregg prevented him from undertaking it by holding him fast to his lines, thereby retaining the cross-roads at the Tavern and securing the left of the field.

At one o'clock Humphreys tells Sheridan that Hancock's flank had been turned, and that Meade thought he had better draw in his cavalry so as to secure the protection of the trains. Accordingly Sheridan drew in from Todd's Tavern and the Brock Road. Wilson at Piney Branch Church was brought back to Chancellorsville, and the enemy by dark pushed forward almost to the Furnaces, about halfway between Todd's Tavern and Sheridan's headquarters at Chancellorsville. Thus by the time Field was ready, the Brock Road beyond Hancock's left, covering ground at once dangerous to the army if it stood still, and absolutely essential if it tried to go ahead, was abandoned. In regaining it the next day, which had to be done to carry out Grant's onward, offensive movement, Sheridan had to do some hard fighting, and met with very severe losses, the responsibility for which became the occasion of an acrimonious dispute that broke out between his own friends and the friends of Meade as soon as Sheridan's autobiography

THE BATTLE OF THE WILDERNESS 285

appeared. Death had overtaken Meade some years before the book was published. Perhaps he was misled by Sheridan's despatch as to positions of the cavalry, but I have never felt that Meade's friends were quite fair to Sheridan in blaming him for falling back, since the plain purport of the orders, as I interpret them, was for him to take no responsibilities that would endanger the safety of the trains by being too far extended. To be sure, it so happened that the trains were secure; Lee's great chance, that hovered for a moment like a black thunder-cloud over the Army of the Potomac, passed by; and if Sheridan had left Gregg at Todd's Tavern, which, as we see now, he might have done, the door to Spotsylvania would in all probability have been wide open for Warren the following night. As it was, Warren found it shut.

The trains at Chancellorsville as soon as Hancock's disaster reached them took time by the forelock and started for Ely's Ford. And, in explanation of their movement, allow me to say that no one scents danger so quickly as quartermasters in charge of trains. While the commander is thinking how he can get ahead through danger, they are busy thinking how they can get back out of danger. For, as a rule, quartermasters hear very little of the good, but all of the bad news from the slightly wounded and the skulkers who, sooner or later, drift back to the trains, the latter invariably telling the same sad, unblushing story, that their commands are literally cut to pieces.

A real adept skulker or coffee-boiler is a most interesting specimen; and how well I remember the coolness with which he and his companion (for they go in pairs) would rise from their little fires on being discovered and ask most innocently, "Lieutenant, can you tell me where the —— regiment is?" And the answer, I am sorry to say, was, too often, "Yes, right up there at the front, you damned rascal, as you well know!" Of course, they would make a show of moving, but they were back at their little fire as soon as you were out of sight.

Not only the skulkers but many a good soldier whose heart was gone, made his way to the trains at Chancellorsville after Hancock's repulse; and the quartermasters had good reason to take their usual initiative toward safety, northward in this case, to Ely's Ford, for there was presageful honesty in the face and story of more than one who came back. As a matter of fact, they came in shoals. Even the ammunition-train of the Second Corps, affected by the contagious panic, had joined the swarm of fugitives. At about six o'clock Sheridan, impressed by the state of affairs, told Humphreys that unless the trains were ordered to cross the river, the road would be blocked and it would be impossible for troops to get to the ford. What would have happened that afternoon among the trains had Longstreet not been wounded and had his troops broken through?

Meanwhile Field, under the immediate eye of Lee,

was getting his men ready to renew the contest. Knowing the situation and the country as we do, it is not surprising that there was delay, or to learn from the report of the First South Carolina, one of the regiments which planted their colors on Hancock's first line of works, that there was much wearisome marching and counter-marching before they all got into place for the attack. Kershaw, by Lee's direct orders, was, with three of his brigades (Humphreys's, Bryan's, and Henagan's), moved to the south, till his right rested on the unfinished railway. His other brigade (Wofford's) was detached to help Perry stop Burnside, who had finally gotten under headway. The only good, so far as I can see, that Burnside did that day was to detach these two brigades from Lee at a critical time.

Field put what were left of the Texans, G. S. Anderson's and Jenkins's brigade of South Carolinians (commanded by Bratton since Jenkins's sudden death), in several lines of battle on the south side of the Plank Road, where the main assault was to be given; and along with them was R. H. Anderson's fresh division of four brigades.

By this time three or four precious hours had flown by; for it was almost four o'clock when the line was reported ready to move. This delay — I have no doubt that on its account Lee did not promote Field to the command of his corps in Longstreet's place — but, however that may be, the delay must have been keenly disappointing and vexing to Lee. For he knew well what advantage Hancock was making of the respite, that every minute order was taking the place of disorder, confidence of panic, and that breastworks were growing higher and more formidable.

But now these seasoned veterans of Antietam, Fredericksburg, Malvern Hill, and Chancellorsville, they who broke through Sickles at Gettysburg and Rosecrans at Chickamauga, are ready for another trial — their last of the kind as it turned out, for, with but one or two feeble exceptions Lee never tried another such deliberate assault. Had he had as many men as Grant, however, I have but little doubt that his fighting spirit would have inflamed him to repeat and re-repeat Malvern Hill and Pickett's charge. But this time Pickett was not with him — his immortalized division was at Petersburg looking after Butler; nor could Alexander bring up his artillery, as on the famous day at Gettysburg, to shake the lines along the Brock Road.

At last Field got them arrayed, and brightened here and there by blooming dogwoods and closely overhung by innumerable throngs of spring-green leaves, leaves on slender branches that gently brush faces and colors as the soft breezes sigh by, is the long line of gray, speckled at short intervals by the scarlet of torn banners. Little did those men dream as they stood there that Fate only a few hours before had for good and all sealed the doom of the Confederacy, that their cause was lost, and that the sac-

THE BATTLE OF THE WILDERNESS

rifices they were about to be called on to make would be a waste.

On my visit to the field last May, I sat a while on a knoll not far from where their left lay, — the spot is quite open and gloried with more of the stateliness of an oak forest than any point in the Wilderness, — and as my mind dwelt on those battle lines waiting for the command, "Forward," that would blot out this world for so many of them, I felt one after another the tender throbs of those human ties which stretch back to the cradle and the hearth. When, on the point of yielding to their pathos, at the behest of Imagination, if not of Truth itself, the background of my meditations became a vast, murky-lighted expanse, and from a break in its sombre depths a Figure — perchance it was Destiny — beckoned me to come and look down on the struggle-to-the-death. On gaining the edge of the rift three spirits were standing there. The Republic, with an anxious look, her eyes fixed on the combatants; below at her left was one with a radiant, glowing face; and standing apart, with swimming averted eyes, was another of sweet gentleness. I asked Imagination who these two were. She answered: "The radiant one is the Future, the other with the heavenly countenance is Good-will." And while I gazed, the war ended and at once Good-will knocked at the doors of conqueror and conquered, and at last, under her kindly loving pleading, they joined their hands, and lo! she won for civilization, democracy and religion their greatest modern triumph.

XI

BESIDE throwing up near the junction two or three additional lines, Hancock had slashed a border of the woods in their immediate front. His troops were posted from right to left as follows, their order showing the haste with which they were assigned to position. First came Kitching's heavy artillery that the Alabama brigade threw back from the slopes of the Widow Tapp field as they came forward to help Gregg and Benning, its right opposite the knoll heretofore mentioned; then Eustis's brigade of the Sixth Corps; then, in three lines of battle, two brigades of Robinson's division of the Fifth; then Owen's brigade of the Second; then Wheaton and L. A. Grant of the Sixth, their left resting on the Plank Road at the junction which the day before they had saved. Immediately in rear of them lay Carroll of the Second with his fearless regiments; and behind Carroll, in a third line, stood Rice of the Fifth; the remnants of his brigade all waiting for the attack that they knew was coming. In the road at the junction was a section of Dow's Maine battery under Lieutenant W. H. Rogers. Then came Birney in three lines of battle, then Mott in two lines, and on his left Smyth with his gallant Irish, flying with the Stars and Stripes the golden Harp of Erin on a green field.

THE BATTLE OF THE WILDERNESS 291

Webb was next to Smyth, then Barlow. The other four guns of Dow's battery were in an opening behind the left of Mott's second line, and next to him Edgell's six guns of the First New Hampshire.

At 3.15, all being quiet, kind-hearted Lyman asked permission of Hancock to go back to the hospital and look after his boyhood friend, "little" Abbott. The gallant fellow was then breathing his last, and died about four.

A half-hour later Field's doomed line came on. The point which he had chosen to drive it through was Mott's and Birney's front, just to the left of the junction. It was a lucky choice, for a part of the former's division had behaved badly on both days, its conduct in marked contrast with that when Kearney and Hooker used to lead it.

Surmising from the skirmish-line reports that the main assault would be south of the Plank Road, a bugler was stationed on Mott's breastworks, with orders to sound the recall for the skirmishers at the enemy's first appearance. Soon his notes rang out, and Dow's and Edgell's guns opened at once with spherical case. But on they came, marching abreast to within one hundred paces of the Brock Road. There, confronted by the slashing, they halted, and for a half-hour poured an uninterrupted fire of musketry across the works, our lines replying with deadly effect. The incessant roar of these crashing volleys, and the thunder of the guns as they played rapidly, struck war's last full diapason on the Plank Road in the Wilderness.

Meantime fire, that had crept through the woods from the battle-ground of the forenoon, had reached the bottom logs of the breastworks in some places and was smoking faintly, waiting for a breath of wind to mount and wrap them in flames. And now, while the battle was raging to its culmination, on came a fanning breeze, and up leaped the flames. The breastworks along Mott's and Birney's front soon became a blazing mass. The heat grew almost intolerable, and the wind rising — what desolated Southern home had it passed! — now lashed the flames and hot blinding smoke down into the faces of the men, driving them, here and there, from the parapets.

Soon one of Mott's brigades began to waver and then broke, retiring in disorder toward Chancellorsville. At its abandonment of the works, South Carolinian and Texan color-bearers rushed from the woods, followed by the men, and planted their flags on the burning parapets, and through the flame over went the desperate troops. At this perilous sight Rogers at the junction began to pour double canister into them, and Dow and Edgell crossed his fire with case and like charges of canister. The former must have had his eye on a particular battle-flag, for he speaks in his report of shooting one down five times. Meanwhile his own breastworks get on fire, and the

THE BATTLE OF THE WILDERNESS

extra charges that the gunners have brought up from the limbers explode, burning some of the cannoneers severely. Still he keeps on, his guns belching canister.

As soon as the break was made through Mott and his own left, Birney in great haste rode to Robinson, his next division commander on his right, telling him what had happened, that Hancock was cut off, and suggesting that proper disposition be made to receive an attack on Robinson's left and rear. Lyman, who when the assault began had gone to notify Meade, was met on his return by one of Hancock's aides, who told him that the enemy had broken through, and that there was no communication with the left wing. He rode on, however, and found Birney at the junction, who confirmed the aide's story. It is said that when Birney's aide came to Grant and reported that the enemy had broken the lines, he and Meade were sitting together at the root of a tree, and Grant, after hearing the story, did not stir, but looking up said in his usual low, softly vibrating voice, "I don't believe it."

Meanwhile Birney had called on Rice, and Hancock on Carroll; the batteries ceased firing, and together those two fearless commanders with their iron-hearted brigades dashed with bayonets fixed at the enemy and soon hurled them from the works, leaving colors, prisoners, and over fifty dead and many wounded within the burning entrenchments.

To the south in front of our lines for four or five hundred yards from the junction, clear to where Webb was posted, Confederate dead and helpless wounded dotted the ground. They had charged with great valor.

I have always thought that if Grant had been with Hancock at the time of this repulse, he would have ordered an immediate advance. For the Army of the Potomac never had another commander who was so quick as Grant to deliver a counter-blow.

Field's losses were heavy, he had signally failed to carry the works, and soon drew his shattered lines back almost to the Widow Tapp field, and at about sundown reformed them perpendicular to the Plank Road, their left resting on it, and bivouacked about where Gregg first struck Wadsworth.

That night the Texans who had suffered so severely collected the dead they could find, dug a trench near the road, and buried them. And when the last shovelful of reddish clay and dead leaves was thrown, they tacked a board onto an oak whose branches overhung the shallow trench, bearing the inscription, "Texas dead, May 6th, 1864." Field said in a letter to his friend, Gen. E. P. Alexander, that a single first lieutenant was all that was left of one of the companies.

W. R. Ramsey, of Morton, Pa., who was in Wadsworth's front when the Texans charged, and was wounded so he could not move, says that some South Carolina men brought blankets and covered him that night besides making and bringing coffee to him, and that one of their little drummer boys staid with him till his leg was amputated. Who can doubt that the Good Samaritan reached a hand when the little drummer boy entered Heaven's gates!

As this is the end of the fighting of these Confederate troops in the Wilderness, here is how General Perry, who commanded one of the brigades, closes his reminiscences of the battle: "Many a day of toil and night of watching, many a weary march and tempest of fire, still await these grim and ragged veterans; but they have taught the world a lesson that will not soon be forgotten, and have lighted up the gloom of that dark forest with a radiance that will abide so long as heroism awakens a glow of admiration in the hearts of men." True, well and beautifully said.

And now for the narration of some personal experiences, not because they were of any great consequence in themselves, but one of them at least, as it so happened, had a part in the history of the day. During the forenoon — from official dates of various orders I know it must have been not later than ten; at any rate it was after my return from trying to find Wadsworth — Warren, who was standing in the dooryard of the Lacy house, saw a guard that had charge of a small squad of Confederates just in from the front halt them near the bank of the run. He told me to go down and find out who they were. Noticing a young officer among them, I asked him what regiment he belonged to. He and his companions were tired and not in good spirits over their hard luck, with its long period of confinement before them, for Grant had suspended the exchange of prisoners; and he answered me with sullen defiance in look and tones, "Fifteenth Alabama!" which, if I remember right, was in Law's brigade of Longstreet's corps. Not being very skillful at worming valuable intelligence out of prisoners, I was getting very little from them, when a mounted orderly came to me from my immediate commander, the Chief of Ordnance, Captain Edie, to report at Meade's headquarters. On reaching there, Edie told me I was to start at once for Rappahannock Station with despatches to Washington for an additional supply of infantry ammunition to be sent out with all haste. The wagons going to meet the train for the ammunition and other supplies were to be loaded with wounded, who would be transferred to the cars, and thence to the hospitals in Alexandria and Washington.

How the notion got abroad that the supply of ammunition was exhausted I cannot explain, except by the heavy firing. As a matter of fact, we had an abundance; but, somehow or other, Humphreys or Meade was made to think we were running short, and, as early as seven o'clock, a circular was issued to all corps commanders: —

The question of ammunition is an important one.

THE BATTLE OF THE WILDERNESS 297

The Major-General commanding directs that every effort be made to economize the ammunition, and the ammunition of the killed and wounded be collected and distributed to the men. Use the bayonet where possible.

By command of Major-Gen'l Meade.

S. WILLIAMS,
Adjutant-General.

Humphreys in a despatch to Warren said, "Spare ammunition and use the bayonet."

At nine o'clock, corps commanders were told to empty one-half of the ammunition-wagons and issue their contents to the troops without delay, sending the empty wagons to report to Ingalls at Meade's headquarters.

I asked Edie what escort I was to have. He answered, "A sergeant and four or five men." I exclaimed, "A sergeant and four or five men! What would I amount to with that sort of escort against Mosby?"

For those who have been born since the war, let me say that Mosby was a very daring officer operating between the Rapidan and Potomac, his haunt the eastern base of the Blue Ridge. I think every staff officer stood in dread of encountering him anywhere outside the lines, — at least I know I did, — from reports of atrocities, perhaps more or less exaggerated, committed by his men. I must have worn a most indignant expression, possibly due to just having escaped capture, for Edie roared with laughter. But I declared that it was no laughing matter, that I had to have more men than that, and I got them, for they sent a squadron of the Fifth New York Cavalry, in command of Lieutenant W. B. Cary, now the Reverend Mr. Cary of Windsor, Connecticut, and may this day and every day on to the end be a pleasant one for him! And besides, they supplied me with a fresh horse, a spirited young black with a narrow white stripe on his nose.

When I was ready to start, I heard General Grant ask some one near him, "Where is the officer that is going back with despatches?" Those that I had received were from Meade's Adjutant-General. I was taken up to him by some one of his staff, possibly Porter or Babcock. Grant at once sat down with his back against a small pine tree, and wrote a despatch directed to Halleck.

While he was writing, E. B. Washburne, a prominent member of Congress, who, as a fellow townsman of Grant's, having opened the door for his career, had come down to see him start the great campaign (on account of his long-tailed black coat and silk hat the men said that he was an undertaker that Grant had brought along to bury "Jeff" Davis), gave me a letter with a Congressman's frank, to be mailed to his family. A number of the staff gave me letters also. A telegraph operator was directed to go with me, and my final instructions were that, if I found communication broken at Rappahannock, I was to go to Manassas, or the nearest station where the operator could find an open circuit.

I set out with my despatches, several correspondents joining me, and I remember that I was not half as polite to them as I should have been; but in those days a regular army officer who courted a newspaper man lost caste with his fellows. Soon after crossing the Rapidan we met a battalion of a New Jersey cavalry regiment that had been scouting up the river. It was a newly organized regiment, one of Burnside's, and on account of its gaudy uniforms was called by all the old cavalrymen "Butterflies," and most unmercifully jibed by them. But the "Butterfly" soon rose to the occasion, and paid the old veterans in coin as good as their own. As we were riding by them, one of our men inquired if they had seen anything of Mosby, and, on being answered in the negative, observed sarcastically in the hearing of the "Butterfly," "It's mighty lucky for Mosby," and rode on with the grin of a Cheshire cat.

We followed the road to Sheppard's Grove and then across country to Stone's or Paoli Mills on Mountain Run. From there we made our way to Providence Church on the Norman's Ford Road, passing over a part of the field where the lamented Pelham was killed. The old church, with some of its windows broken, stood on a ridge; desolated fields lay around it. When we reached it the sun had set, and I remember how red was its outspread fan in the low western sky. Rappahannock Station was in sight, and over the works which occupied the knolls on the north side of the river, which the Sixth Corps had carried one night by assault after twilight had fallen, the preceding autumn, to my surprise a flag was flying. I had supposed that the post had been abandoned, but for some reason or other Burnside had left a regiment there. Our approach being observed, the pickets were doubled, for they took us for some of the enemy's cavalry.

I went at once, after seeing the officer in command, to the little one-story rough-boarded house that had served as the railroad station; and, while the operator was attaching his instrument, which he carried strapped to his saddle, I opened Grant's despatch and read it. In view of its being his first from the Wilderness, I will give it entire: —

WILDERNESS TAVERN,
May 6, 1864 — 11.30 A. M.

MAJOR-GENERAL HALLECK,
Washington, D. C.

We have been engaged with the enemy in full force since early yesterday. So far there is no decisive result, but I think all things are progressing favorably. Our loss to this time I do not think exceeds 8000, of whom a large proportion are slightly wounded. Brigadier-General Hays was killed yes-

THE BATTLE OF THE WILDERNESS 301

terday, and Generals Getty and Bartlett wounded. We have taken about 1400 prisoners. Longstreet's, A. P. Hill's, and Ewell's corps are all represented among the prisoners taken.

U. S. GRANT,
Lieutenant-General.

Meanwhile the operator's instrument had clicked and clicked, but could get no answer, and he decided we should have to go on possibly as far as Fairfax Station. Thereupon I talked with the commander of the escort, who thought the march should not be resumed till the horses had fed and had a good rest, as it was at least thirty miles to Fairfax Station. We agreed to start not later than half-past ten.

The colonel gave us some supper and wanted to know all about the battle; but I was very tired, and in those days with strangers very reserved, so I am afraid I disappointed him, and soon went to sleep. My reticence is reflected in the following despatch from C. A. Dana, Assistant Secretary of War, whom Lincoln had asked to go to Grant and tell how the day was going; for that merciful man could not stand the strain of uncertainty any longer. Dana arrived at seven o'clock the following morning, and reported: "An officer from General Meade was here at 2 o'clock this morning seeking to telegraph to Washington, but was recalled by a second messenger. They report heavy fighting, etc. . . . The battle is believed here to have been indecisive, but as the officer said but little, I can gather nothing precise."

Well, why should I have particularized or boasted? The fact is I had seen nothing like a victory. Naturally prone to take a dark view, and equally anxious to avoid conveying half-developed information, I do not believe that the colonel could have pumped with any chance of success in getting either favorable news or full details.

Saddling had begun when I was waked up by the officer of the guard, who said that a civilian had just been brought in from the picket-line, claiming to be a scout from Grant's headquarters with orders from him to me. I did not recognize the man, though I may have seen him about the provost-marshal's headquarters. He handed me a small envelope containing the following order: —

HEADQUARTERS, ARMY OF THE POTOMAC,
May 6, 1864 — 2 P. M.

LIEUT. MORRIS SCHAFF,
        Ordnance Officer.

The commanding general directs that you return with your party and despatches to these headquarters, the orders directing the procuring of an additional supply of ammunition having been recalled.

I am, very respectfully, your obedient servant,
        S. WILLIAMS,
            Assistant Adjutant-General.

THE BATTLE OF THE WILDERNESS 303

The original in the same little envelope is lying before me now; it is beginning to wear an old look and is turning yellow. You, envelope, and your associations are dear to me, and as my eye falls on you, old days come back and I see the Army of the Potomac again. In a little while we shall part; and I wonder if in years to come you will dream of that night when we first met on the Rappahannock, hear the low intermittent swish of the water among the willows on the fringed banks as then, and go back under the dim starlight to the Wilderness, with a light-haired boy mounted on a young black horse that had a little white snip on its nose.

As there was no occasion for hurry, and the scout and his horse both called for rest, I waited till two o'clock and then set off on our return, the scout taking the lead. There was a haze in the sky, and in the woods it was very dark. We had been on our way some time, and I had paid no attention to the direction we were going, when, for some reason or other, I asked the scout if he were sure of being on the right road. He answered that he was, and we rode on. But shortly after, I heard the roaring of water falling over a dam away off to our right, and asked, "Where is that dam?" He said on the Rappahannock. "If that's the case," I replied, "we are heading the wrong way; it should be on our left."

Well, he reckoned he knew the road to Germanna Ford; but I was not satisfied, and, after going a bit farther, told the lieutenant to countermarch. At this the scout was very much provoked, declaring we should soon be completely lost in the woods. He went his course and I went mine, and within a mile I struck a narrow lane which led to a house with a little log barn or shed just opposite, and in a flash I knew where we were.

It was really a great relief, as any one will appreciate who has tried to find his way in a dark night across an unfamiliar country.

The water we heard that still night was Mountain Run flowing over the dam and lashing among the boulders below it at Paoli Mills. On my visit to the Wilderness last May I went to the dam, and then to the old, weather-beaten, forsaken mill that stands alone some two hundred yards off in a field. Its discontinued race was empty and grass-grown, and some of the members of a small, scattered flock of sheep ready for shearing were feeding along its brushy banks. By the roadside, below the boulders, is a shadowed, gravelly-edged, shallow pool, and as I approached it a little sandpiper flitted away.

Daylight had just broken when we reached Madden's, and, as we were passing a low, hewed log-house, a powerful, lank, bony-faced woman appeared at the door combing a hank of coarse gray hair.

I said, "Good-morning, madam, how far is it to Germanna Ford?"

She replied surlily to my question, and then with a

THE BATTLE OF THE WILDERNESS 305

hard smile added, "I reckon you 'uns got a right smart good whipping last night."

"What do you mean?" I asked.

"Well, you'll find out when you get back." And she gave me a spurning look as she turned in the doorway that as much as said, "You caught h—l and deserved it."

The other day when I traveled the road I made some inquiries about the old lady and found that her name was Eliza Allen, and that she had long since died; a catbird was singing in the neglected garden.

Reader, to fully comprehend what Eliza denominated as a "right smart good whipping" necessitates my going to the right of the army during the late afternoon and evening of the first day. And as the narrative is drawing towards its close I'd like to have you go with me. For I want to take a walk with you before we part, for we have been good friends, and I want you to see moreover the Wilderness as it is. We will follow up the Flat Run Road from where it joins the Germanna, and thence to where Sedgwick's right lay. Before we set out let me tell you that the darkish, weather-worn roof and stubby red chimney coming up through the middle of it, that you see a half-mile or more away across the deserted fields, are those of the old Spottswood manor-house. Its lower story is concealed by that intervening heave in the ground; its mistress, Lady Spottswood, is buried on the plantation known as "Superba," near Stevensburg.

In a few steps this fenceless road, a mere two-wheeled track winding among the trees, will quit the fields and lead us into deep and lonely woods. I passed over it twice last May, azaleas and dogwoods were blooming then as now, and I think I can point out the identical giant huckleberry — it is on the left of the road — whose white pendulous flowers first caught my eye with their suggestion of bells tolling for the dead. And I venture to say that no finer or larger violets are to be seen anywhere in the world, or more pleasing little houstonias, than you see now. Later on I can promise you the sight of cowslips gilding patches of shallow, stagnant water; for as we draw nearer to where Sedgwick's line was first established (the maps show it) we shall come to the swampy heads of Caton's Run and the upper waters of the tributaries of Flat Run. The road is between them, the former on our left, the latter on the right. Hark a minute! that must be the same herd of cattle I met with last year: I came on them at this sudden turn and up went every head wildly. Yes, the same lonely *kling, klung.* I recognize the bells. We shall not see them; they are feeding off toward the Pike and Warren's lines.

"I thought you said it was not very far, but we have walked at least a mile. How much farther?" Only a short way; a new road is always long. "What is this

THE BATTLE OF THE WILDERNESS 307

low, continuous mound that we see on both sides of the road?" halting suddenly, you ask. That is all that is left of Sedgwick's entrenchments. Let us follow it to the right, if for nothing else on account of its soliciting lonesomeness. I am sure it will enjoy our presence, for think of the days and nights it has lain here dreaming. "Do you imagine the spirits of those boys ever come back, who fell here?" Oh, yes, over and over again in line with flags flying and the roses of youth in their cheeks. Think of the fires, though, that swept through the woods that night! "I wonder if spectral ones break out with the reappearance of the dead?" No, and if they should, the trees would shiver down the fallen dew and quench them; for timber dreads to hear the snapping march of fire.

"Shall we go on?" Yes, a bit farther; the walking is not easy, I know, for the limbs are low and the trees are thick. Moreover it is growing rougher and swampier; more and more, too, the green vines impede our way. Test their strength if you care to do so. But here at last is the right of the line near the head of a branch. If we were to follow it till it meets the run, and then a bit farther northward, we should come in sight of some old fields; but we will not penetrate deeper; let us pause and rest a moment for we are in one of the depths of the Wilderness. Notice the rapt, brooding, sullen stillness of the woods, the moss in tufts tagging those forlorn, blotched young pines, those dark shallow pools with their dead-leaf bottoms, that leaning stub with only one limb left, those motionless fallen trees, and those short vistas scrutinizing us with their melancholy gray eyes. Were you ever in a quieter spot or one where you felt the living presence of a vaster, more wizard loneliness? "Never, never." Your voice even sounds strange; and, excuse me, if I remark a glint of wildness in your eyes, — that atavistic glint which comes only in places like this.

Well, on the afternoon of the first day, about here the right of Keifer's brigade formed — it ought to be known in history as Keifer's, for Seymour had just been assigned to it. It consisted of the Sixth Maryland, One Hundred and Tenth, One Hundred and Twenty-second, One Hundred and Twenty-sixth Ohio, Sixty-seventh and One Hundred and Thirty-eighth Pennsylvania; and Ohio, Maryland, and Pennsylvania may well be proud of their record on this ground. On their left were those sterling brigades of Russell and Neill of the Sixth Corps, only a few of the men visible, the bulk completely buried by the thick undergrowth. Let us imagine that this is the day of battle, that the sun is on the point of setting, and that orders have come to go ahead.

If you care to go forward with them I'll go with you. "Go! why, yes, yes, let us go by all means!" For the sake of my old state, let us join the One Hundred and Tenth Ohio under Colonel Binkley. The first line under Keifer is made up of that regiment

THE BATTLE OF THE WILDERNESS

and the Sixth Maryland, the latter on the left, connecting with the Fourth New Jersey. Behind us in a second line are the One Hundred and Twenty-second Ohio, then the One Hundred and Thirty-eighth Pennsylvania, and then the One Hundred and Twenty-sixth Ohio. Colonel John W. Horn, commanding the Sixth Maryland, is sending out skirmishers to cover his front; they are under Captain Prentiss, a very gallant man. (In the final charges on the forts of the Petersburg lines Prentiss led a storming party, and, as he crossed the parapet, had his breastbone carried away by a piece of shell, exposing his heart's actions to view. The Confederate commanding the battery which had just been overpowered fell also, and the two officers lying there side by side recognized each other as brothers. They were from Baltimore.) Captain Luther Brown of the One Hundred and Tenth Ohio is in charge of the skirmishers in his regiment's front. Now the order comes for the first line to move forward. The colors advance; let us go with them. That firm, earnest-eyed man commanding the regiment is Binkley; and there is McElwain, one of the bravest of the brave. The fire is terrific, men are falling, but colors and men are going ahead. Did you see the look in that sergeant's face as he fell? And now comes a horrid thud as a shot strikes a corporal full in the breast. (Pushing aside the low, stubborn limbs and scrambling over these wretched vines, on goes the line.

310 THE BATTLE OF THE WILDERNESS

There is no silence in the dismal Wilderness now. Smoke is billowing up through it, the volleys are frequent and resounding; bullets in sheets are clipping leaves and limbs, and scoring or burying themselves deep in the trunks of the trees. On go the sons of Ohio and Maryland.) I wonder how much longer they can stand it. Look, look how the men are going down! But don't let us cast our eyes behind us; as long as those brave fellows go ahead, let us go with them.

The lines are slowing up under that frightful, withering fire. Now they stand, they can go no farther, for just ahead (behind logs hurriedly assembled) on that rising ground are the enemy, and they mean to hold it. Moreover, it has grown so dark that their position is made known only by the deep red, angrily flashing light from the leveled muzzles of their guns. Although Keifer has reported that unless reinforced he doubts being able to carry the position, yet back comes the command to attack at once. The line obeys, but is checked by a terrible fire. Some brave fellow cries out, "Once more"; they try it again, but the fire is too heavy.[1] Here for nearly three hours they

[1] Captain W. W. Old of General Edward Johnson's division (Southern Historical papers) says that the fighting was so intense that night that General Johnson sent him to get two regiments to take the place of as many men in Pegram's brigade whose guns were so hot that they could not handle them. He arranged to slide the fresh regiments along the breastworks, but was told that there was no room for more men, that all they wanted was loaded guns, and details were made to load and carry them in.

THE BATTLE OF THE WILDERNESS 311

stand that scourging fire, bullets at highest speed, for it is very close range, converging across their flank from right and left. Keifer, although seriously wounded, is staying with them. Who is this riding up in the darkness to Keifer, saying sharply, "Support must be sent, for the enemy are flanking us"? It is the daring McElwain; down goes his horse. (That is the last of the gallant fellow; he and many others are burned beyond recognition.)

At last the men are falling back; but let us take this little fellow with us and help him along. We lift him, he puts his arms around our necks, and, colliding with trees, limbs raking our faces, we stagger along over the uneven ground in the dark. Now we stumble headlong over a body, and, as we fall, our friend moans piteously, and so does the unfortunate man our feet have struck, who says faintly, "I belong to Stafford's brigade [Confederate]; will you get me some water?" I hear you say right heartily, for I know you are gallant men, "Yes, indeed, we will. You, Captain, take the little corporal along and bring a canteen and I'll stay here till you come back." On my return, "Where are you?" I cry. "Here we are; come quickly, for the fire in the woods is making this way fast." And the soldier in gray is borne to the rear.

Let us close our eyes to the scene and our ears to the cries, and leave this volley-crashing and heart-rending pandemonium. The Sixth Maryland has lost, out of 442,152 officers and men; and the One Hundred and Tenth Ohio, 115 killed and wounded.

Grant, through misinformation, reported to Halleck two days later that Keifer's brigade had not behaved well, and for years and years they have had to stand this bitter injustice. It is true that the next night this brigade, as well as Shaler's, which was sent to its right, was swept away by Gordon in the discomfiture referred to by Mrs. Allen; but let us look into the facts.

The impetuous attacks of Russell's, Neill's, and Keifer's brigades on that first night were met by those of Hays, Pegram, and Stafford, during which, as already told, Pegram was severely and Stafford mortally wounded. The losses on both sides were heavy, and toward the close of the action Gordon was sent for by Ewell to go to the support of his staggering troops. Owing to the darkness and the nature of the wood, it was well along in the night, and the fighting was over, before his brigade reached a position on the extreme left of Ewell's line, which at this point swung back a little northwestwardly. Gordon directed his men to sleep on their arms, and at once sent out scouts to feel their way and find the right, if possible, of Keifer's position. At an early hour these scouts reported that his lines overlapped it and that it was wholly unprotected.

This news was of such importance that he sent the scouts back to verify it. Satisfied on their return that

THE BATTLE OF THE WILDERNESS 313

they had not been deceived, and keenly appreciating what his adversary's unprotected flank invited, he waited impatiently for daybreak. As soon as it broke, he mounted his horse and was guided by his explorers of the night before to a spot from whence, creeping forward cautiously some distance, he saw with his own eyes our exposed flank. The men, unconscious of danger, were seated around little camp-fires boiling their coffee. Colonel Ball of the One Hundred and Twenty-second Ohio says that General Seymour, then in command of the brigade, was repeatedly notified during the night that the enemy were engaged cutting timber for their works and moving to our right. For some reason or other General Seymour did not give heed to this significant information and throw up a line for the safety of his right. Gordon rode at once, burning with his discovery, to his division commander, Jubal A. Early, a sour, crabbed character, who, unlike Gordon and the big-hearted and broad-minded Confederates, bore a gloomy heart, a self-exile cursing his country to the last. What is bleaker than an old age a slave to Hate! Our higher natures have each its dwelling place — and how often they invite us up, and how rarely we accept! But I cannot believe that they extended many invitations to Jubal A. Early — who, after the war was all over and Peace healing the wounds, still kept on with increasing bitterness — to join them around their hearths. No, there as here, the Spirit loves the man and soldier who takes his defeats and disappointments with a gentleman's manliness.

Gordon laid the situation before Early, expecting him to jump at the chance to strike a blow such as that which made Stonewall famous. But, to Gordon's amazement, Early refused to entertain his suggestion of a flank attack, alleging as a reason that Burnside was on the Germanna Road directly behind Sedgwick's right, and could be thrown at once on the flank of any attacking force that should try to strike it. If this interview took place between daylight and seven o'clock, Early was right as to the presence of a part, at least, of Burnside's troops on the Germanna Road, for, as we have already seen, the head of his rear division, the first, did not reach the Pike till about seven o'clock.

Early declining to make the attack, Gordon went to Ewell and urged it upon him; but he hesitated to overrule Early's decision, and so Gordon had to go back to his brigade, cast down and doubtless disgusted through and through with the lack of enterprise on the part of his superiors and seniors. He was only thirty-two or three, while Ewell and Early were approaching fifty years of age. By the time Gordon had returned from his fruitless mission, Shaler's brigade had been sent to Seymour's right. Thus Ewell's lines lay quiescent throughout the livelong day behind their entrenchments, while Longstreet and Field desperately battled to the southeast of them. To his

THE BATTLE OF THE WILDERNESS 315

failure to grasp the golden opportunity Ewell owes his fixed place in the rank of second-rate military men; but he is not alone; it is a big class. The truth is that next to hen's teeth real military genius is about the rarest thing in the world.

Stung by disappointment over his failure to carry the Brock Road, Lee set off for Ewell's headquarters, the declining sun admonishing him that only a few hours remained in which to reap his expectations of the morning. The course he takes, if one cares to follow him, is, for a mile or more, through a wandering leaf-strewn, overarched wood-road to the Chewning farm, his general direction almost due northwest. At Chewning's he passes Pegram's and McIntosh's batteries; they salute, — the Confederates cheered rarely, — he lifts his hat, carries his gauntleted left hand a little to the right, presses his high-topped boot against Traveller's right side, and the well-trained gray, feeling rein and leg, changes to almost due north, and with his strong, proudly-daring gallop brings his master to the Pike.

When Lee reined up at Ewell's headquarters, he asked sharply, — I think I can see the blaze in his potent dark brown eye, — "Cannot something be done on this flank to relieve the pressure upon our right?" It so happened that both Early and Gordon were with Ewell when this guardedly reproving question was put. After listening as a young man and subordinate should to the conference of his superiors,

316 THE BATTLE OF THE WILDERNESS

Gordon felt it his duty to acquaint Lee with what the reader already knows. Early, with his usual obstinacy, vigorously opposed the movement, maintaining that Burnside was still there; Lee, having just thrown Burnside back from the Plank Road, heard him through, and thereupon promptly ordered Gordon to make the attack at once. By this time the sun was nearly set.

XII

GORDON set off, moving by the left flank, with his own and Robert D. Johnston's North Carolina brigade (the one that claims it made the march of sixty odd miles in twenty-three hours!), and, after making a détour through the woods, brought his men up as rapidly and noiselessly as possible on Shaler's flank. Pausing till Johnston should gain the rear of Shaler's brigade, and then, when all was ready, with a single volley, and the usual wild, screaming yells, he rushed right on to the surprised and bewildered lines, which broke convulsively, only to meet Johnston. Seymour's right was struck, panic set in, and the men fled down the lines to the left, and hundreds, if not thousands, back to the Flat Run and Germanna roads. When those following the breastworks reached Neill's steadfast brigade, Colonel Smith of the Sixty-first Pennsylvania gave the command, "By the right flank, file right, double-quick, march!" This brought him right across the retreating masses, and he told his men to stop the stampede as best they could; but the disorganized men swept through them in the gathering darkness, the Confederates on their heels.

But, meanwhile, Morris and Upton had come to Smith's aid, and between them they stopped Gordon; not, however, without losing a number of men and prisoners, among whom was F. L. Blair of Pittsburgh, a member of the Sixty-first Pennsylvania, to whom I am indebted for a vivid account of what happened. Shaler and Seymour, trying to rally their men, were both taken prisoners.

As soon as the break occurred, Sedgwick threw himself among his veterans, crying, "Stand! stand, men! Remember you belong to the Sixth Corps!" On hearing his voice in the darkness, they rallied. Meanwhile the panic was at its height, and several of his staff flew to Meade's headquarters, — Meade at that time was over at Grant's, — telling Humphreys that the right was turned, the Sixth Corps had been smashed to pieces, and that the enemy were coming up the road. Humphreys, with that promptness and cool-headedness which never deserted him, let the situation be as appalling as it might, at once made dispositions to meet this unexpected onslaught, calling on Hunt, the provost guard, and Warren, all of whom responded briskly. Lyman says in his notes, "About 7.30 P. M. ordered to take over a statement of the case to General Grant in the hollow hard by. He seemed more disturbed than Meade about it, and they afterwards consulted together. In truth, they [the enemy] had no idea of their success." Meade then returned to his headquarters, Grant going with him.

On hearing some of the panicky reports from Sedgwick's aides, Meade turned to one of them and asked fiercely, "Do you mean to tell me that the Sixth

THE BATTLE OF THE WILDERNESS 319

Corps is to do no more fighting this campaign?" "I am fearful not, sir," quoth ——. I think I can see and hear Meade, and I cannot help smiling, for it reminds me of a little interview I had with him myself a few days later, the first morning at Spotsylvania. I happened to be in the yard of the Hart house, gazing across the valley of the sleepy Po at a long Confederate wagon-train hastening southward amid a cloud of dust, when he rode up. I ventured to say to him that a battery would easily reach that train. He gave me a deploring look and then said, "Yes! and what good would you do? scare a few niggers and old mules!" That was the only suggestion I made to him for the management of his campaign.

Well, Sedgwick, having thrown himself into the breach, rallied his men, and the danger was soon over; for Gordon's troops were in utter confusion, engulfed by the Wilderness, as ours had been in every one of their attacks; and he was mighty glad, and so were his men, to get back to their lines.

Gordon's attack, brilliant as it was, and thoroughly in keeping with his exploits on so many fields, fields whose sod I am sure cherishes his memory fondly, has never seemed to me to have had the importance that he, in his frank, trumpet-breathing reminiscences, attached to it. He contends that, if he had been allowed to make the attack earlier in the day, it would inevitably have brought complete victory. But how easy for him, how natural for us all, to be deceived by retrospection! For chance sows her seed of possibility in the upturned earth of every critical hour of our lives; the mist of years quickens it, and in due time the clambering, blossoming vines are over the face of Failure, hiding its stony, inexorable stare. The past of every one, of armies and empires, as history tells us well, is dotted with patches of this blooming posy; and I can readily see how Gordon's reverie-dreaming eye, floating over the sad fate of the Confederacy which he loved so well, should fall on that day in the Wilderness; and how at once possibility reversed the failure beneath the lace-work of this apparently so real, so comforting and illusive bloom.

Yet, as a matter of fact, there was only one hour on the sixth, as I view it, when his attack would have been determining, — but, fortunately for the country, that hour never came; — namely, when Longstreet should have overwhelmed Hancock, which, as I believe upon my soul, he would have done had not Fate intervened. Hancock would probably have met the end of Wadsworth, inasmuch as he never would have left that key of the battle without pledging his life over and over again, — I say, had Gordon struck at that hour, nothing, I think, could have saved the Army of the Potomac. But so long as we held the Brock Road, I doubt very much if it would have been attended with any results more serious than it was.

But let that be as it may, by half-past nine the tumult died down and the Wilderness resumed her

THE BATTLE OF THE WILDERNESS 321

large, deep silence. So great, however, was the confusion, and so keen the consciousness that a disaster had just been escaped, it was decided to establish a new line for Sedgwick; and accordingly the engineers proceeded in the darkness to lay one. Starting on the right of the Fifth Corps, they swung the line back along the ridge south of Caton's Run, resting its right across the Germanna Road, thus giving up all north of Caton's Run, including the Flat Run Road. The map shows the new line. It was near midnight when Sedgwick's men began to move into their retrograde, and obviously defensive position.

This acknowledged attitude of repulse, together with the dismaying experiences of Warren and Hancock, threw the shadow of impending misfortune, which found expression far and wide that night in sullenly muttered predictions that the army would recross the Rapidan within the next twenty-four hours.

And what should be more natural? For hitherto two days of conflict with the Army of Northern Virginia south of the Rapidan and Rappahannock had marked the limit of the Army of the Potomac's bloody stay. The two days were up, between sixteen and seventeen thousand killed and wounded, the fighting in some respects more desperate than ever, and as a climax, the right flank crushed, as in Hooker's case!

Was history to repeat itself? Already three long years of war! When will this thing end? Must we go back defeated, as in years gone by, and then try it over again? No, sorely and oft-tested veterans, you have crossed the Rapidan for the last time. At this hour to-morrow night you will be on the march toward Richmond; for, dark as it looks to you and to us all, the Rapidan will never hear your tread again till you are marching home from Appomattox. And I am sure the river will ask you, as you are on your way across it then, "Army of the Potomac, what has become of Lee's bugles that we used to hear on still nights? the singers of the hymns, and the voices of those who prayed in such humility for peace, for their firesides, and their Confederacy, — it is almost a year since we have heard them. What has become of them all?" And I think I can hear you reply tenderly, "We overcame them at Appomattox, have given them the best terms we could, have shared our rations and parted with them, hoping that God would comfort them and at last bless the Southland." And so He has. O Hate, where was thy victory? O Defeat, where was thy sting?

To revert to Gordon's attack: the rumor was started that night — my friend, "Charley" McConnell of the Fifth Artillery, heard it and reported it to Sheridan — that Meade was ready to take the back track. Later in the campaign, when the burdens were lying heavy on his shoulders, and everybody should have stood by him, for the awful slaughter of Cold Harbor had just occurred, unscrupulous staff officers

THE BATTLE OF THE WILDERNESS

and newspaper correspondents whom he had offended declared the rumor to be a fact. Meade's temper! How much it cost him, and how long it kept the story going! Oh, if Fortune had hung a censer on his sword-hilt, and he could have swung the odor of sweet spices and fragrant gums under the nostrils of his fellow men, including cabinet officers, then, oh, then, his star would not be shining, as now, alone, and so far below Sheridan's and Sherman's! His chief trouble was that he always made ill-breeding, shrewdness, and presuming mediocrity, uncomfortable.

But as for his taking the back track, on the contrary he is reported to have exclaimed, "By God! the army is across now, and it has got to stay across!" If the oath were uttered, heard and recorded, then, at the last great day, when the book shall be opened and his name in order be called, "George Gordon Meade!" and he shall rise and, uncovering, answer in his richly modulated voice "Here!" I believe, as the old fellow stands there at the bar of judgment, bleak his heart but unfaltering his eye, he will look so like an honest gentleman in bearing, that the Judge, after gazing at his furrowed face a while, will say with smothered emotion, "Blot out the oath and pass him in." I really hope at the bottom of my heart, Reader, that he will include you and me, and the bulk of the old Army of the Potomac; and, to tell the honest truth, I shall be unhappy if we do not find the old Army of Northern Virginia there, too.

324 THE BATTLE OF THE WILDERNESS

Sheridan, the great Sheridan, for, whatever may have been his mould or the clay that was put in it, he was the one flaming Ithuriel of the North, by dark had drawn back from Todd's Tavern to Chancellorsville, and was encircling the disquieted trains. Custer on going into bivouac near Welford's Furnace had scattered his buglers far and wide through the woods, with instructions to sound taps, to make the enemy believe that cavalry was there in thousands; and every little while up till midnight these notes would peal through the silent timber. Wilson was camped between Grant's headquarters and Chancellorsville, and that night Sheridan's chief of staff, Forsyth, shared his blanket with him.

Well, with Gordon's attack over, the second day of Lee's and Grant's mighty struggle for mastery in the Wilderness ends, and great majestic night has fallen again. The losses of each have been appalling; and from Maine to the far-away Missouri (for Sherman was moving also), there is not a neighborhood or a city where awe and anxiety are not deep, for all realize that on this campaign hangs the nation's life. The newspapers have proclaimed the armies in motion, and the thousands of letters written just as camps were breaking have reached home. The father has been to the post office, he has a letter from Tom, the family assembles, and his voice trembles as he reads his brave boy's final tender message to him and the mother, who with uplifted apron is quenching her tears, and saying, struggling with emotion, "Perhaps our Tom will be spared; perhaps he will be." "Do not give way, mother; do not cry! Old Grant will win at last," exclaims the husband, as he puts the letter back into the envelope and goes over and strokes with loving hand his wife's bended brow. But let him or the North be as hopeful and consoling as might be, they could not drown the memory of the long train of consuming and depressing vicissitudes of the Army of the Potomac, which, with the other armies in Virginia, up to this time had lost, in killed, wounded, and missing, the awful aggregate of 143,925 men, the majority of them under twenty-two.

Yes, two days of awful suspense for the North have gone by, and city is calling to city, village to village, neighborhood to neighborhood, "What news from Grant?" Hour after hour draws on, and not a word from him. The village grocer has closed, and his habitual evening visitors have dispersed, the lights in the farm-houses have all gone out. Here and there a lamp blinks on the deserted, elm-shaded street, and in the dooryard of a little home on the back road off among the fields — the boy who went from there is a color-bearer lying in Hancock's front — a dog bays lonelily. The halfway querulous, potential, rumbling hum of the city has died down, "midnight clangs from the clocks in the steeples," and the night editors of the great dailies in New York, Philadelphia, Boston, and Chicago are still holding back their issues, hoping that the next click of the fast operating telegraph will bring tidings, glad tidings of victory from the old Army of the Potomac.

Mr. Lincoln cannot sleep, and at midnight, unable to stand the uncertainty any longer, asks Dana, Assistant Secretary of War, to go down and see Grant and find out how it is going. At that very hour Grant's staff and all about headquarters, save a newspaper man, are asleep, and Grant, with the collar of his coat upturned, is sitting alone, with clouded face, looking into a little dying-down camp-fire, nervously shifting his legs over each other. Of all the tides in the remarkable career of this modest, quiet man, that of this midnight hour in the Wilderness is easily the highest in dramatic interest. What were the natural reflections, as he sat there alone at that still, solemn hour?

Two days of deadly encounter; every man who could bear a musket had been put in; Hancock and Warren repulsed, Sedgwick routed, and now on the defensive behind breastworks; the cavalry drawn back; the trains seeking safety beyond the Rapidan; thousands and thousands of killed and wounded, — he can almost hear the latter's cries, so hushed is the night, — and the air pervaded with a lurking feeling of being face to face with disaster. What, what is the matter with the Army of the Potomac? Was an evil, dooming spirit cradled with it, which no righteous zeal or courage can appease? And he shifts his position.

THE BATTLE OF THE WILDERNESS

Let there be no mistake: Grant had reached the verge of the steepest crisis in his life; and I think under the circumstances he would not have been human if the past had not come back. He sees himself rising from obscurity, and the howl of the wolf that has never been far from his door, drowned in the cheers of his countrymen over victories he had won; rising from a cloud of painful, uncharitable disrepute up to the chief command of all the armies and his country pinning its last hopes on his star. What a retrospect! Was it all a dream, a dream to be shattered by an unrelenting Fate? and did he deserve it? Self-pity is moving. He had done his best, he was conscious of no harm in thought or deed to any of his fellow men in his upward flight. He had loved his country as boy and man. And now was he to follow in the steps of McDowell, McClellan, Pope, Hooker, and Burnside, and land in his old home in Galena, a military failure? Was the sky that hung so black and lasted so long to cloud over again? The tide of feeling was up: he leaves the slumbering camp-fire for his tent, and I am told by one to whom it was confided, one of his very close aides, that he threw himself on the cot-bed, and something like stifled, subdued sobs were heard.

But before dawn broke, the cloud that had settled on him had lifted, and, when his attached friend, General Wilson, who was a member of his military family while at Vicksburg, disturbed over rumors, rode to his headquarters at an early hour, Grant, sitting before the door of his tent, said calmly, as Wilson, having dismounted some paces away, started towards him, with anxious face, "It's all right, Wilson; the Army of the Potomac will go forward to-night." And at 6.30 A. M. he sent the following order to Meade: —

GENERAL: — Make all preparations during the day for a night march, to take position at Spotsylvania Court House with one army corps; at Todd's Tavern with one; and another near the intersection of Piney Branch and Spotsylvania Railroad with the road from Alsop's to Old Court House. If this move should be made, the trains should be thrown forward early in the morning to the Ny River. I think it would be advisable in making this change to leave Hancock where he is until Warren passes him. He could then follow and become the right of the new line. Burnside will move to Piney Branch Church. Sedgwick can move along the Pike to Chancellorsville, thence to Piney Branch Church, and on to his destination. Burnside will move on the Plank Road, then follow Sedgwick to his place of destination. All vehicles should be got off quietly. It is more than probable the enemy will concentrate for a heavy attack on Hancock this afternoon. In case they do, we must be prepared to resist them and follow up any success we may gain with our whole force. Such a result would necessarily modify these instructions.

THE BATTLE OF THE WILDERNESS 329

All the hospitals should be moved to-day to Chancellorsville.

U. S. GRANT,
Lieutenant-General.

To take up the thread of my return with the despatches. Impressed by Mrs. Allen's story and ominous satisfaction, I left the escort with directions to come on at its own marching gait, and hastened to Germanna Ford, crossed the river on the pontoon bridge, and, having gained the bluff, gave my horse the bit. He bore me speedily along the densely wood-bordered road, spotted by cast-away blankets and deserted now, save that here and there lay prone a sick or completely exhausted Negro soldier of Ferrero's over-marched colored division. They were not ordinary stragglers, and I remember no more pleading objects. Most of them had lately been slaves, and across the years their hollow cheeks and plaintive sympathy-imploring eyes are still the lonesome roadside's bas-reliefs.

The dewy morning air was steeped with the odor of burning woods, and the fire, although it had run its mad course, was still smoking faintly from stumps and fallen trees. This side of Flat Run it had come out of the woods and laid a crisp black mantle on the shoulders of an old field.

Beyond the run (no one can cross it now without pausing, for, its large, umbrella-topped water-birches standing in clumps will capture the eye with their sombre vistas), suddenly (and much to my surprise), I came squarely against a freshly-spaded line of entrenchments with troops of the Sixth Corps behind it; and in less time than it takes to tell, I was in the presence of General Sedgwick and his staff. The rather stubby, kindly-faced general was dismounted, and with several of his aides was sitting on the pine-needle-strewn bank of the road. His left cheek-bone bore a long, black smudge which I suspect had been rubbed on during the night by coming in contact with a charred limb while he was rallying his men. From Beaumont or Kent of his staff, or possibly from "Charity" Andrews of Wilson's class (for I remember distinctly having a short talk with him either then or later on the way to Meade's headquarters), I got an account of what had happened.

In a few minutes I was at the Pike,—the fog and smoke were so deep one could barely see the Lacy house,—and turned up to Grant's headquarters on the knoll. Meade was standing beside Seth Williams, the adjutant-general, when I handed the latter the despatches, saying that I had received his orders to return with them and that I had not been able to make telegraphic connection with Washington. Meade asked, "Where did you cross the Rapidan this morning?" I replied, "At Germanna Ford, on the pontoon bridge." "Is that bridge still down?" he demanded sharply. "Yes, at least it was when I

THE BATTLE OF THE WILDERNESS 331

crossed only a little while ago." Whereupon he turned and in a gritty, authoritative tone of command called out, "Duane!" Duane was chief engineer on his staff and was eight or ten feet away, talking with some one. I had noticed him particularly, for his back was literally plastered with fresh mud, his horse having reared and fallen backward with him. On his approaching, Meade, looking fiercer than an eagle, wanted to know why the bridge was still down, orders having been given at half-past eleven the night before for its immediate removal to Ely's Ford. I was mighty glad that I was not in Duane's shoes, for Meade did not spare him.

It seems that immediately after Gordon's attack, Humphreys or Williams sent Charles Francis Adams, of Boston, then in command of a squadron of the First Massachusetts Cavalry, with orders to the officer in charge of the bridge, directing him to take it up and proceed with the pontoons to Ely's Ford. For some reason or other, for which Duane was not at all responsible, the orders were not obeyed.

Having returned the letters which my friends had given me to their respective writers, I got a little something to eat, then went to Edie's tent and was soon fast asleep.

The chronicle of the third day, whose early hours I had passed on my way from Rappahannock Station, is about as follows. Some time during the night it was reported to Hancock that the enemy could be heard moving, and General Barlow, on whose picket line the report probably originated, thought, as Gibbon the day before had thought, that the enemy was massing to attack him. Stonewall Jackson's exploit still hung like a spectre around the left of Hancock's corps. On the strength of Barlow's alarming chirp, so to speak, Birney ordered each of his divisions to put three-fourths of their commands in the front line of entrenchments and the balance in the second (at this point just south of the Plank Road it will be remembered that there were three or four lines of breastworks, the outcome of Field's assault). Hancock's despatch conveying Barlow's news and impression reached Humphreys at 4.40, and by that hour daybreak had passed on.

About the same time Burnside sent in a report that his pickets too had heard wagons and troops of the enemy moving busily toward the south through the night, this in a way confirming Barlow's report. As a matter of fact the enemy were not leaving Burnside's front, nor were they massing to attack Barlow.

But to illustrate the nervous state of our corps commanders, Warren, a little later, at 7.40 A. M., reported to Humphreys that Roebling had heard cheering in the direction of Parker's store, — they probably had just been told of Gordon's success the night before, — that he had no doubt the enemy was passing a heavy force along his front, and if they were to concentrate upon him, in the fog and smoke they might break through. In view of this possibility he urged the construction of a line on the ridge east of Wilderness Run, and that Hancock should make a determined attack — the suggestion obviously springing from Burnside's report of the enemy leaving his front, which must have been communicated to Warren. Warren ended his despatch with, "You know how much more important our right is to our army just now than the left." Here we have another instance of Warren's tendency to put his finger in the pie. The only way I can account for this nervousness is by the experiences of the two days' fighting and the presence of the looming fog and smoke. We are all more or less apprehensive if not cowardly when wrapped in a heavy fog and unseen danger close at hand. Warren, fearing they were forming to come down the Pike, had Griffin shell the woods. Even Meade seemed to have been flustered, for just after hearing from Warren he despatched Hancock: "It is of the utmost importance that I should know as soon as possible what force, if any, of the enemy is on your left. Please ascertain by any means in your power. . . . There are indications of the enemy massing in front of Warren; either you or he is to be attacked and I think he, from their abandoning the Plank Road." Here we have the re-reflection of Burnside's report.

In accordance with Warren's suggestions Comstock and artillery officers were sent to select a line on the elevated ground east of the run; and Warren, to make sure of getting back to it if compelled to do so, set some of the engineer battalions and detachments of the Fifteenth New York Engineer Regiment to making bridges across the run. But from all we can learn, his anxiety was wholly unfounded, for there is no evidence that Lee at any time during the day entertained a thought of attacking. The fact is, he had shot his bolt, and so had Grant. Nor is it at all likely that Lee seriously considered making a strategic move; his disparity of numbers was too great for risking wide manœuvring. Moreover, he knew that in the nature of things Grant would have to choose within the next twenty-four hours between renewed assault, retreat, or advance, and hoping he might choose retreat, he left the door to the Rapidan wide open behind him. But, as illustrative of how the Army of the Potomac credited Lee's fighting spirit, Wilson, before the sun was very high, was directed by Sheridan to send a brigade toward Sedgwick's right and find out if the enemy had made any movement in that direction. Meade became restless on not getting word promptly from the cavalry, and at 8.45 A.M. said in a despatch to Sedgwick, "I cannot understand the non-receipt of intelligence from your cavalry. Single horsemen are constantly arriving from the ford signifying the Plank Road is open." — I was doubtless one of the single horsemen referred to. — How inconsistent is all this nervousness with the claim that we won a victory in the Wilderness.

THE BATTLE OF THE WILDERNESS

By ten o'clock, the fog and smoke having lifted, and Warren being able to see everything, he tells Crawford that he thinks Lee is retreating! Lee retreating! Did he not wait defiantly a day after Antietam and a like time after Gettysburg, inviting assault? No, he was not given to abandoning fields, and the men knew it; so, the army, crouching, confronted its dangerous adversary with vigilance unrelaxed, prepared to meet a lunge as a tiger which had felt another's teeth and claws.

Hancock, in receipt of Meade's anxious despatch, sent Miles along the unfinished railway, and Birney up the Plank Road. Miles executed his orders with his usual vigor, and located Lee's right about five hundred yards south of the railway. Birney found Field behind strong entrenchments this side of the Widow Tapp's field, practically on the spot where he went into bivouac after his unsuccessful assault the evening before. Both Miles and Birney, in pushing their lines hard up against the enemy, met with considerable losses.

Sheridan had, on his own initiative, pushed Custer back along the Furnace Road to the Brock; and, at noon, having gained the import of Grant's order to Meade for his night move, sent Gregg and Merritt to drive the enemy from Piney Branch Church and Todd's Tavern, so as to clear the way for Warren and the trains. This was not accomplished till after sundown, and only by the hardest and most resolute kind of fighting. Sheridan won the hotly contested field, Stuart leaving, among his dead, Collins, Colonel of the Fifteenth Virginia Cavalry. But Stuart still held the road to Spotsylvania, and never did his cavalry or any other do better fighting than was done the next morning resisting Merritt and Warren.

Out of a tender memory of Collins's fate, — he had been our tall, light-haired, modest, pink-cheeked adjutant at West Point, — while my horses were crunching their dinner of corn on the ear, I walked over the ground last May where he fell. It had lately been raggedly ploughed; and catching sight of a couple of daisies in bloom, I went to them. And now if those to whom sentiment in prose is unpleasing — and there are many such in the world, and too, too often have I offended them already — will excuse me, I'll say that as I stood over the daisies, a gentle wind came along, they waved softly, and with a heart full of auld lang syne, I said, "For the sake of my West Point fellow-cadet, and for the sake of days to come, and for the Southern sweetheart he married, wave and bloom on, Daisies!"

Could Sheridan have made his attack with all of his cavalry (Wilson had gone with a part of his division to look after Sedgwick's right), it might have put links of an entirely different character in the chain of events.

Wilson went far enough with McIntosh's brigade to satisfy himself that the Germanna Ford Road was

THE BATTLE OF THE WILDERNESS 337

clear, and then, to be doubly sure, sent McIntosh to the ford itself.

At a quarter to one McIntosh in a despatch to Sedgwick from Germanna Ford reported: "The road is all open. One battalion of the Fifth New York Cavalry crossed the ford this morning at 7 A. M. They came from Rappahannock Station and left that station at 2.30 this morning." This, of course, was my escort.

And now, a strange thing happened. Just after McIntosh's despatch, announcing a clear road, was received, one came to hand from Colonel S. T. Crooks, of the Twenty-second New York, picketing between Flat Run and the ford, saying that the enemy's pickets were on the road, and that a short distance down the Rapidan large columns of dust could be seen, McIntosh meanwhile having moved to Ely's Ford. Thereupon Meade grew furious, and sent this message to poor Crooks: "You will consider yourself under arrest for having sent false information in relation to the enemy. You will turn your command over to the next in rank, directing that officer to report to Colonel Hammond commanding Fifth New York Cavalry for orders."

What were the facts? General A. L. Long, chief of artillery of Ewell's corps and late biographer of Lee, says: "I was directed by General Ewell to make a reconnaissance in the direction of Germanna Ford. Taking one brigade of infantry and two battalions of artillery, I advanced to the Germanna Road, striking it about a mile from the ford. Two or three regiments of cavalry were occupying the road at this point. They were soon driven away by a couple of well-directed shots. It was discovered that the enemy had almost entirely abandoned the ford and road. It was evident that they were leaving our front." I do not know what ever became of Colonel Crooks, but I hope he was righted at last.

I do not recall seeing Grant during the day, but he is reported by one who was near him to have been deeply absorbed, and to have visited the line between Burnside and Warren, his eyes resting on the Chewning farm on the Parker's Store Road. As to his antagonist, Gordon says Lee invited him early in the forenoon to ride with him over the ground of his movement of the night before. While on the ride, Lee expressed his conviction that if he could check Grant, such a crisis in public affairs in the North would arise as might lead to an armistice; and I am almost sure he was right. Gordon says he referred to the rumors that Grant was retreating, and that Lee gave them no credit, predicting, on the contrary, that he would move toward Spotsylvania.

Meanwhile the rear of both armies contrasted sharply with their fronts. Scattered over the dulled, impoverished fields, amid flooding sunshine, — for after the smoke and fog had broken up and gone, it was a beautiful, serenely smiling day, — lay the ar-

THE BATTLE OF THE WILDERNESS 339

tillery and the multitudinous trains, their animals harnessed and hitched, dozing where they stood. Men and drivers lounged in groups near their guns and teams, some sound asleep, some playing cards, here and there one writing home, and here and there, too, a bohemian dog that had been picked up and adopted, curled down, nose on paws and eyes half-closed, but out for what was going on. Yes, a battle-field has a wide compass, very human and interesting.

About noon orders were issued for the wounded to be loaded in trains, and, under an escort of thirteen hundred cavalry, taken across the Rapidan at Ely's Ford and on to Rappahannock Station, there to meet cars that were to be sent out from Alexandria. The wounded were divided into three classes, those who could walk, those able to ride in the wagons, and, third, the most severely wounded, including those suffering from fractures, or from some recent amputation, and, most unfortunate of all, those whose wounds had penetrated the breast or abdominal cavities. The wagons, having assembled at the various hospitals (there were 325 of them and 488 ambulances), were thickly bedded with evergreen boughs on which shelter tents and blankets were spread. Dalton was put in charge of the train, Winne and other corps inspectors aiding at the respective hospitals in getting the necessary supplies together, and selecting and loading the wounded. It was approaching midnight before the train, with its seven thousand souls, either on foot or being carried, was ready to move; nearly a thousand had to be left on account of lack of transportation. No one can appreciate, unless he has been witness of such scenes, the strain upon the surgeons that night. I have often thought that they never received a full measure of recognition for their humane services.

Let us not follow the train in the darkness, for almost every wagon is a hive of moans, and we should hear horrible cries of agony breaking from the men as the wheels grind on boulders or jounce across roots, the piercing shrieks mingling with the shouts of drivers and clanking of trace-chains. Before Dalton got to the ford, orders came to countermarch and proceed to Fredericksburg with the poor fellows. Whenever an unrighteous war shall be urged upon our country by the unscrupulously ambitious or thoughtless, I wish that the Wilderness, Spotsylvania, and Cold Harbor would lay bare all that they remember.

In this connection here is what Keifer says: "On my arrival at hospital about 2 P. M. I was carried through an entrance to a large tent, on each side of which lay human legs and arms, resembling piles of stove wood, the blood only excepted. All around were dead and wounded men, many of the latter dying. The surgeons, with gleaming, sometimes bloody, knives and instruments, were busy at their work. I soon was laid on the rough-board operating-table and chloroformed."

THE BATTLE OF THE WILDERNESS 341

Notwithstanding this frightful record, I think I can hear the Wilderness exclaim with holy exultation, "Deep as the horrors were, the battles that were fought in my gloom were made glorious by the principles at stake ; and I cherish every drop of the gallant blood that was shed."

Lee, after his ride with Gordon, went back to his headquarters and directed Stuart and Pendleton to thoroughly acquaint themselves with the roads on the right, which the army would have to follow should Grant undertake to move, as he thought he might, toward Spotsylvania; the latter, to cut a path through the woods to facilitate the infantry's march in reaching the Catharpin Road. The filing of our ammunition and headquarters trains past the Wilderness Tavern in the forenoon, preliminary to clearing the way for Warren and the general movement, and visible from Lee's lines, make the sources of these precautions plain. Lee established his headquarters for the night at Parker's store, and between sundown and dark directed Anderson, whom he had assigned to Longstreet's command, to go to Spotsylvania either by Todd's Tavern or Shady Grove Church, and Ewell to conform his movements to those of the troops on his right; and if at daylight he found no large force in his front, to follow Anderson toward Spotsylvania. It is obvious from these orders that Lee was not fully informed of the situation, for at that very hour Sheridan was in full possession of Todd's Tavern, and "Charley" McConnell of Pittsburg was probably burying Collins, the friend of his youth. It may interest some readers to know that he cut off a lock of Collins's hair before he laid him in his narrow bed, and that that lock at last reached loving hands and is preserved.

General Pendleton went to see Anderson, described the route he was to take, and left one of his aides as a guide, Lee having directed Anderson (his despatch is dated seven P. M.) to start as soon as he could withdraw safely. Anderson, rather a slow but valiant man, had fixed on starting at three, but was under way by eleven, and those four hours gained were mighty valuable to Lee.

Meade's orders for the movements of the night were issued at three P. M., and, like all those written by Humphreys, are models of explicitness. Sedgwick was to move at 8.30, by way of the Pike and Chancellorsville and thence to Piney Branch Church; Warren was to set off for Spotsylvania by way of the Brock Road. Their pickets were to be withdrawn at one A. M. Burnside was to follow Sedgwick, and Hancock was to stand fast. The sun was just above the tree-tops when Warren with his staff left the Lacy house. For some reason that I do not know, instead of following the Germanna Road to the Brock, he took the Pike, and just as we gained the brow of the hill at the old Wilderness Tavern there was borne from the enemy's lines on the still evening

THE BATTLE OF THE WILDERNESS 343

air the sound of distant cheering. I halted and turned my horse's head in the direction whence it came, that is, up the run, whose trough-like valley, with its timbered head, lay resting against the upheaved openings of the Widow Tapp and Chewning farms. The sun was now lodged halfway in the tree-tops, and looked like a great, red copper ball. I think I can hear that Confederate line cheering yet. At the time I supposed that, seeing us on the move, they thought we had had enough of it, and were seeking safety at Fredericksburg. It seems, however, to have been unpremeditated and to have been started by some North Carolina regiment in the right of their line cheering Lee, who happened to go by them. Assuming that it was a cry of defiance, the adjacent brigade took it up, and, like a wave on the beach, it broke continuously along their entire line. And after dying away, from their right beyond the unfinished railway to their extreme left resting on Flat Run, it was followed by two more like surges.

Cheers never broke on a stiller evening. There is not a breath of air, the flushing west is fading fast, the world is on the verge of twilight, and trees, roads, fields, and distances are dimming as they clothe themselves in its pensive mystery. Where now are the scenes and the sounds of only three evenings ago? Where are all the men who were singing in their bivouacs along Wilderness Run? Where are Wadsworth, Hays, Jenkins, Jones, Stafford, McElwain,

Campbell Brown, Griswold, and "Little" Abbott? And where are the hopes and plans of Grant and Lee when the sun went down on the first night in the Wilderness. Well! well! and all will be well!

The Pike to Chancellorsville is packed with moving trains. The resolute batteries that stood on the slope, where the little chapel stands now, have pulled out, crossed the run, and their heavy wheels are rolling over and muttering their rumbling jars; they will hear no bugle-calls for taps to-night, nor will three thousand dead. The sunset flush has ebbed from the west, the lone, still trees are growing black, and the overhead dome vaulting the old fields of the Lacy plantation is filling with a wan hushed light.

Wilderness Run now utters its first audible gurgle, night is falling fast on the earth, and weary day is closing her eyes. Grant's and Meade's headquarters tents are struck, the orderlies are standing by the saddled horses, the men are waiting behind the breastworks in the already dark woods for the word silently to withdraw. A few minutes more and the Lacy farm will be hidden. Now it is gone; and here comes the head of Warren's corps with banners afloat. What calm serenity, what unquenchable spirit, are in the battle-flags! On they go. Good-by, old fields, deep woods, and lonesome roads. And murmuring runs, Wilderness, and Caton's, you too farewell.

The head of Warren's column has reached the Brock Road, and is turning south. At once the men

THE BATTLE OF THE WILDERNESS 345

catch what it means. Oh, the Old Army of the Potomac is not retreating! and in the dusky light, as Grant and Meade pass by, they give them high, ringing cheers.

And now we are passing Hancock's lines, and never, never shall I forget the scene. Dimly visible but almost within reach from our horses, the gallant men of the Second Corps are resting against the charred parapets, from which they hurled Field. Here and there is a weird little fire, groups of mounted officers stand undistinguishable in the darkness, and up in the towering tree-tops of the thick woods beyond the entrenchments tongues of yellow flames are pulsing from dead limbs lapping the black face of night. All, all is deathly still. We pass on, cross the unfinished railway, then Poplar Run, and then up a shouldered hill. Our horses are walking slowly. We are in dismal pine woods, the habitation of thousands of whippoorwills uttering their desolate notes unceasingly. Now and then a sabre clanks, and close behind us the men are toiling on.

It is midnight. Todd's Tavern is two or three miles away. Deep, deep is the silence. Jehovah reigns; Spotsylvania and Cold Harbor are waiting for us; and here we end.

The Riverside Press
CAMBRIDGE · MASSACHUSETTS
U · S · A